UNDER PRETEXT OF PRAISE

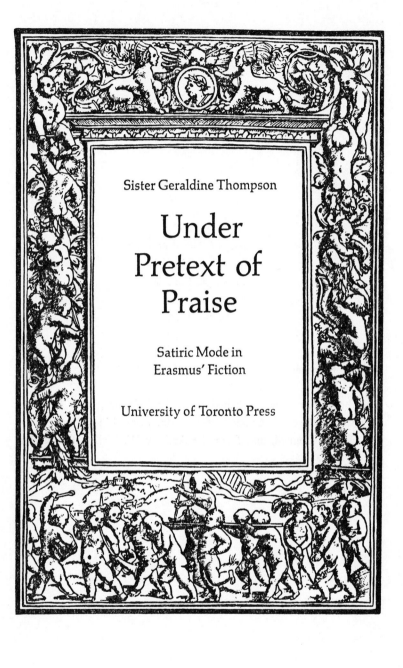

Sister Geraldine Thompson

Under Pretext of Praise

Satiric Mode in
Erasmus' Fiction

University of Toronto Press

Erasmus Studies: A Series of Studies
concerned with Erasmus and Related Subjects   1

This book has been published with the help of grants from the Humanities Research Council of Canada, using funds provided by the Canada Council, and from the Andrew W. Mellon Foundation.

In this respect I had exactly the same principles in the *Praise of Folly* as in my other works, although my method was different. In the *Enchiridion* I have a straightforward pattern for the Christian life ... In the *Praise of Folly* I did in a jesting fashion exactly what I had done in the *Enchiridion*. I wanted to admonish and not to carp; to do good, not harm; to have regard to men's character and not to be a stumbling block to it.

From a letter to Martin Dorp 1515
Allen Ep 337: 86–94

❧ Contents ❧

❧ Preface ❧

IT IS NOW MANY YEARS since a well-known classicist advanced the suggestion that it was Erasmus who had re-introduced irony into European letters and that this had been his great contribution thereto.[1] It is even a long time since I read the book and pondered the question of whether irony was really Erasmus' great contribution or if some other quality of thought or style might not be more significant. I still do not know the answer to that question, but the quest provided me at that time with a thesis, and set alight in me an interest that has endured, and been often rekindled, through many years of teaching.

The last five years, since the five-hundredth anniversary of his birth, have seen a great renewal of interest in Erasmus. Many excellent studies of the great humanist have stimulated that interest, and at my own university a project to translate into English all Erasmus' works and letters has been initiated and is well under way. This, then, is one more study. And perhaps a teacher of English literature, one who has small Latin and less Dutch, should be diffident about nosing into the ranks of the exegetes, historians, and classicists who write so well of Erasmus. I am. And my only reason for writing this book is the consideration that much less has been written about Erasmus' fictional work and its literary excellence than about the educational and editorial writings. My book is about the fiction and what it contains of instruction and delight.

1 J.A.K. Thomson *Irony: An Historical Introduction* (London 1926) 66

Most of Erasmus' fictional work is satiric, entirely or in part –
The Praise of Folly, many of the colloquies, and the two long
dialogues *Julius secundus exclusus* and *Ciceronianus*; and it is to
these four writings that I have directed my chief attention in this
study, though in the process of explication and analysis I have
sought for analogues and amplifications in the educational and
exegetical works. This is especially so in the introductory and
concluding chapters where the necessity of intruding into areas
of scholarship not quite in my own neighbourhood proved to be
for me a kind of precious bane – more bane than precious perhaps
for my generous friends in the Classics Department; but for the
reader I hope the reverse will be true.

In the course of bringing to boil the ingredients of Erasmus'
satire, I have become preoccupied with three things which, willy-
nilly, have become the focal points of my analyses. The first of
them is Erasmus' remarkable belief in the teachability of man,
and in the educator's role in bringing him not only to humane
learning but to goodness. Learning and virtue Erasmus sometimes catches together under the one word 'wisdom,' though this
is not always so. In any case, this faith in the teacher's ability to
convert the ignorant, the foolish, and even the iniquitous into
wise and good citizens of Christendom is basic to an understanding of Erasmus' satire. It is the purpose of it; it dictates the choice
of subject matter and of form; it even conditions the style – the
way signs and symbols are used, for instance, and the timing and
duration of the irony, for the ironic inversion rarely covers the
entire work.

The second point is close to the first: it is Erasmus' notion of
what man is and to what end he is to be educated. Man differs
from all other creatures because he has reason and is moral. So
many biographers of Erasmus and critics of his work have drawn
attention to his dominant interest in man as a moral being, one
who is constantly behaving – often badly, sometimes virtuously,
always with the possibility of betterment – that one hardly needs
to point again to the moralistic emphasis in all Erasmian writing.
I have pointed to it, however, and often, but have been aware
also of two characteristics of his moralism: first, when Erasmus

makes a satiric presentation of some activity, good or bad, he is less interested in the act itself than in the thinking that preceded it, and even the bystander's judgement of it: the attitudes and climates of opinion in and around the act are paramount. Secondly, morality to Erasmus is more than mere ethics, or even mere reasonableness sometimes: it is a part of man's imaging of God and of his search for Christian perfection; and so it can hardly be separated from the devout life. If spiritual exhortation is less manifest in his fiction than is moral directive, if love of neighbour looms larger than love of God, nevertheless the life of the spirit is usually discernible either explicitly or by implication in most works. And so, in these pages, I have tried to present an Erasmus who recognizes in his reader a man of catholic appetite, a lover of literature who savours a story, finds delight in its words, metaphors, and patterns of thought, and a moral man who can be – and wants to be – taught how to think and act according to right reason, and a pilgrim to the heavenly Jerusalem who is glad to see the signposts on the way; for I think that the reader of ample appetite will find Erasmus trying to satisfy his every taste – not, however, by providing within a single text a stratification of various readings: the one figure that Erasmus never uses is the *aenigma*. It is rather his way to move from the merely ethical into the Christian-moral, and eventually into the realms of the devout life.

Irony and its significance, which had long since supplied the leverage for this study, is my third emphasis. And Erasmus' irony is indeed something to admire. Both dramatic and satiric, it is tantalizing in its subtlety, various in its techniques, and often doubly pronged so that it not only damns what it praises (as one expects it to do) but also damns the too-obvious alternative, cozening the reader's expectations and leaving him pondering the whereabouts of the right and the perimeters of truth – even, perhaps, pondering the nature of man. Whether or not irony is the most significant attribute of Erasmus' satire is another matter. There are many other arresting qualities in his thinking and his style: the peculiar relation between his reverence for, and cautious use of, symbol and sign is worthy of note; his professed repudiation of over-nicety in style (analogous to his rejection of the precisions of speculative philosophy) is significant too; and above all, his ability to impale on his pages with a dramatist's facility the all too recognizable posturings of silly people – the people of his own times, but of course of ours too, for the follies of human nature do not change much.

So all-inclusive are the facets of Erasmus' thinking that often what one says about him can be mooted and modified. One can say, for instance, that he reveres education and erudition above all else and calls learning the handmaid of virtue; yet he can repudiate the sophistications of scholarship and laud the simple untutored good man in page after page of directive. He wants the scriptures read with a spiritual meaning, he says often enough, but he can write at length of the perils of moving far from the safe and sure literal-moral sense. He writes monographs on the proper use of words and the most eloquent modes of amplification, and even proffers a guideline to the minute niceties of letter-writing; yet he protests vehemently in another place that he has too much to say to be bothered with the flowers of rhetoric, which might indeed in some cases be just a kind of 'perfume in the porridge.' And this adoption of many viewpoints – or, one might better say, this avoidance of any one extreme position – is something anyone writing about Erasmus must grapple with. The 'buts' and 'yets' and 'althoughs' that have proved to be my most ubiquitous conjunctions will not, I hope, weaken the points I have made about Erasmian satire, and especially the three here outlined: that man, a reasoning creature, can, by good teaching, be brought to reasonable and virtuous action, and that satire must function as an adjunct to that good teaching; that the writing must from time to time satisfy all the reaches of man's being – his delight in story and style, his desire for instruction, and his immortal longings; that the irony in Erasmian satire is remarkable, that it yields often enough to more directly persuasive writing, and that it is implemented by other tropes and techniques also remarkable.

In the colloquy called 'The Godly Feast,' Erasmus has one of the characters, a city man longing for a rural holiday, speak dis-

paragingly of a certain blind beggar who 'rejoiced in the jostling of a crowd because, he would say, where there were people there was profit.'[2] But that is just what Erasmus himself provides in the satires – a jostling crowd. My hope is that those who meet that crowd at one remove in these peopled pages will likewise find that in them 'there was profit.'

2 *The Colloquies of Erasmus* trans Craig R. Thompson (Chicago 1965) 48

❧ Acknowledgements ❧

My warm gratitude goes out to those who have helped me in various ways: to Professor A.E. Barker, once of the University of Toronto, now of the University of Western Ontario, without whose assistance and encouragement I should never have ventured to write even an article, much less a book; to Professor D.F.S. Thomson, of the University of Toronto, who first led me into the intricacies of Erasmian Latin; to Professor Norman Endicott, also of Toronto, whose lectures and conversations have so often given me new insights into the Renaissance mind. To Professor Craig R. Thompson, who has written so well of Erasmus, I owe special thanks for his gracious and careful reading of a chapter of my manuscript, and for his scholarly advice. I am indebted too to many members of the Classics Department of the University of Toronto for their generous help – among them I should like to single out for special thanks the three members of my own congregation: Sister St John (who was my first Latin professor, long ago) and Sisters Blandina and Mechtilde; and I am also most appreciative of the help of Father Reginald O'Donnell, of the Pontifical Institute of Mediaeval Studies, who has taught me more than paleography. I also want to thank my cousin, Adelle Shirriff, who faithfully gave many a Tuesday to helping me proofread my typescript and compile an index. And to the long-suffering members of my community and my family, who have never yielded to exasperated outcries at my long-winded Erasmian cogitations, I offer thanks and a promise of amendment.

A grant from the Canada Council enabled me to spend a year

in London, using the library of the British Museum. For this, and for the help of librarians both there and at the libraries of the University of Toronto, I am indeed most grateful.

SISTER GERALDINE, CSJ

UNDER PRETEXT OF PRAISE

Cognitio verborum prior...

KNOWLEDGE BEGINS WITH DEFINITION, so Erasmus counsels;[1] things, he concedes, are of more importance, but the words that name and define them have at least temporal priority in the order of learning. One might then curry favour with the Dutchman's ghost by beginning with definition, hoping to find, through rejecting and including, some norms that will include the wide varieties of Erasmian satire, from the lamentations of *The Complaint of Peace* to the blustering shafts of the colloquy 'The Shipwreck.'

The definition offered by the Oxford English Dictionary, that satire is 'a poem, or, in modern use, sometimes a prose composition, in which prevailing vices or follies are held up to ridicule,' is perhaps less than satisfying. Its three elements, that the mode is ridicule, the subject matter prevailing folly or vice, and the dominant form poetry, are questionable norms for many of Erasmus' satires: to see the follies attacked in some of the colloquies as 'prevailing,' one would have to twist and attenuate them; ridiculing irony Erasmus usually employs as an initial device, but often enough, before the work ends, this is transmuted into something more sweetly and reasonably persuasive; and

---

1 *Principio duplex omnino videtur cognitio, rerum ac verborum. Verborum prior, rerum potior. De ratione studii* (1512), in *Omnia Opera* (Leyden 1702) I 521A. Further references to untranslated passages will be to this edition unless otherwise stated, and will be designated as LB, followed by volume and column numbers; where feasible, documentation will be bracketed into the text.

poetry, at least in its narrower sense, is not the form of any of the satires, though if we accept (as Erasmus would have accepted) the Sidneian notion of poetry as being an 'arte of imitation ... a representing, counterfeiting, or figuring foorth,'[2] all Erasmian satire is poetry.

Erasmus himself would surely have quarrelled with the defining of any kind of writing, and especially satire, without reference to its purpose. His own satires – and perhaps those of any Christian humanist – can best be understood in terms of purpose; and it is noteworthy that most satirists, when they reflect upon their work, appraise it in terms of its moral purpose and effect. Donne, for instance, moots the question of whether or not railing can cure certain 'maladies,' yet hopes his words will be ancillary to those of the preacher; he is apprehensive, in later years, lest the scorn that 'cuts deeper than a sword' may do more harm than good to the things of God. Dryden speaks of the satirist's business as being 'to reform vice,' and notes that the ancients wrote satire for the amendment of vicious men, or failing that, for the dissuading of others from such vice; he approves Heinsius' opinion that satire is 'a kind of poetry invented for the purging of our minds; in which human vices, ignorance, and errors ... are severely reprehended.' Swift protests in one place that he wants only to vex the world, yet admits his desire to persuade all honest men to be of his opinion; he refers to his wit as his 'method of reforming,' and in one instance conjectures that satire may have been introduced into the world so that scoundrels impervious to the demands of religion or virtue might be kept within the bounds of morality through fear of having their crimes 'exposed to open view ... and themselves rendered odious to mankind.' Pope thinks satire arises from the 'strong antipathy of good to bad,' calls it a sacred weapon left for the defence of truth, the 'sole dread of folly, vice, and insolence'; and although Johnson doubts Pope's highminded intentions – at least as applied to the *Dunciad* – he gives favourable judgement to that poem

2 Sir Philip Sidney *An Apology for Poetry,* in *Elizabethan Critical Essays* G. Gregory Smith (ed) (Oxford 1904) I 158

because, in spite of its petulancy and malignancy, it aims to re-establish some needed poetic norms.[3]

For Erasmus, certainly all satire, perhaps all fictional writing, is just as good as, and no better than, its capacity to effect or sustain good thoughts and godly living. The Praise of Folly may masquerade as a mere *jeu d'esprit*, yet Erasmus likens it to the *Enchiridion*, a work overtly didactic; the colloquies are addressed to schoolboys (and sometimes to their older brothers) to famil-iarize them with conversational Latin and the ethics of godly Christian living; *Julius exclusus* purposes to awaken a Christian church and its hierarchy to the disparity between apostolic ideals and worldly ones; *Ciceronianus* begins by censuring exaggerated imitation of literary models, then moves on to exhorting to godliness a Christendom too easily beguiled by pagan formal perfection.

It needs no great flight of imagination to envision Erasmus as seeing himself as some wise man from the sky (or from the the Netherlands) similar to the wise man who disturbs the theatre scenes in the *Praise of Folly*, hoping to awaken the apathetic Christians of his day to right thinking and sober reality.[4]

In the interest of lessoning his victim, or, more often of stirring up a climate of opinion hostile to some vice or folly, the satirist creates a work wherein some indirection stands between the reader and the stark criticism; for there must be pleasure or interest for the reader if he is to read on and, through the reading, be convinced of the writer's rightness. What is *utile* must also be *dulce*, though often the little bit of honey that makes the medicine

3 John Donne, Verse Satires III and IV, and Sermon given at Chilsey in 1627 (Simpson and Potter edition of the Sermons, University of California 1953–61 VII 65–6); Dryden *The Original and Progress of Satire* passim; Swift, Letter to Alexander Pope, 29 September 1725, and lines from 'To a Lady who Desired some Verse in Heroic Style,' and from *Examiner* paper 38; Pope, from the dedication of the *Dunciad* to Lord Middlesex; Johnson *Works* Arthur Murphy (ed) (London 1820) IX 187

4 *Moriae encomium declamatio* (1509) trans Hoyt Hopewell Hudson as *The Praise of Folly* Modern Library 1967, 38. The original edition of the Hudson translation was from the Princeton University Press 1941.

go down is mixed with vinegar. To achieve his end the satirist makes use of certain figurative devices, and so, in a sense, does make a poem; and since the way of satire is usually to show the folly attacked as absurd, the figures most often used are those of ridicule: irony and the perquisites of irony – hyperbole, litotes, zeugma, incongruity, parody, and sometimes fiction or story.

To think of 'lessoning a victim,' or even of activating a climate of healthy opinion, as being the whole driving power of a satire, is, of course, an over-simplification. True, some moral indignation is usually the impulse or ignition spark, but the energy so generated is often carried forward by the sheer delight of creation. It is so with John Donne, with Dryden, and surely with Pope. But with Erasmus the urge to better his fellow men is paramount. Although there is surely nothing pedestrian about the lively *Praise,* nor about *Julius* or the colloquies, the good counsellor's method never quite gives way to the artist's élan, and this is especially evident in his choice and manipulation of figure and scheme. When he uses irony, it may be finely toned or brashly exaggerated, doubly pronged or simple and incisive, deceptively sweet or drenched in acid; but it nearly always gives way in the end to the direct statement of what he means or the direct exhortation to the good he envisions. His own excitement in the act of artistic creation must be disciplined, and so must the readers'; otherwise the lesson might be lost.

And, as we shall see, this is still more the case when Erasmus uses the non-ironic figures. He who is so alert to the hieroglyphics of nature, who sees the emblematic in all his surroundings, and who is so eager to teach all Christendom to see what God is showing them in nature and art and circumstance, and above all, in men and their doings, rarely trusts his own meaning to a symbol, or even to an obscure metaphor. Symbol may be used, or metaphor or allegory, but it is explained. God creates, hiding his lessons in the crevices of his creation; and man can do the same, creating another nature and hiding his meaning within it; but that is not the way of a teacher: his way is to help the spectator or reader to find the meanings. Erasmus would be a teacher.

Erasmus has been credited with having reintroduced irony into European literature[5] – a questionable tribute surely: one has but to think of Chaucer's Pandarus or Pertelote or Skelton's Parrot among many such early or contemporary ironic creations to counter the notion. But it is true that the delight of Erasmus' satiric writing comes often enough from its ironic ingenuity, though this is not at all the unique or even the prime cause of the endurance of his work. Yet, because he was so well aware of the power of irony, and because those who followed in his wake, and thought they were imitating him, were much less perceptive and competent than he in the devious ways of irony, it is perhaps well to detail some of the techniques and purposes of irony and the wry figures in its retinue.[6]

More than a device or a deliberately established trope, irony is a total arrangement of thought, a state of mind; and paradoxically, although it stands as part to the whole when considered in the embrace of satire, it has its own wholeness, of which satire is in turn just a part. It did not begin as a figure of ridicule certainly. Its complex development both as a figure and an attitude can be traced through the ages of Greek drama and dialogue, on into Roman literature, and up to its renewal in the Renaissance.[7] In its early significance it was a quality, first of the

5 J.A.K. Thomson *Irony: An Historical Introduction* (London 1926), 66
6 These figures – hyperbole, *meiosis* (which Erasmus would call *diminutio*), zeugma, mimicry, and the simple inversions of irony itself – are only wry, of course, when used within a covering mood and context that is satiric. For instance, the hyperbole in 'he could split the rocks with his eloquence' (Erasmus' own example) is not ironic at all, but when his Moria says 'my morons are as plump and sleek as the hogs of Acarnania,' the exaggeration is brought to the support of satiric intention, for the context assures the reader that the meaning is censorious. So too with zeugma: one can speak of taking 'one's hat and one's departure' without any irony, but Pope's coupling of lap-dogs and husbands has the good ironic bite, saying the one thing, that dying pets and dying husbands are equally lamentable, and giving to understand the contrary. Thus it seems to me that such figures as these are ironic only when the context makes them so.
7 Thomson *Irony* chapters 1 and 2; Northrop Frye *Anatomy of Criticism* (Chicago 1961) 40ff; G.G. Sedgewick *Of Irony, Especially in the Drama*

self-deprecatory man who feared to let the gods see him well-endowed; then of the man of fine perception, the Socrates, who, by deceptively innocent questioning, confounded his interrogators; and finally of the comic satirist who said one thing, but, well aware of his double tongue, gave to understand some other thing.

Because some remnants of early and later connotations still cluster around the word, and because its function may be dramatic or satiric, and its mood tragic or comic, irony resists definition. Professor J.A.K. Thomson, who writes so well of it, refrains from proffering one, though he describes it often and well, as do Rosemond Tuve, Northrop Frye, John Peter, Alvin Kernan, and many others.[8] The cryptic (and over-simple) definition given by Erasmus's contemporary, Wynkyn de Worde, that irony is 'that figure by which a man sayeth the one thing and giveth to understand the contrary,' however much it leaves unsaid of the fine sensibility that irony bespeaks, and of the history and philosophy behind it, seems to be at least loosely applicable to all irony's faces.

For our purposes in the present study there are two kinds of irony: dramatic and satiric. Both spring from double meanings and variations in awareness, real or assumed. That is why the ancient definition is so apt. With dramatic irony, which holds the mimetic mirror up to the irony inherent in life itself, the author is the omniscient god, though when he has occasion to speak in his own person, he is careful to appear as uninformed as his fictional mouthpiece. He assumes some awareness in his reader or listener; and to his created characters he gives unequal degrees of perception.

(Toronto 1935) 9ff; Earle Birney, 'English Irony before Chaucer' *University of Toronto Quarterly* VI (1937) 538ff

8 Thomson 212–13; Frye *Anatomy* 30–5, 176ff; 'The Nature of Satire' *University of Toronto Quarterly* XIV (1944) 75–9; Rosemond Tuve *Elizabethan and Metaphysical Imagery* (Chicago 1947) 205–8; John Peter *Complaint and Satire in Early English Literature* (Oxford 1956) 10–13; Alvin B. Kernan *The Cankered Muse* (New Haven 1959) 3–15 and 81–140

The effectiveness of dramatic irony depends on many things: the activating or the merely informative quality of the ironic speech, for instance. Sophocles' *Oedipus Rex* illustrates this well: when Oedipus misinterprets his wife's plea to cut short his inquiry, and deplores her snobbish anxiety about his birth, the audience's horror is given new point, but the progress of the play is neither impeded nor propelled: the words neither aggravate nor accelerate the miserable end. But when he invokes the gods and urges them to bring ruin to the man who has brought sorrow and shame to Thebes, the tragic dénouement is indeed brought nearer its full complement of anguish; this is more than irony of speech; it is operative irony.[9] Moria, the speaker of *The Praise of Folly*, makes an oration that curdles with irony, but the words are not operative, because there is no plot to provide such movement; Julius, in a dialogue having some slight movement towards decision or judgement, damns himself with every speech which advances the wrong reasons for consideration; and Julius' irony, though it is in many ways less satisfying than Moria's, is operative. Another aspect of dramatic irony is one that can wrinkle itself into a title or name. Whether we call Sophocles' play *Oedipus Rex* or *Oedipus Tyrannus*, there is irony in the title – not of speech, nor of action, yet with some bearing on situation and understanding, for Oedipus is on the defensive because he is, or thinks he is, only *tyrannus* and not *rex*, and when at last he knows he has always been *rex*, it is bitter knowledge. Moria's praise is *of* folly and is also Folly's praise, and there is a pleasant irony in the double genitive – triple, when we think of its glancing reference to Erasmus' friend, Thomas More.

In all these instances a faulted awareness (real or pretended) makes the speech or action or situation poignant and ironic. Irony that is not dramatic but only satiric may co-exist in dialogue or drama; when a speaker knows the full import of his words, and for reprehensive or didactic purpose makes the speech

9 Sophocles *Oedipus Rex* (Fitts and Fitzgerald translation, Harcourt, Brace 1949) lines 1003–19 and 223–40

literally less than true, it is satiric irony. The author is providing not dramatic irony, but a character who knows how to be ironic or sarcastic. Moria, for instance, is, in the early parts of the *Praise*, unaware of her false reasoning, but later on is either half aware or fully aware of the undesirability of falsity, and her word of commendation is simply scornful.[10] One of the three speakers in the *Ciceronianus* is truly beguiled by a literary fashion, and speaks with dramatic irony (and satiric, of course, from the readers' standpoint), but his two companions are well aware of his false position and only pretend to agree with him in order to overthrow his logic in the end; and Erasmus takes care that the reader knows this from the beginning and recognizes a simple portrayal of deception.[11]

The effect of dramatic irony is related too to the congruencies of time. Sometimes a sequence of events is required to shape the disparity between the thing said and the idea communicated. Thus, when the temple-haunting martlet bespeaks the peace of Macbeth's castle (I, vi, 4), it is not a false symbol at that moment; the castle is peaceful enough then, and only in the light of later disturbances is the phrase ironic. At other times the unequal faces of irony are simultaneously operative, as when Oedipus invokes the retributive gods: the utterer of the curse is already the killer of Laius when the dreadful words are being spoken; or as when Julius tries to bluster away the judgement that is leaving him *exclusus* at heaven's gate: the deeds that sanction the judgement are already done and his words are ironic confirmation of its justice. But Erasmus, whose satiric irony is often dramatic too, provides few examples of the irony involving time-lapse. The reader of the *Praise of Folly*, for instance, does not think of

10 Compare, for instance, Moria's praise of a sensuous old age (p 17) with her sarcasm when she attacks the greed of supposedly devout churchmen (p 87 and 97–9).

11 *Ciceronianus, or a Dialogue on the Best Style of Speaking* trans by Izora Scott, ed by Paul Monroe (Columbia University Teachers' College Series, no. 21, New York 1908); the opening speeches articulate the speakers' true positions.

Moria's early scorn for the life of reason or of faith (which she is later to judge desirable) as a ploy of irony: whatever irony inheres in each part is bolted in to that part. In 'The Apotheosis of Reuchlin,' a colloquy wherein there is certainly potential for such time-sequenced irony, there is no evidence of it. Only perhaps in the first of that series of colloquies in which Eubulus and Catherine win through to a happy married life does Erasmus exploit this kind of opportunity, and then it is trifling. Catherine would 'rather die,' she says, 'than give up [her] ... resolution of virginity,' though she is to discover very soon how readily she can give it up.[12]

Still, the consideration of dramatic irony is not irrelevant to our study, for Erasmus, as we have said, does like to play doubledutch, keeping the two ropes of satiric irony and dramatic playing into each other. In both kinds the speaker (or doer) says or does foolish things, and the listener knows better. Little is needed to make dramatic irony satiric: censorious intention and a shift in the position of the percipient. The ironist, whether it be Sophocles or Erasmus or Dryden, is the one who sees and judges rightly and hopes for matching percipience in the reader: the difference between Oedipus and Moria, each speaking from a position of unawareness, is in the intention of the author, sympathetic or critical. If the satirist does not speak through a fictional mouthpiece and his irony is therefore non-dramatic, he himself pretends to the false stand, or at least talks in devious ways.[13] Erasmus' best satires have always something of dramatic irony in them. But many of those who followed in his wake failed to use his techniques. The minor satirists of the mid-century, writers of paradox and poetry and controversy, are for the most part

---

12 *Colloquia familiaria* (1516–28) Trans and ed by Craig R. Thompson as *The Colloquies of Erasmus* (University of Chicago Press 1965) 106 and 112–14. The two colloquies are 'The Girl with no Interest in Marriage' and 'The Repentant Virgin.'

13 Here and throughout, the term 'satirist' is meant to apply to the author, unless otherwise stated, and not, as Alvin B. Kernan has used it, to refer to the chief voice or character of the satire. See *The Cankered Muse* (Yale 1951) chapter 1, 14–28.

unaware of the rich and subtle shades of meaning Erasmian irony can suggest. Even Nashe, whose references to Erasmus are so abundant as to persuade one that he is a kindred spirit, has little of the Erasmian finesse: fictional figures are few in his work, and so the satiric irony is rarely dramatic too. Donne, perhaps, comes close to the Erasmian temper, and since he often speaks through fictional characters (a man-about-town, a lecherous lover, a claimant for Lucifer's hospitality) he uses an irony both satiric and dramatic.

If irony can be said to be more than a technique, this is especially true of satiric irony. It may appear as concentrated in an image or may ride the entire work; but it is, first, in the temper of the mind that creates the image and the work. And this is much to the point, for although Erasmus was not always dominated by the ironic mood, it was often enough resident in his incisive mind. This quality of mind may well be, as Professor J.A.K. Thomson thinks, the reluctance to yield to intense feeling, so that 'feeling more deeply than his words, taken at their face value suggest,' the ironic man is open to misunderstanding. 'He asks more of his readers than some can give ... they honestly find it hard to believe that a man *can* feel strongly on a matter on which he will not let himself go' (p 66).

This unwillingness to let himself go Professor Thomson calls 'a passion for moderation.'[14] Irony may, and often does, go hand in hand with moderation, but the relation is perhaps rather one of affinity than of cause and effect, as Thomson would have it. Both irony and the tendency to moderation are often found in a mind perplexed in some measure about the good thing it does not quite bring into focus, though not at all perplexed about the evil things it sees too well. One who clearly envisions the good life, or some choice within it, is more likely to express himself in straight exhortation than in irony, because his message is too urgent to be trusted to the ambivalences of irony – or he thinks it is. Professor Frye, in the article already quoted, carries this idea into a slightly different channel:

For better or worse [he says], it is the tiny David with his sudden
and vicious stones who goes out to battle now, and the great
Rabelaisian bellow has dropped out of literature. For that kind
of satire flourishes in a world of solid assurances and unshak-
able values; the whole weight of a confident society is flung into
the scales against limp affectation. The less sure society is of its
assumptions, the more likely satire is to take the line of irony, of
the method laid down once for all in the dialogues of Plato. [82]

Satire as an instrument of persuasion is less than a perfect tool,
and often enough fits the hand of a man himself in need of mental
or moral surgery, or at least of healing. But it does contribute to
the healing process, and after the catharsis, we sometimes find a
richer tone as the satire draws to a conclusion. Sometimes – not
always. For most satire, perhaps all pure satire, is characterized
by its static position, its satirist railing to the bitter end, its fools
confirmed in their folly. A recent critic, for instance, can point to
the static character of the satiric situation and the absence of
progress in its plot as being one of the recognized marks of a
satire.[15] But this, as we shall see, is not quite true of Erasmus'
satires, which often do move towards at least a conversion of
mind. Here again it is the indomitable teacher and humanist who
determines the shape of the satire, reasoning, one supposes, that
if the reader can see his own absurdities mirrored and exaggerated in those of the foolish person presented, and then see
his mirrored self turning towards wiser things, the lesson is
doubly rich. Moria, who is certainly the sum of all folly, is herself converted (though her entourage may remain fixed in folly)
and lifts the *Praise* to surprising levels of richness; Nosoponus,
the gull of the *Ciceronianus*, shows signs of becoming reasonable; the colloquies too sometimes move from their brittle opening tone into some fairer shape into which conversion and exhortation can be fitted.

In its absolute form, as an instrument of regeneration (rather
than merely one of reproof) satire is the less effective for being

15 Kernan 30–4

incapable of moving on any level but that of reason; for reason may lead to the life of good behaviour, even good Christian behaviour (since it is folly to jeopardize future blessedness if one believes in it); but it can only commend this good life in moderation. When faith and charity interpose to direct that goodness into the area of perfect love, irony is not a part of the loftier environment: it simply does not operate on that level.

But Erasmus does concern himself, even in the so-called satires, with man at all his levels of being, and does try to provide sustenance for all. Therefore, just as there is small warrant for saying he re-introduced into European literature the figure of irony, so also it would be unwarrantable to say that irony was his greatest legacy to English (or European) letters. The fact that it is a legacy at all invites two questions in any case: where did irony go during the next half-century? For, outside the drama, there is little irony in the literature of England during these years, and what little there is is not used in Erasmus' way. For the most part there is invective, lament, and plaintive allegory; late in the century there is a resurgence of dramatic irony – which indeed Erasmus' near-dramas may have helped to promote; false *encomia* and paradox abound too in the mid-century, their frivolities claiming sanction through Erasmus' *Praise*; some of them are ironic, but again the irony is not used as Erasmus had used it, fused with other figures and bent to serious purpose. And this, of course, leads into the second question: if his imitators only partially recognized the ironic techniques he was using, what were the other qualities, more easily discerned and imitated, that kept the satires alive and influential during those years?

Of the figures not ironic in themselves but proceeding towards irony or supplying for it, some might be singled out for what Erasmus would call *amplificatio*: story or fictional form; allegory and symbol; and verse form.

Story and plot and character seem so obviously linked with creative writing as to need little comment. One need only think of what *Gulliver's Travels* would be without Gulliver, or *The Praise of Folly* without Moria, or Donne's *Conclave* without

Ignatius and Machiavelli to realize what liveliness is given to satiric attack by being bounded and particularized in character and situation and the suspense of story. It is not just that the 'satirist' is not now the author or even the author's *persona* – indeed Gulliver is far more naive than Swift, and Moria often a witless and wanton creature. But fiction gives a new dimension to satiric irony by making it dramatic. Moria, for instance, can proffer an irony both dramatic and satiric – dramatic because of her impercipience, and satiric because the matter of her discourse is made up of morals and manners, and her judgements of them call for rebuttal. Throughout much of the declamation she earnestly opts for folly, not always because she mistakes it for wisdom (for sometimes her vision is clear enough), but because she cannot but choose it anyway; and flexible and fictional as she is, she can do what Erasmus cannot do: she can adopt three or four positions within as many pages, now witless but full of good will, now clear-visioned but perverse, loving her fools one minute, scorning them the next.

Rhyme and rhythm, used without the wry satiric figures, are weak surrogates for them. But there are satires, recognized as such since the prevailing folly or vice is attacked in a form obviously literary, that do not use the indirections of irony. Many of the poems of the mid-century are non-ironic, but because they are censorious and because they are rhymed and metrical (and usually slightly allegorical) they are thought of as satires; William Roy's *Rede Me and Bee not Wrothe*, ironic now and then, has pages and pages of what is hardly more than rhymed invective; Gascoigne's *Steele Glas* is compounded of allegory and rhyme; Hake's *Newes Out of Paules* is rarely ironical but the rhyme marches on. Even the simplest rhymster, however, usually conscripts at least one of the other figures: alliteration, simile, personification. At least when one sees verse one knows that the critic has intended to be more than a mere fault-finder; he wants his work to be enjoyable. In certain parts, for instance, of Skelton's *Colyn Cloute*, where verse is almost the only indirection, it does put a dab of literary icing on the censure, though the coating is meagre:

What care they though Gill sweat
Or Jack of the Noke
The poore people they yoke
With summons and citacyons
And excommunications ... [323–7]

But metrical form, with sometimes a little allegory, alliteration, or a bit of dialogue, seems to be the only literary element in much of the satire of the mid-century. Surrey, Heywood, Roy, Gascoigne, Hake, Guilpin, Weever, Rowlands – verse with allegory, verse without allegory, dialogue in verse; there is not much else. This is not to say that rhyme and allegory do not provide real pleasure, but only that, separated from irony or cognate indirection, they do not provide effective satire. Used in conjunction with the satiric figures, all these techniques, even rhyme, can mightily enhance and implement denunciation. Dryden, for instance, in his *Absalom and Achitophel*, voices much the same complaint as does Skelton when he speaks of the Jebusites' having proselytized and

> ... raked for converts even the courts and stews
> Which Hebrew priests the more unkindly took
> Because the fleece accompanies the flock. [127–9]

Here the rhythmic form adds much to the satiric thrust, though, of course, the effect does not depend on this alone: there is lively fiction and allegory, the allusive verbal ingenuity, the understatement ('the more unkindly'), and the irony in the double meaning of 'fleece.'

Allegory and symbol are close kin to each other, both of them related to the metaphor.[16] Metaphor has two terms: the tenor, which signifies the literal meaning, and the differential, which is the analogue or vehicle in which the meaning is offered. To say that the road is a ribbon of moonlight leaves no one in doubt

16 For saying so there is good precedent: Erasmus speaks of metaphor as being the source of several tropes, and in his *De ratione concionandi*, or *Ecclesiastes*, lists some of them: *collatio* (or simile), *abusio*, *aenigma*, *imago*, *allegoria*, *proverbia*, and *apologia* (LB V 1033F).

about the solidity of the road. The symbol, on the other hand, at least in its modern and sophisticated sense, presents only the differential or analogue, letting the reader discover for himself the subtler meaning; tenor and differential are both in the symbol – otherwise it would not be a symbol – but the tenor is not to be sought in the words themselves (or actions, if the symbol is one of action). The total meaning of the symbol and the assertion made of it must be real in its own order – an order that is often other than the one signified. Thus, for instance, Browning's 'Nay, sir, we'll go together down' is what the Duke actually says, referring obviously to the staircase. That is solidly so, whatever we may infer about its darker implications. Robert Bolt's *A Man for All Seasons* opens with talk about a falcon, a 'royal bird' that swoops, sometimes blindly, ruthlessly, and from incredible heights, on his prey, a fact that any toxophilus may corroborate before he even begins to wonder if this hawk may be differential for another royal bird. When James Joyce lets a Jesuit sit in the shadows playing with a curtain cord, the attempt to rope in young Stephen is suggested in a symbol that almost moves into allegory, for the symbols proliferate and reappear for some paragraphs. In an allegorical work, the vehicle, or what is literally said, often has less reality and certainly less interest than has the deeper meaning, though lovers of *The Faerie Queene* and *Gulliver's Travels* may reasonably dispute this opinion.[17]

Erasmus' use of symbol is, in any case, less than sophisticated or subtle, for he uses his symbols as an educator, not as poet or teller of tales.[18] His own imagination is alert enough to see the

---

17 See C.S. Lewis' introduction to the section on Spenser in *Major British Writers* (New York 1954) I 97, for the opinion of one who is scholarly enough to be simple in his approach to *The Faerie Queene*.

18 A caveat may be given here: Erasmus' *symbolum* does not translate our word 'symbol'; rather he uses it in its theological sense as an element of a creed or catechism (see *Colloquies* C.R. Thompson [ed] 51, 180, 516; and the dialogue *Symbolum sive catechismus* LB VII 1136A ff), where the term has no reference at all to any figure of speech or thought as we understand it. A cognate word, *symbola*, is a sign of another kind – a piece of negotiable currency (see *Colloquies*, 189n). The words he does use to denote the figure of speech or its allied tropes are: *mysterium*,

parallels in nature and circumstance and art, and to apply them; indeed he urges all his readers to familiarize themselves with nature and acquire like perceptiveness.[19] But his own symbols he rarely allows to stand unbuttressed: the meaning must be made quite clear. I say 'rarely,' for there are places even in his soberest tracts where he can shore up a long precedent argument in a terse figure that is closer perhaps to symbol than to metaphor: a long polemic, for instance, on the interpretation of scriptural mysteries ends with a reference to the unveiling of Moses' face; and again he comments that scriptural soundings are so many and so varied that they provide waters wherein 'elephants may swim and lambs may wade'; in another place, he asks if there are some who think the scriptures fit only for the perfumed, the *'balsamo unctis'* (LB V 30B; IX 783D; and IX 786c).

Usually, however, Erasmus takes care that the reader has explicit directions for reading his metaphors or symbols right. If he had been telling the story of the real Princess he would surely have provided a chorus character to tell the reader that the unhappy girl so sensitive to the pea under the twenty mattresses and twenty ticks was really but the image of the sensitive soul quick to shrink from the slightest deviousness in matters of moral or spiritual moment; he would have had his Gulliver explain the eggs and the heels. He may let his Eutrapelus talk of wheat in an alien field, but it is not for the reader to apply the meaning to Fabulla, who has delegated the care of her child to another. No: the speakers in the colloquy ('The New Mother') put vehicle and tenor carefully together, and what might have been symbol be-

allegoria, similitudo, collatio, the verb *repraesentare,* and the periphrastic *genus figuratum dictionis.* For the kind of symbol discussed above (the falcon's swooping, the Duke's stairs, the curtain cord), I suspect Erasmus would have used the word *aenigma,* as he does in *De copia,* cap. 18, LB I 19A, or in the King and Rix translation (documented below, p 19) 30.

19 See, for instance, 'The Godly Feast' (*Colloquies* 51ff); the *Enchiridion militis christiani* (trans R. Himelick, Bloomington, Ind. 1963) 49ff and 101ff; *Ratio verae theologiae* (LB V 81A and 82B–C); and *De ratione concionandi* (LB V 1028D and 1033F); the last two refer, however, almost exclusively to scriptural interpretation and not to perception of the natural symbols in everyday life.

comes something close to epic simile: just as the wheat ... so the child ...

Even in his *De copia*, where one might expect to find a freer illustration of symbol or metaphor, he either prefaces the figure with an explanation or subjoins one:

> for example you may say: if uneducated people censure and condemn your writings, do not be troubled; they will certainly be approved by the most learned. For is it to be wondered at if the Aesopian Cock scorns a precious stone?[20]

Strangely enough, Erasmus does recognize that the ancient writers themselves expected the reader to understand. 'Who does not understand,' he says, '... that the story of Icarus' fall into the sea warns one not to go higher than one's destiny?' (LB I 91A; King and Rix translation, p 70)

Erasmus seems to think of the human person as the great symbol[21] – in a religious sense, surely, for man's word is the prolongation of God's Word, but experientially too, since God wrote large his messages through the human beings whose activities make up the scriptures, and even, so Erasmus ventures to say,

20 *De duplici copia verborum ac rerum* LB I 99C–D. From the translation by Donald B. King and H. David Rix (Milwaukee 1963) 85
21 I have been unable to track down any text in which Erasmus explicitly speaks of the human being as the prime symbol, and indeed the adages (especially 'Festina lente' and 'Herculei labores' with their animal and floral emblemology) might make one think non-human nature was more significant (*The Adages of Erasmus: A Study with Translations* Margaret Mann Phillips [Cambridge 1964] 171–209). More than once, too, Erasmus recommends studying nature so that one may recognize its symbolism, for 'nature is not silent but speaks.' See especially *Colloquies* 48, 51, 310, 360, and the editor's note on 516, with its citing of the *Ratio verae theologiae* (LB V 805C–D) and the *Ecclesiastes* (LB V 825C–F, 866A–867B); also *De ratione studii* (LB I 527A–F). Still, his own most cogent and frequent figure is that of a human being standing in for a virtue or vice, or for a class of people; thus Joseph, he says, is the symbol for governance, Aaron for prayer, and Moses for knowledge (*Adages* 193, and *Enchiridion* 47), his Peace is a woman and twice she speaks of the human body's shape and texture as emblematic of peace; Folly is a woman too, and Vanity is her friend Philautia. In his *De ratione concionandi* he uses Abraham, Sara, the three guests, and the busy servants to illustrate what is meant by allegory (LB V 1031A–1038F).

taught his creatures through the fictional activity of classical myth and story.[22] What Erasmus says through these human symbols would, however, have nothing of the nature of *aenigma*, whether he explained it or not, for the human symbol, being of the same order as its tenor, operates through expansion rather than transference, and is more archetype than symbol. Anyone can see that Julius, for instance, a greedy man, is all greedy men, that Moria is more than a foolish woman – she is all foolish folk. The Silenus Box, on the other hand, is *not* of the same order as that for which it stands (man's double image), nor is the phoenix, nor the perfume in the porridge.

Symbolism, imagery, and fiction are effective leaven in any writing; and just as they raise any kind of prose to the level of poetry, so they raise criticism or denunciation to the level of satire. And all the embellishing figures have, as we have said, a kinship with irony in any case, a kinship recognized by rhetoricians throughout the ages, and by Erasmus himself.[23] A satiric

22 In the *Enchiridion* (p 50) he explicitly recommends knowledge of the classics as part of the armour of a Christian knight, and in a later chapter refers to St Augustine's appreciation of the Platonists and Pythagoreans, 'not only because they hold a great many views fully harmonious with our religion, but also because their very manner of using a language figurative, and, as I have said, appropriate to allegory, comes closer to the style of Holy Scriptures' (p 107). In the colloquy called 'The Godly Feast' Eusebius, an Erasmus-figure, says Cicero was inspired by God; about this colloquy, its editor, C.R. Thompson, comments that Erasmus, here as always, shows his conviction that 'the best that has been thought and said in pagan literature contributed far more to moral enlightenment than did the dreary dialectics of philosophers or most of the metaphysical speculations of modern theologians' ('Better Teachers than Scotus or Aquinas,' in *Mediaeval and Renaissance Studies* II [1966] 116. See also *Adages* 214, 230, 231, 356; and *De ratione studii* passim.).

23 *Rhetorica ad herennium* IV, xxxiv, 45–6 (Loeb edition, 345); Quintilian, *Institutio oratoria* IV 1, 39, and VI 2, 15. Geoffrey of Vinsauf, in his *Poetria nova* (ed. Sister Margaret Nims, Toronto 1967, lines 928ff), following both Cicero and Quintilian, gives as his example of *permutatio* (or allegory), a ridiculing example. Erasmus, in his *De ratione concionandi*, lists allegory as one mode of biblical interpretation and notes, as an *obiter dictum*, its ancient (non-exegetical) meaning: 'Allegoria Graecis dicta est, quod aliud dicitur, aliud intelligitur, quae ratio

scale of sorts might be predicated here: one may have a kind of satire without any irony at all but with some other literary figure – William Roy's *Rede Me and Bee Not Wroth* has already been noted; and one may have satire with irony and not much else: one can find an example of this in one of Erasmus' adages, which anathematizes a petty quarrel between a Franciscan (whom the author scorns) and a member of the Servite Order (whom he also scorns). He speaks of these Servites as being so called because 'as I understand ... they serve the Virgin Mary alone and have nothing to do with Christ or any other of the saints.' In the course of the narrative he goes on to call the Franciscan a 'devout and high-minded man ... filled with righteous indignation.'[24] And finally, one may have a more complex and satisfying satire wherein the ironic figures are implemented with all the others. Sometimes the process of expressing satiric dissatisfaction has so sanative or cathartic an effect on the writer that a mood of greater tranquillity issues from, and follows, the ironic one, as seems to be the case in *The Praise of Folly*; and sometimes a full poetic, with symbol and metaphor and other amplifying figures, runs tandem to the ironic tone, as, for instance, in the colloquy called 'The Well-to-do Beggars.'

The articulation of these concepts of ridicule and poetry has led to the probing of some notions more cognate to subject matter than style; and already it has become evident that, although Erasmus is much preoccupied with the folly that prevails, he is just as much concerned with the wisdom that does not.

Lest we lose sight of our *via media*, however, I should like to recapitulate and amplify what has been said of Erasmus' revitalizing of irony. One cannot, for instance, forget his interest in the

competit et in Ironia ...' In an earlier paragraph the connection between allegory and metaphor had been noted: 'Rhetores, ut ante diximus, Allegoriam definiunt perpetuam Metaphoram ...' (and the rest of the sentence had pointed out that exegetes have given the word a wider interpretation) (LB V 1034D and F).

24 From the adage 'Esernius cum Pacidiano' (*Adages* 304).

salebrosus Hieronymus,[25] which must have included delight in the saint's salty ironies. Nor can we shrug aside as youthful trifles the translations and imitations of Lucian made by More and himself. One critic, H.A. Mason, mulling over the exceeding popularity of the new translations of Lucian in the early sixteenth century, and burrowing into the whys and wherefores of this popularity, argues that, whatever the reasons, it was a true and right instinct that led More and Erasmus to Lucian, and not any inability to recognize his minor position in the rostrum of classical writers. Mason sees Lucian as becoming a sort of catalyst (for More and Erasmus, and through them, for other humanists) in the gradual movement towards a truer understanding of the spirit of the classics and of their diffusion within European letters. The two humanists found in Lucian – and Mason quotes More's letter (*Lucubrationes*, 273–6) to substantiate this – not only a rare and finely blended combination of wit and instruction, but abundant grist for the mills of Christian reflection.[26] Certainly that is true of what we find in Erasmus' borrowings: it is the ironic situation with its capacity for ironic dialogue he borrows, transferring into it a Christian content. Another critic, Martha Heep, points out that Erasmus sometimes borrows and uses, with little mutation, whole situations, sometimes deliberately and voluntarily, sometimes because the Lucianic formula was becoming so familiar to him. But, like Mason, Professor Heep sees the strongest similarity to be in the form and situation, not the content, so that even in the two Erasmian colloquies wherein the borrowing is most evident ('Charon' and 'The Imposture') the subject matter is of Christian Europe in the sixteenth century – an indictment of unscrupulousness in affairs of State and Church, and a ridiculing of charlatanry in language.[27]

25 Erasmus' great admiration for Jerome is everywhere evident. His calling him salty comes in a letter to Johann Eck (*Opus epistolarum Des. Erasmi Roterodami* P.S. Allen [ed] Oxford 1906–58 III 334). Subsequent references to Erasmus' correspondence will be designated by 'Allen' followed by volume and page number, and where possible bracketed into the text.
26 H.A. Mason *Humanism and Poetry in the Early Tudor Period* (London 1959) 60, 67–72
27 Martha Heep 'Die Colloquia Familiaria des Erasmus und Lucian'

And so, granting the Lucianic flavour and the ironic bite to much that Erasmus wrote, one must, I think, still say that not all of Erasmus' satire is Lucianic, nor always quite Jerome-like. He himself allocates Lucian's works among those which delight the spirit by being 'far from the truth,' and couples them with the arguments of ancient comedy, which 'please not by imitation of reality, but by allusions and allegories.'[28] But Erasmus does, for the most part, try to imitate reality and is sparing in the use of allegory. His most memorable characters, the Innkeeper, Fabulla, Nosoponus, Julius, Catherine, the Dominicans, are plain folk, recognizable, earthy, and particularized. Moria, allegorical enough in her inception, becomes an individual and real before her speech is well begun; the Lady Peace cannot hold her author's attention or interest, and he lets her shrivel and die; Charon and Alastor are unreal people in an unreal situation, but I venture to say that Erasmus is in better fettle when he puts real people, like Peter and Julius the Second, into the Christian parallel to that other-worldly situation. He is unlike Lucian, in any case, of course, because nothing of Christian faith or hope emerges from the Lucianic dialogues, whereas almost no satire of Erasmus' is quite without these qualities.

He himself said that the Praise of Folly, his most recognizably satiric work, attempted to say the same things the Enchiridion said – and the Enchiridion is an openly didactic work.[29] For such a

Hermaea xviii (1927) 28, 29. Miss Heep's sentence concluding what she had to say of 'The Imposture' is a significant generalization: 'So scheint mir gerade dieses Gesprach den Beweis zu liefern, dass Erasmus zwar unbedenklich bei Lucian entlehnt, wenn ihm etwas passt, dass er aber das Entnommene auf personliche Weise verarbeitet und daher von einer Nachahmung nur in beschranktem Sinn gesprochen werden darf.'

28 LB I 99F–100A; King and Rix translation 86–7
29 In a letter to Martin Dorp, who had censured the Praise, he says of it: 'In this respect I had exactly the same principles in the Praise of Folly as in my other works, although my method was different. In the Enchiridion I have a straightforward pattern for the Christian life ... In the Praise of Folly I did in a jesting fashion exactly what I had done in the Enchiridion. I wanted to admonish and not to carp; to do good, not harm; to have regard to men's character and not to be a stumbling block to it' (Allen ii 93).

man and such a purpose, to rely on only the devices of pagan literature would be out of character. Erasmus' irony may be a classical legacy; his other figures owe much to the Christian tradition, and especially to the patristic writings which had intervened between Lucian's day and his, writings he laboured long to restore and make available for Christendom.

The exegetical modes of interpreting Scripture have long since been the perquisite of the literary historian – since Dante's day at least; and of late, have been so well revived as to have become household words.[30] Erasmus' satire rarely lends itself, it is true,

30 Both in a letter to Can Grande della Scala and in the introduction to the *Convivio* (ed. Brusnelli and Vandelli [Florence 1934] 96–7), Dante explains his understanding of the senses and his own use of them. In the letter, which is the more explicit, he reflects that there are two kinds of allegory, that of the poets and that of theologians, and two kinds of so-called literal or historical meanings. Poets create, he notes, while theologians interpret what God has created. For poets then the historical sense is a fiction, the allegorical true. (Toynbee edition of the letter [Oxford 1920] 173). Pre-dating Dante, of course, there had been the counsels of St Augustine in Book III of the *De doctrina christiana*, and the many interpretations and elaborations of it through the early centuries, culminating in the twelfth-century *Didascalicon* of Hugh of St Victor.

Among scholars more recently interested in the modes of mediaeval exegesis are: Henri de Lubac *Exégèse médiévale: Les quatre sens de l'écriture* (Paris 1963); Walter Burghardt, 'Early Christian Exegesis,' in *Theological Studies* XI (1950) 78–116; Beryl Smalley *The Study of the Bible in the Middle Ages* (Oxford 1941); also her 'Stephen Langton and the Four Senses of Scripture' *Speculum* VI (1931) 60–75. Writing about the literary use of the scriptural senses are: R.P. Blackmur *The Expense of Greatness* (New York 1950); M.W. Bloomfield 'Symbolism in Mediaeval Literature' *Modern Philology* LVI (1958) 73–81; Helen Gardner *The Business of Criticism* (Oxford 1959); Bernard F. Huppé and D.W. Robertson, Jr *Fruyt and Chaf: Studies in Chaucer's Allegories* (Princeton 1963); W.F. Lynch *Christ and Apollo* (New York 1960) chapter 7 and supplement 4; Rosemond Tuve *Allegorical Imagery* (Princeton 1966); Ruth Wallerstein *Studies in Seventeenth-Century Poetic* (Madison, Wisc. 1950).

The idea of the historical sense resting in the fiction, and the allegorical being the true sense, is important in this study, since we are ultimately concerned with Erasmus' fiction. What Moria says at the rostrum, for instance, is only literally true within the illusion of the

to an obscure or recondite reading, and because of this, it is tempting to shrug aside any discussion of the exegetical modes acceptable to the mediaeval and early Renaissance writer. Two considerations, however, militate against such a by-passing. The first is that Erasmus himself has much to say on this topic, and although what he says is applied directly to scriptural readings, the general tenor of his attitude to teaching and writing is revealed in these comments. And the second is that, although he does not laminate his fiction in such a way as to permit uncovering obscure allegorical meanings, he does provide nourishment in these writings for all of Christian man's modes of thinking and acting and being. For these reasons I propose to consider the much-mooted levels of interpretation and especially what Erasmus himself has to say of them, explicitly and by implication. Two pieces of writing, in particular, offer the ransacking reader some illumination concerning both Erasmus' inclusiveness and his emphases: one of them is a work of instruction, the *De ratione concionandi*, or *Ecclesiastes* (*Liber* III); the other is one of the non-satiric colloquies, 'The Godly Feast.'

The idea of God's generation of things and his manipulation of them in order to communicate his teaching to man is as old as recorded religious history, and is indeed the coping stone of the whole system of levelled interpretation. It is the exegete's warrant not only for seeking the hidden and profound meanings in certain scriptural passages (the Book of God's revealed word), but also for his belief in the very obvious literal and historical facts recorded therein. It is also every man's sanction for seeing divine lessoning in the activities and people that touch him (the Book of nature – also revealed, though in another way). As words serve man, so events and things and people serve God as a mode of making ideas visible. St Paul had said so, as had many of the

fiction: there is no Moria, there is no auditory. It is the moral sense that is really true and intentionally so; sometimes this is found through an allegorical or figurative reading, more usually through expansion of the particular so that it applies not only to the fictional followers of Moria, but to all the readers of the book.

Fathers, up to and including St Augustine. Thomas Aquinas too had been very explicit, speaking of God's power not only to accommodate words to whatever is to be signified (for man himself can do as much), but to accommodate things and events themselves.[31]

This doctrine may have different emphases for different men: all Christians should be alert not only to the lessons of Scripture, but also to those of history and circumstance; the artist may imitate the creative act and thus share in it; the teacher (and Erasmus would have everyone a teacher) must awaken perceptiveness in others to recognize what is being taught in Scripture, in nature, and in art.[32]

Never a lover of excessively neat distinctions, Erasmus says (in the *De ratione concionandi*) that the older writers classified by using only two senses, the literal and the spiritual, 'which they called by various names – tropology, allegory, anagogy – but without much distinguishing between them' (LB V 1034E). It is the new breed, he says, the *recentiores*, or *neoterici*, who have codified and catalogued so that we must now distinguish four senses. Erasmus does not quote, though he must have known it, the familiar couplet:

> Littera gesta docet, quid credas Allegoria,
> Moralis quid agas, quo tendas Anagogia,[33]

nor does his explanation of the senses quite match the ditty's. In any case, he damns with faint praise any over-nicety about the

31 'in cujus potestate est non solum voces ad significandum accommodet (quod etiam homo facere potest) sed etiam res ipsas.' *Summa theologica* I q 1, a 10
32 St Augustine, to whose *De doctrina christiana* Erasmus is often indebted, also distinguishes between the role of the interpreter and that of the teacher. Eloquence, he says, is not to be used for ascertaining the meaning but for setting it forth once it has been ascertained. Perspicuity is the great essential of style, and the prime requisite for instruction, 'though other qualities are required for delighting and persuading the reader' (translation by John J. Gavigan OSA, from the series *Fathers of the Church: Writings of St Augustine* IV (New York 1947) Book II cap. 7, and IV foreword and cap. 10.
33 *Patrologia Latina* J.-P. Migne (ed) CXIII col. 28. The couplet did not

words one applies to the various readings.[34] The early Fathers
had easily interchanged the names, and Paul himself had not
been over-precise in his use of the term 'allegory.'[35] And not only
is early tradition against such distinctions but the very logic of
semantics too, for all non-literal ways of interpreting have names
capable of similar definition. He had already noted that metaphor was the fountainhead of all the tropes; now he recapitu-
lates by pointing out how closely related are the three non-
literal ways of interpreting (LB V 1034F–7035A). Yet, for the sake
of those whose teaching requires them to use the precise terms,
he undertakes to supply both definitions and a carefully worked
out paradigm for each. Tropology is the mode, he says, that,
keeping always close to the literal, applies the scriptures to the
morals to be taught; allegory accommodates the text to Christ
and the Church Militant;[36] anagogy transports one from here to
the Church Triumphant, out of the body up to the summit, the
Trinity, beyond which there is nothing further.

originate with Nicholas of Lyra, though it is often attributed to him.
It is given succinct explanation by W. Burghardt in the article referred
to above, and in Henri de Lubac, 'Sur un vieux distique: la doctrine du
"quadruple sens",' in Mélanges offerts au R.P. Cavallera (Toulouse
1948), as also in the introduction to his Exégèse médievale. See also
Rosemond Tuve, Allegorical Imagery 45 n20. Erasmus himself makes
ironic comment on Nicholas in the adage 'The Sileni of Alcibiades'
(Adages 283), but does not refer to the couplet.

34 His indifference to naming the various readings does not mean he disparaged the readings themselves, provided, as he says, they do not strain
the common sense. Professor Roland Bainton notes that even the usual
four senses are too few for Erasmus, who would allow a proliferation
of tongues or interpretations, as many as there are serious readers
(Erasmus of Christendom [New York 1969] 141–2). And Professor C.R.
Thompson notes that Erasmus is running true to form in 'The Godly
Feast,' inasmuch as his dinner guests refer now and then to the early
exegetes, but never to the mediaeval ones, although he was 'familiar
with these, as his notes to the New Testament show ...' ('Better Teachers
than Scotus or Aquinas,' in Mediaeval and Renaissance Studies II [1966]
138).

35 St Paul had spoken of allegory (in Galatians 4) when the New Jerusalem
or the Church Triumphant is symbolized in Sara; the recentiores, one
supposes, would have called this anagogy.

36 In the illustration he submits, this seems to be what exegetes now call
typology.

Amplificandum est! The story of Abraham's entertaining of the heavenly guests is used as illustration of the four modes. To show the literal meaning the text is paraphrased; then, as moral lessoning, Erasmus comments on the three social virtues evidenced: simplicity, hospitality, good order in the home. As we might expect, the moral level is the one most abundantly amplified. In the few paragraphs devoted to the allegorical interpretation, Erasmus follows his own definition (and the couplet's) precisely, making the story yield a message about Christ and the Church Militant. Abraham here becomes more than the kind host whose hospitality one might imitate: he is now the Church receiving Christ as guest, sacrificing to Him the best and rarest fruits of the earth.[37]

Under the heading of anagogy, Erasmus is again jejune, and the commentary occupies only a fraction of one column. Nor does this part advance very far, one thinks, into the *quo tendas* of man's questing spirit. Abraham not only recognizes the divine in the three visitors but, together with the exegete, he recognizes that the three are one: and Erasmus probes the intricacies of the syntax to show that verbs and adjectives are now singular, now plural, and from this argues Abraham's — or the inspired writer's — recognition of the Trinity of Persons in one Nature.[38] To the simple vision of God, however, Erasmus returns in the end, and

37 This kind of allegory Erasmus sees as a mixture of allegory and tropology, for the elements in it may be redisposed so that the tender calf is Christ Himself sacrificed for man — and so, one supposes, man is taught to love and honour the redemptive act; and the three cakes eaten by the three guests, but not by the Jews, configure the Trinity, recognized only by the Christian to whom revelation has come so that he is no longer under the veil of Moses. Perhaps the lesson is to value the gift of revealed truth and the consequent freedom to interpret the law according to the spirit. But Erasmus does not make very clear why he thinks this part *mixta*. Certainly he provides two distinct allegories, the latter *sublimior*, but the tropology seems capable of being fitted into, or excluded from, both or either of them.

38 He singles out these phrases and suffixes: in oculis *tuis*. ... laventur pedes *vestri* ... ad *te* ... dixit ... potero ... scio; and finally (in the pleading for Sodom) numquid per*des* ... (LB V 1037C; italics limited to the significant word or suffix).

on this good anagogical note almost closes the paragraph. Almost, not quite: for he must reiterate his initial conviction: 'But about terminology we will not be anxious; it is the thing that matters.'

The thing that matters most to Erasmus is the moral sense. And he is at his best when he speaks of this. His insight into Abraham's treatment of the guests is penetrating and sensitive, and the lessons on true hospitality are easily applicable to his contemporaries.[39] In this part too he commends and recommends the older exegetes, especially Origen and Chrysostom, who, like himself, consider this mode the most useful. To support his own conviction he cites Chrysostom, who preferred to stress the sober certainties, since this way is more immediately useful in teaching morals, moves men more effectively, is understood by, and pertinent to, all men, and finally is heard with greater faith than are the allegories and anagogies discovered by the ingenuities of an interpreter, which may be 'in a sense arbitrary, and thus of no value in strengthening the dogmas of one's faith' (LB V 1036E).

Erasmus' unfolding of the moral level does not so limit itself to ethical practicalities as to exclude the *quid credas* of allegory or even the higher sublimities. Abraham recognizes the supernatural in his guests, he prays for Sodom; he is given a son by the God who will not be outdone in generosity – *pro vitulo filium accepit!* And Erasmus sees Chrysostom's moral reading as deepening not just the morals of the people but their faith. Indeed, for Erasmus, all morality seems to be fused with religious belief and dependent on it for sanctions, as conversely, all faith is evident in the good life.

Erasmus concludes this part with a sentence that again shrugs

---

39 As a citizen of Christendom, Erasmus was to some extent a homeless man, and thus dependent on hospitality, which is, therefore, to him a virtue of great excellence. Here, for instance, he speaks of a man's delight in talking long at the dinner table without fear of his wife's showing resentment, as did Xanthippe, Socrates' wife (mentioned also in 'The Godly Feast'); and of the sensitivity of the host who respects his guests' desire to leave at a fixed time, and does not detain them with idle gestures – even to pressing on them the inevitable 'one for the road.'

aside terminology, praises this kind of interpretation, and undercuts to some extent the other kinds even before he comes to the
point of explaining them.[40]

This emphasis on the moral lesson, so evident here (as it is to
be evident in all the fictional works) is perhaps doubly activated.
Erasmus considers the substance of the non-literal modes less
universally acceptable and less necessary for good living; and
the manner of ascertaining what such substance is is not quite
verifiable. The moral sense he values supremely because he is by
nature and experience a moralist and teacher. Good living and
firm faith are inseparables for him, but the first is the guarantee
of the latter. Too often perhaps he had seen that a species of
pseudo-godliness was apparent in an unprincipled man, and that
godliness unbuttressed by the strengths of disciplined and un-
selfish living could go soft or superstitious or even greedy. Julius
was a case in point, or the Dominicans who devaluated Reuchlin,
or the superstitious mariners in Adolph's tale of shipwreck.[41]

This same preference can be easily seen in his fictional works
where he is concerned with what people do and think, especially
what they think about what they do. It is true that Moria's praise
of fools seems eventually to be moved by faith and love and the
hope of things to come – the beatitude of the anagogical readings.[42] But this entry into the transports of divine love comes not
by way of an allegorical or symbolic reading of what otherwise
has been interpreted more simply: it follows the other parts and
is lucidly, unmistakably clear. And this is Erasmus' way. He

40 'If we accept the distinctions of the modern exegetes, these things can
be regarded as tropology, adhering as they do pretty closely to the literal
meaning, yet for all that providing no less pleasure than usefulness,
pouring into the minds of the unlearned examples of devout men whose
actions the scriptures commend' (LB V 1036D).
41 Examples from *Julius secundus exclusus* 'The Apotheosis of Reuchlin,'
and 'The Shipwreck' (*Colloquies* 81–6 and 139–46)
42 A beatitude, one might venture, more inspiring than the *beatitudo
Ecclesiae triumphantis* of the *De ratione concionandi*, which, though
theologically sound, seems to make heaven not much more than an
extension of this world.

values the things that are *sublimior* and 'beyond which Scripture cannot penetrate,' but he likes to present them without obscurity. For all man's cravings the nourishment is provided: a story for his imaginative self, a moral lesson for the moral man, the life of faith within a divinely constituted Church for the Christian man, and the yearning for things to come for the pilgrim to eternity – but with a simplicity of presentation that will not lend itself to false readings. And all this is at least partially explained by considering these same convictions as they are applied to the reading of scripture and the preaching of the word of God.

The *Praise* is not unique in its providing of imaginative energy, moral lessons, and spiritual sustenance, nor in its giving predominance to the moral teaching. Most of the satiric colloquies, perhaps because of their original purpose, emphasize the moral life rather than the spiritual, but it is a moral life fitted to the demands and sanctions of a Christendom more than a little conscious of its religious values; the *Ciceronianus*, which begins by exploding the vanities of literary artifice, moves very soon into deeper reflections on sincerity and right reason, and comes in the end to be an exhortation to make the truth of religion properly articulate; *Julius* too is generous in its offerings: the errant pope is *exclusus*, of course, and in some sense the reader too, for he is never permitted to see over Peter's adamant shoulder into the glory that Julius cannot quite gain. But one is made well aware that if Julius' *quo* on earth had been a question more insistently asked, the *ubi* might have been happier.

The other reason for his preferences Erasmus also provides in this tract on homiletics. Not only is the substance of the recondite meanings less satisfying, but the mode of establishing it is often unreliable. He urges the preacher to choose and use his texts carefully, 'lest in any way the true sense of the scripture be distorted' (LB v 1027A). It is all too easy, he says, to torture scripture to our own purpose, and he gives a telling illustration of an ingenious allegory's violation of both the sense of the text and the logic of its parts. A forceful enunciation of principle follows: allegory that does not bear out the proper (*rectus*) sense of the text is faulty (LB V 1027D).[43] Yet extreme literalism is also to be censured, and ludicrous examples are presented of those who, excluding tropes and allegories altogether from Scripture, make of the law, which St Paul calls spiritual, something carnal. This 'judaism' is an extreme just as flawed as that of the exegetes who reject the literal sense without necessity, and subverting the very strength and basic meaning of the Bible, offer what may be only human, not divine.[44]

If the learned scholar then may so easily mishandle the re-vealed word of God when he mines it for recondite meanings, how much the more easily may the common reader fail to find the true import of the humanly creative word, even the satiric word, if the writer fails to make quite clear what the *sensus rectus* is. And so Erasmus prefers fable to allegory, simile to metaphor, and archetype to symbol; the archetype need only be expanded to universal stature, but the symbol may need to be transferred to something of another order of being; it is for God the Creator and Artist to clothe the earth in symbols and allegories; less dar-ing is Erasmus the teacher.

Thus, in a treatise openly didactic, Erasmus offers his theories of communication and of teaching. In 'The Godly Feast,' a fic-tional colloquy, he touches on the same ideas, but with the artis-

43 A fuller generalization comes a few sentences further on: 'That way is best, if one can manage to achieve it, that does not turn from the true understanding of the Scriptures. Thus, when various interpretations of the same passage are found, you should not seize on the one best suited to the exigencies of your present thesis, but on that which is in your judgement the true one' (LB V 1028C).

44 The Anthopomorphites are cited, for instance, who make the Almighty too human, subject to whims and fancies and changes of mind; and the Euchitians, who use the injunction to pray without ceasing as warrant for idling through their days, muttering an endless number of psalms; the Chiliastes, who find in the word of God an imperative for unreason-able fasting and girding of limbs, even for carrying at all times a small wooden cross in the hand. A censorious word is found too for those who are, as John Donne would say, 'hungry of an imagined martyrdom,' deliberately provoking civil authority and asking for trouble; and for those who 'hate mother and father' so literally as to take the text as mandate for leaving parents destitute in order to answer a questionable call to desert or monastery.

try of a creative writer. In this long dialogue, published in the 1522 editions of the colloquies,[45] seven men, devout and literate laymen, are luncheon guests at the country home of one Eusebius, and there find in the house, the gardens, frescoes, statuary, food, and scriptural readings ample food for reflection. The reflections show the ability of these men to see the symbolic and emblematic in all aspects of life, for 'nature is not silent,' nor is artefact. The garden proclaims the bounty of God, the fountain symbolizes the heavenly stream that refreshes the soul thirsting for God, guests wash their hands before the meal and are thus reminded of the Last Supper and the cleansing of heart and mind, the gold inlay on a book symbolizes the wisdom of its pages, and so on. But this is not an allegorical or symbolic colloquy; it is a colloquy about eight men who see and explain the emblems and symbols of nature and circumstance.

One might, of course, consider whether or not Erasmus means the whole colloquy to be read as an allegory of the well-disposed soul's relation with certain qualities suggested by the names of the speakers, with love of God and fear of the Lord, with godly counsel and the prudent love of moderation.[46] And one might say that surely at least the inner court is the garden enclosed of the soul consumed with the love of God. But one encounters difficulties in such a reading. In the inner garden, for instance, we find fragrant flowers, choice herbs and a fountain, all appropriately ordered in it; but not so appropriate is the talk of the fine economy of the irrigating waters which drain off the refuse, *after* delighting the soul, thus putting the purgative moment (if it is that) after the unitive. Then too this fountain is compared (unfavourably) with the 'fountain of Sacred Scripture' as if it were no more than a simple artefact; and the marble that turns out to be not pure marble but painted cement, a cheaper substitute, is well suited to the moral lesson of non-extravagance, but

45 Froben brought out two editions of the colloquies in 1522. The earlier one contained only the introductory part; the whole as we now have it was first published in the later edition.
46 Theophilus, Timothy, Theodidactus, Sophronius, and Chrysoglottus are some of the names.

not very well suited to the idea of the inner sanctuary of the pure soul.

And Erasmus might well say that that is just the point: the reader, allowed to puzzle out a hidden meaning, is too often uncertain. Indeed, in this very colloquy, in one of the rare instances of his using a symbol without explaining it, he points this up. In one of the pictures the 'painter has made the water wonderfully clear' so that amphibians swimming therein are easily seen, and Eusebius explains: 'He *had to* [paint it thus] or we should have needed other eyes' (p 55; italics mine).

This colloquy, not satiric and, therefore, not surveyed in the chapter on the colloquies, is nevertheless greatly relevant to this study, inasmuch as it is a compendium of almost all Erasmus' theories and preferences. His conviction that the Christ-life shows itself most clearly in charity and especially in the social virtues is seen all through the fictional works, but nowhere more convincingly than in his portrayal of Eusebius, the perfect host, sensitive to the wants of each guest, graciously and modestly indicating the points of interest in his house and on his estate, gently controlling the conversation so that each one is drawn out, and giving each one the greatest compliment: his intelligent and appreciative comment. Eusebius has Erasmus' ironic mind too and can be playful: his wife, whom he loves (from subsequent comments, we know this), is not present at this stag dinner, of course, and he explains her absence in a joking way, saying he fears she might be like Socrates' wife, unsympathetic to philosophical talk and ready to upset the table in anger. He is fond of a paradox, and notes the pictured scorpion as a poisoner poisoned, and the polypus as a captor captured; reflections on celibacy are brought to a close by some airy persiflage about the fowl he is serving, who had 'long lived celibate, yet is not of the company of the blessed.' Like Erasmus too, this genial host loves a tidy aphorism that encapsulates a longer wisdom: under one of the gallery's frescoes depicting the life of Christ, the caption 'I will: be thou clean' summarizes, he says, the whole story.

Erasmus' love of moderation is seen in this colloquy too. Timothy points out that the Lord had said 'Seek ye first ...' not 'seek ye only ...' the kingdom of God, and that care for material goods is thus not condemned but only disciplined; some half-dozen pictures on the dining room walls warn us, Eusebius says, to be temperate at feasts. And when Timothy, exulting in the feast of spiritual delights, proclaims his willingness to forgo all bodily nourishment for spiritual banquetting, Eusebius counters:

> Rather let us learn from Paul both to abound and to suffer hunger. When there is lack, let us thank Jesus Christ for supplying us with means of self-control and patience; when there is plenty, we should thank the generosity of him who freely invites us. ... Enjoying in moderation what the divine goodness has provided, we ought to be mindful of the poor ... [69]

Although here, as in all Erasmus' writings, the emphasis is on practical Christian charity and sound principles of behaviour, the various modes of interpretation come into play as the scripture readings draw out the discussion. A boy of the household reads a passage from Proverbs 21: 1–3:

> The King's heart is in the hand of the Lord, as the rivers of water: he turneth it whithersoever he will. Every way of a man is right in his own eyes; but the Lord pondereth the hearts. To do justice and judgement is more acceptable to the Lord than sacrifice.

Eusebius himself interprets it according to the moral sense; in the course of his talk we note Erasmus' own tenets about the rights (divine and otherwise) and the responsibilities of the king; strongly Erasmian too are the views Eusebius advances about the power of education and prayer in the moulding of the royal (or other) disposition. Timothy finds a deeper or more arcane meaning and sees the king's heart as that of the perfect man, freed in some measure from the laws that govern the less perfect. This is allegory of a kind, perhaps *mixta tropologia*, and not quite the *allegoria* of Erasmus' definition. The *quid credas* is presented later, however, by Theophilus's interpretation of justice and judgment as more acceptable to the Lord than sacrifice. Strangely enough the anagogical *quo* (though it is present by implication all through) is given explicit consideration only in the interchange of opinions about Socrates and the other good pagans who must surely have attained to final glory and be now with the saints of the Church.[47]

One of the most significant exchanges in this dialogue – at least for our purposes – is that one which concerns the value of creative art. In this case it is the art of painting and sculpture that focuses the talk, but what Eusebius and Timothy say of this can be easily transferred to the modes of literature. About the frescoes decorating the walls of the galleries above the inner court, Timothy has some reservations:

TIMOTHY: Wasn't so neat and trim a garden good enough for you unless you painted other ones besides?

EUSEBIUS: One garden wasn't enough to hold all kinds of plants. Moreover, we are twice pleased when we see a painted flower competing with a real one. In one we admire the cleverness of Nature, in the other the inventiveness of the painter; in each the goodness of God, who gives all these things for our use and is equally wonderful and kind in everything. Finally, a garden isn't always green, nor flowers always blooming. This garden grows and pleases even in midwinter.

TIMOTHY: Yet it doesn't breathe.

EUSEBIUS: But on the other hand it needs no attention.

TIMOTHY: It pleases only the eyes.

EUSEBIUS: True, but it does that forever.

TIMOTHY: A picture, too, grows old.

EUSEBIUS: Yes, but it's longer-lived than we are, and age commonly adds to it a grace we lose. [137]

47 It is in this colloquy that the famous phrase *Sancte Socrates* appears. If this seems a daringly ecumenical canonization for a sixteenth-century writer, it must be remembered that the author of *Piers Plowman* has Trajan speak to the poet, saying that, pagan as he had been, and initially condemned to hell, St Gregory's tears, prompted by his knowledge of Trajan's many acts of justice and mercy, have released him from eternal punishment (W.W. Skeat edition, London 1886; B-text, passus xi, 1, 136ff; and C-text, passus xiii, 1, 74–87). A prime source for this advanced thinking is Paul the Deacon's *S. Gregorii magni vita* cap. 27 (PL 75, 56–7); and another, almost contemporary work, John Damascene's *De his qui in fide dormierunt* (PG 95, 262–3). See also James of Voragine's *Legenda aurea*.

Thus Eusebius (and Erasmus) proffer three recommendations for man-made beauty: 1/ it proclaims the glory of God no less than does nature, for God made the maker of it; 2/ it is constant and enduring; and 3/ once in being, it needs no sustaining care.

All Erasmus' colloquies, this one especially, proclaim the glory of God not only by being works of art but by being consciously directed to this end; and 'The Godly Feast' has been one of the most enduring colloquies, eliciting appreciative comment right up to the present;[48] my treatment of it has not been in the nature of any 'sustaining care'; I have simply found it rewarding in its presentation of Erasmian preoccupations, and delightful in the presenting of them.

His role of teacher Erasmus never forgets. If man needs to be perceptive in order to rightly read the scriptures, still more does he need to be able to read life wisely. For revelation is a constant as well as a piece of history. Scripture and the Incarnation teach man the divine plan of life, but nature and the things of every day have their meaning too. Erasmus had pointed to the tree of Mambra as being not only a tree but also a sign of vision, first a thing, then a sign; he had noted the choice of the best calf as first a simple action, then a type of hospitality, then a sign of the supreme deserts of God. Here the teaching was exegetical, but Erasmus does the same thing as a writer of fiction: he points out that things and actions – clothes, for instance, or the making of pilgrimages – are signs as well as things and activities, and that the sign-value must be recognized and studied. It is no simple equation, however. Erasmus' concern reaches out beyond the mere recognition of sign to the propriety of the sign and the validity of the thing signified, and he excoriates the retention of any sign whose meaning is withered. For him the greater part of morality is concentrated in such things, and the man of great percipience

48 One of the most recent is Professors John Meagher's and Richard Schoeck's 'On Erasmus' "The Godly Feast,"' in *Erasmus in English* 1:3 (1971) 10–12. This is a witty and informative dialogue between these two professors, 'conducted by mail between Toronto and Washington in the summer of 1970: a procedure which might well have both pleased and amused Erasmus ...'

(and with a modicum of good will) cannot but be a man of Christian morality. Even sins of pride he sees as violations of reason; and for those of passion he has (at least as satirist) only a passing concern, for these are transgressions that do not yield to the rationale of satire. Thus it comes about that often enough the substance of what he tells so unsymbolically is concerned with the use and misuse of the symbols of life and nature and the Church.

One might hazard a guess that this preoccupation with men and events as being the alphabet of divine communication derives from Erasmus' frequent reading of Augustine,[49] whose *De doctrina christiana* had long since christened the Ciceronian reflections on things and signs, bending them to the exigencies of Christian homiletics and teaching. All teaching, says St Augustine, is a matter of either signs or things, a dictum redolent enough of Cicero, and one which Erasmus must surely have had in mind as he began his *De ratione studii*. Although the *De doctrina* is ultimately, and primarily, concerned with words (the only 'things' whose unique value is as 'sign'), his introductory chapters articulate a general theory of things and signs, and present some considerations about things, which he subdivides into things that are ends in themselves and thus lovable, and those that are means to an end, and so merely usable. St Augustine modified the Ciceronian ordering here so that the end is always the Christian life of the Spirit, and the means comprises all that is used in the progress thereto. This categorizing of things is not irrelevant to the analy-

49 In a somewhat acrimonious letter to Johann Eck, Erasmus scoffs at Eck's impugning his knowledge of Augustine. If he had belittled only his understanding of him, Erasmus complains, it might have been excusable, but to doubt his having read the Augustine canon is nonsense. He points out that in his more than fifty years he has always been a disciple of the older theologians, that he had read through the canon in his early days, that he has been citing the texts of Augustine almost daily ever since, whenever the work in hand demanded it, that there is hardly a work of Augustine's which he has not mined for texts to substantiate his own expressed convictions, or for commonplaces; and finally that the more he reads of Augustine, the more he appreciates his worth (Allen III 335).

sis of Erasmus' satire, as we shall see. But it is his treatment of the sign that is still more significant.

If we consider this theory of words and things, eternal and changeless on the one hand, temporal and mutable on the other, in conjunction with the accepted view of Scripture as not just an allegorical account of ethical ideas but a true account of things divinely made to happen with a moral and persuasive purpose, we come easily enough to the further consideration that things may be useful to interpret signs, as well as signs to interpret things. Thus used, the thing is a logical and organic symbol. The calf, for instance, in the story of Abraham and his guests, was (with no detriment to its real calf-quality) the measure of Abraham's generosity and even the prefiguring of the sacrificed Son of God; and the story itself was not simply an inspired fable, but rather a piece of history guided into being by the Author of all things so that its lesson might be revealed by such people as the writer of Genesis, and Erasmus, his interpreter.

Similarly, when Erasmus tells the story of a worldly pope seeking admission to heaven, there is a humanly dramatic quality to the story, and through humanly real symbols the moral is conveyed. But Julius is a 'thing' interpreting a concept or sign, a thing before he is a symbol; and when this thing is seen as a natural symbol of materialism, we have an example of a thing being useful to interpret a sign. Erasmus is using his imagined figure as God had used Abraham, guiding him into being, providing him with dialogue and situation and action, for moral and spiritual purposes.

These are the organic signs, surely, of Augustine's predilection, springing directly from thought. Such symbols need not, of course, be human beings. Erasmus' usually are, but other orders of being serve also: the shadows in the cave, the vestments of a prelate, the sign on the inn door, a fetid weed. All of these are things mutable and temporal, but signs too of things changeless and eternal.

As a man of letters Erasmus chooses the precise things that will signify his purpose and he delights to give them life and energy; as a moralist he is concerned that his readers recognize these signs and all signs for what they are. So Julius, for instance, is created to stand as sign for certain things; and one certain thing he stands for is, paradoxically, the proud prelate's inability, or reluctance, to see in his own vesture the sign of his tremendous predilection and responsibility; and thus poor Julius, dull and damned, teaches the reader two ways: by being himself a sign, and by talking and so revealing his own attitude (or lack of attitude) to things and signs. Many of the follies and vices Erasmus decries stem from this reluctance to see – a form of *acedia*. A monk is reputed to have had a holy death because he had clutched in his dying hand a fold of his habit, though what the cowl and cincture stood for had been long forgotten; a husband and father makes a pilgrimage of idle thanksgiving for safe journey, neglecting home and family to do so; an imitator of Cicero will use no phrase that his eloquent exemplar had not used, though the essence of true eloquence is lost in the slavish mimicry. These are the things that drive Erasmus to the whips and scorns of satire: the failure of man to understand significance, and consequent upon this, the failure of significance itself.

In his relation to eloquence, the Christian writer may fail in two ways, by neglecting eloquence or by overstraining it. He may neglect it altogether, leaving truth 'unarmed' against a false position defended 'briefly, explicitly and plausibly.' These are Augustine's words, but Erasmus might have written them. He does, indeed, say much the same thing often – for instance, in the *Antibarbari*, the *De ratione studii*, and the early columns of the *De ratione concionandi*.[50] Eloquence, Augustine had said, must

50 *Antibarbari* LB X 1753E–1734C; *De ratione studii* LB I 523 B and F;
De ratione concionandi LB V 900A–C; indeed, the last-named presents
a full explanation and illustrations aplenty (throughout the work, but
especially in the columns mentioned above) of proper classical rhetorical
procedures of structure and style, not for any mere civic orator, but for
the preacher or teacher of God's word. One might refer too to the letter to Eck, quoted above (Allen III 335–6), in which he admits, after the
long eulogy of Augustine, that he would nonetheless rank him beneath
St Jerome, whose knowledge of both Greek and Roman languages and
literatures makes him the more perfect Christian exegete. He says much

go hand in hand with wisdom and goodness – Cicero's orator had had to be a *vir bonus* as well as *dicendi peritus* – and the serious Christian writer or preacher, however pure his intentions may be, must not shoulder aside the rules of rhetoric. Augustine suggests that he study them rather from the examples of good Christian writing than from the rule-books, so that he learn by imitation rather than rote. Perhaps Erasmus would give only partial agreement to this, preferring the writer to learn both by precept and by example: one cannot forget his strictures (in the *De ratione studii*) about the unwisdom of putting *exercitatio* before *ratio*.[51]

The second way in which Christian instruction may fail, Augustine thinks, is by overdependence on eloquence. Divine grace and a profound knowledge of the scriptures must aid in the finding of the right kind of eloquence (II 10). Even when the Christian speaks from the abundance of his heart, so one with his message that he has no conscious thought for the manner of

the same thing in a letter to Dorp, praising Jerome, Origen, and Augustine for their study of language and letters, which have been, as St Augustine says, 'so useful in explaining Sacred Scripture' (Allen II 113). The *De conscribendis* presents too some long paragraphs urging the study of humane letters as the proper pursuit of the good Christian gentleman (LB I 348D–E).

51 'Natura rationem desiderat, exercitatio nisi ratione gubernetur multis periculis atque erroribus est obnoxia' (LB I 497A). Erasmus, however, following Quintilian (II 5), does not want the boy student (and still less, one supposes, the writer of sermons or satires) to spend long hours memorizing rules of grammar or rhetoric, but would have him, after a moderate period of such study, complete his training by immersing himself in the best examples of such writing (*De ratione studii* LB I 521B–C).
Pursuing this point, we might note that he says of Colet that he 'could not endure that the faculty of speaking correctly should be sought from the trivial rules of grammarians. For he insisted that these were a hindrance to expressing oneself well and that the best result was obtained only by the study of the best authors.' But Erasmus will not condone Colet's rejection of the rules, and thinks Colet 'paid the penalty' for this indifferent scholarship by having to submit to much criticism in this regard and so being reluctant to commit to print his very fine (and otherwise scholarly) thoughts (Allen IV 523; the letter is translated by John C. Olin, in *Christian Humanism and the Reformation* [New York 1965] 187).

his speaking, he finds often enough that his words are in accord with the recommended rules. St Paul is instanced as a splendid example of this natural decorum, and one of Cyprian's works (a letter to Donatus) is slated for mild censure because, Augustine says, it is too overblown with ornament to carry a sober religious message.

Purpose is ultimately the determining factor in judging the quantity and kind of ornament. Augustine speaks of three styles, the low, used for teaching, and largely unornamented, the middle, for delight, and so involving ornament within limits, and the grand or high style for sublime matter and persuasive purpose. This last is the one to be used in handling the things of God. One critic says of this kind of writing that it

> springs from the mind's spontaneous and unconscious activity upon the elements of experience, and thence arises its abundant imagery, for the modes of logic, the topics and tropes of oratory and rhetoric are but explications of the mind's natural working.[52]

If ornament is thus spontaneous and organic to the subject matter, it is a part of persuasion and fit for high purpose, but studied ornament has almost no place in such writing. For the religious writer – and Erasmus is almost always in some sense a religious writer – natural symbols and allegory, already in creation even more than already in Scripture, become part of the matter, God revealing himself to his creatures either in the words he has inspired or the things he creates.

Erasmus himself would have no part with ornament that smacked of affectation. He drives his arguments to conclusion by examples and pithy summarizing statements: he tells a little story, refers to an old myth or proverb, presents an imagined character in an imagined situation and lets him talk. In his adage 'Herculei Labores' he expresses his astonishment that anyone could demand eloquence 'in a work entirely directed to teaching, and to teaching things like these ... so tiny, so humble that not

---

52 Ruth Wallerstein *Studies in Seventeenth-Century Poetic* (Madison, Wisc. 1950) 26

only do they not attract ornaments of speech and fluent writing but they repel everything of the sort' (*Adages*, 203). The particular dismay is expanded then, and Erasmus goes on:

> Tully does not require eloquence from a philosopher, and is anyone going to ask it from a proverb-writer? Seneca never recommends it except when it comes easily or is there of its own accord, so as to treat great subjects in a great manner, and if I were to pretend to the paraphernalia of the Rhetors would it not be a case for quoting the proverb about 'Perfume in the pease-porridge'?
>
> For myself, though I don't despise eloquence in other people, I have never much sought it in my own case, preferring, I don't know why, a sensible style to a highly coloured one, as long as it was not vulgar, and really expressed my thought ...
>
> Indeed, as Cicero says, richness of style must dry up if there is the slightest interruption; if the matter in hand really called for flowers of rhetoric, I had no time for them. And time would always be short for so much looking up, commenting, and memorizing. Although I think that the achievement of expressing these things in not ill-chosen words will seem to be part of eloquence in itself, to anyone who knows what it is. I say nothing of those people (I might call them the apes of eloquence) who judge the art of speaking by a childish jingle of words, and when they have (by dint of many days' toil) interwoven a few flowers of speech into their writings, and scattered over four phrases from Cicero and as many from Sallust, think they have reached the peak of Roman eloquence. They don't think much of the style of St Jerome, they recoil from Prudentius, anything seems inelegant, dumb and stuttering to them unless it holds those four bits of Cicero. If these people ever experienced what it is to chase apparent trifles like these through books, they would perhaps recognise their own lack of fluency and be less impudent in scorning the eloquence of others.[53]

---

53 In the paragraph which follows this one, however, Erasmus seems to weaken his point by conceding that, perhaps, had there been time, he would have provided for the adages more enrichment of language.

Again, in a letter to a Portuguese nobleman, Damian de Goes, he admits his own tendency to extemporize and his reluctance to revise, but in part excuses himself for this, saying:

> the famed beauties of Cicero's style are not suited to the needs of those who are connected with the conduct of education or involved in the business of the Church. ... Religious topics call in fact for an austere kind of style ...[54]

This, it may be objected, is what Erasmus says of the style to be used in teaching and preaching, not what he says of satire's style. But there seems little doubt that Erasmus' satires are often a form of preaching and always geared to education. The *Praise* he likened to the *Enchiridion*, a work of teaching and exhortation; the colloquies were to be used in the classroom; *Julius* is poised between heaven and hell and becomes in places a disquisition on Christian values and choice; the *Ciceronianus* begins by preaching scholarly sincerity and ends by pointing to the great truths of Christian living.

If Erasmus could say, as he does, that he is inclined to extemporize and write in haste, it is with no diffident self-blame that he says so. In the letter quoted above, in the adage quoted, and in the *Ciceronianus*, he admits the characteristic but sees it as suited to the exigencies of his subject matter. In the *Ciceronianus*, for instance, he makes ironic reference to himself as one who 'hurries along, writing a whole volume at a sitting,' and using 'theological words and even vulgarisms,' but one never finds him apologizing: the kind of writing he does abominate is something quite different. Long before, he had formed his habits of thinking and writing, absorbing the prescriptions and the illustrations of Cicero, Quintilian, Jerome, Augustine, and others, so that they were a part of him, controlling his mode of writing without direct advertence. Over-elaboration is distasteful to him, as is anything ornate or affected; the scriptures, old tales, proverbs, and the

---

54 Allen XI 207; trans. by D.F.S. Thomson, in 'The Latinity of Erasmus,' in *Erasmus* T.A. Dorey (ed) (London 1970) 120

prodigal forms of nature provide him with the colours of rhetoric and keep all that he writes lively and intelligible; the writing is rarely abstruse, for its metaphors and symbols either spring so naturally from the thought as to be easily understood or are accompanied with a word of guidance, for clarity is the prime rule of teaching, or preaching, or even of making satires; succinctly he says so in the *De ratione concionandi*: 'concionator frustra auditur si non intelligitur' (LB V 957E).

The quality of a satire bespeaks the satirist's attitude; and the relation between satirist and victim is not the only relation to be considered. To the pamphleteers and controversialists, it is true, this was the important relationship: Nashe hurls his invective at Harvey, let who will listen in; More expostulates with Tyndale in a kind of confrontation. But with literary satire, there is a more complex purpose than the simple reproof. Actually the writing of a satire sets up, or assumes to be already existing, three relationships – six, if we include the responses: satirist to victim, satirist to understanding reader, and reader to victim. We might minimize confusion and the necessity of resorting to algebra if we consider a relatively simple bit of satire.

In his colloquy 'The Abbot and the Learned Woman,' Erasmus presents for ridicule the monk Antronius, a poor thing indeed, both intellectually and spiritually, probably a composite character. The first relationship is certainly that of Erasmus to the monk himself, for the dialogue's impetus probably came from antagonism against such fellows. But it is unlikely that a monk of the Antronius tribe would read the scathing dialogue, still less likely that he would understand its points and percipiences if he did. It is possible that Erasmus was not thinking of any reader at all, but writing to lay the ghost of his own spleen (a further relationship!), since the act of expression may serve as a kind of experience within experience to effect catharsis. But in most cases, certainly most Erasmian cases, the writer does have in mind some reader, a like-minded and understanding one. Erasmus is more likely to be writing for Thomas More or Willibald Pirckheimer than for any Antronius, two readers whose disaffection for all kinds of Antronicism, already existing, will be confirmed and deepened.

Satirists differ in their attitude to the victims of their attack only in degree, not in kind. Erasmus is, of course, wiser than the prejudiced old abbot, and able to present his faults in exaggerated form, to laugh, and make others laugh, at him. Sometimes the laughter is scornful: Erasmus is scornful here. But for the peccadilloes of the Catherines and Fabullas of the colloquies, the scorn is mild and short-lived. But scornful or no, the satirist's business is to keep his readers – even the victim, if he is among them – laughing with him, interested and curious, not retreating in high dudgeon. Dryden's 'fine raillery'[55] is necessary because it does not offend, but 'merely tickles' the victim, delighting the percipient reader, and provoking an unconscious self-appraisal on the part of all readers. There is, as Dryden says, a 'vast difference between the slovenly butchering of a man ... and the fineness of stroke that separates the head from the body and leaves it standing in its place.' The fineness of stroke is the artistry, the trope and figure; in this particular colloquy it is the dramatic presentation, with the absurdities of the monk filtered through *prosopopeia, meiosis*, and *hyperbole*. And even if the satirist's use of such figures should be gauche or inadequate, they are the badge of his urbanity, his civility: he has not been rude or impudent; he has merely written a bit of poetry or drama.

This interposition of an artistic medium between the satirist and his victim creates around the writer a semblance of aloofness or detachment. Semblance only, for the ideal satirist is not actually detached or without sensitivity about his subject. Neither cynical nor skeptical, he is a man of humane spirit, with a modicum of love for his fellows and a basic belief, however submerged, that man is not beyond redemption. Lucian's satires are criticized for being too misanthropic and thus unsatisfying (if the criticism were sound in its particular, the generalization would

55 *Discourse Concerning the Original and Progress of Satire*, Students' Cambridge edition of the *Poetical Works* (Cambridge, Mass. 1909) 313

follow as the night the day); Juvenal is tortured with the conviction that Rome's nobility is passing; Swift is exasperated with British complacency; Pope and Byron writhe under unjust criticism; Erasmus is sickened with the endless instances of humanity preying on itself, in actual war or sterile dispute. Here in the colloquy about the abbot, it is the satirist's personal aversion to prejudice and shoddy scholarship that brings the dialogue into being, and about such a subject Erasmus can write with telling irony. But in every case the emotion is controlled by the effort to pattern and create. Antronius is just far enough removed from reality to be able to deflect that overburden of wrath that the exposition of some actual situation might have carried.

About the victim's attitude to the satirist Dryden may say that it is one of being 'tickled' at the fine raillery, if indeed he recognizes himself at all. But to say that no animosity is ever aroused is hardly true. Dryden, for all his theorizing, did not see fit to attach his name to *Absalom and Achitophel*; and there is reason to believe that, witty and tickled, or foolish and unidentified, both Shadwell and Shaftesbury were not a little piqued at their Drydenic portraits. Not all Erasmus' victims were as magnanimous as Leo x, and outraged clerics fumed and fulminated many times.

The quality of optimism is not lacking in the best satirists – certainly not in Erasmus, but it is perhaps not vested in a hope for amendment on the part of the victim. The ridicule may indeed be directed to someone dead or to a by-gone institution; the past is past, but the writer shows his belief in humanity by recognizing that there are those who will contrive a better future. Donne's *Conclave*, for instance, could never harry Ignatius into good Anglican ways, but its author counted on sympathetic readers who would share his repugnance for what he considered Jesuit wiliness. It was too late for Erasmus to convert Julius, but he could point out to others the weedy odor of any festering lilies.

Ridicule, directed against what cannot be mended because it is no fault of man or society, is hardly satire. Hardy's animus against the President of the Immortals is kin to the old Greek *eironeia,* but not satiric irony; those who ridiculed Pope's stature could hardly have hoped to add a cubit to his size, nor yet to persuade society to banish hunchbacks. The only faith such satirists can have in the right reason of the reader must be faith in a widespread distortion of vision.

Such is not satire in the Christian-humanist sense; and the reflection brings us back to the idea of 'prevailing folly.' If the dram of censure is utterly lacking the ridicule is without moral purpose. This inclusion of purpose outside the intrinsic artistic impulse may make of the writing something less purely aesthetic than lyric poetry, but the double purpose has always been the essence of satire, and commentators seem agreed about this. One must concede, however, that the impulse to such writing may well be born in the ferment of personal indignation. Vice or folly is much more poignantly felt by one who has suffered because of painful experience with it than by the most ardent altruist. Pope would never have been so well aware of injudicious literary criticism if he himself had not writhed under it; Donne's experience of upstart courtiers must have ignited the first and fourth verse satires; Erasmus might have been less concerned with exposing the reactionary quality of monasteries if he had not been apprehensive of being recalled to one of them. In its finished form, however, the satire must be directed to the correction of some folly or vice grave in character and in extent. Otherwise it loses its dignity and even its identity, becoming lampoon or caricature.

All this is relevant to the following chapters inasmuch as it points to a continuing recognition of two things: that satire has a double pulse, aesthetic and didactic, and that this double pulse bespeaks a double heartbeat, emotional and intellectual.

The aesthetic end is the creation of delight, usually through some comic agency, so that the response to the grimmest form of instruction, censure, may be delayed and tempered. The creativity may use the elements of ridicule or may substitute other agencies, provided they act to the same end, balancing pique with pleasure. The satirist who can manipulate not just one but many of the tropes of language and thought can best convince because he can best delight with his variety and because he can even better his instruction by suggesting various aspects of it and various levels of significance.

Generalities are perilous. To say that before the influence of Erasmus came to be felt no English satirist had command of all the satiric weapons would be to ask for trouble. Even to say that Erasmus brought the figure and mood of irony to satire is to oversimplify. But it is surely not too much to say that he established and made popular the ironic way of writing, showing irony to be the most flexible and adaptable of figures, and the only figure capable of conveying a satiric message of complexity or even profundity. Irony did come into prominence during the sixteenth century, first with Erasmus and Thomas More, and then, after some years of arrested growth, with Nashe and Donne and the writers of paradox.

Yet it would be a mistake to assess Erasmus' legacy to satire as one of re-establishing the figures of classical antiquity, and that only; and this chapter has, I hope, made that clear. The symbol was the heritage *par excellence* of the mediaeval poet and preacher; and the scriptural tradition in which it had grown was anything but dormant. But symbolism was capable too of taking on new life, and a new life having some affinity with irony. Erasmus, though he used symbols sparingly, constantly taught the reader to see and appreciate them.

Whether or not one can insist that moral purpose is of the essence of satire (one must remember, for instance, the rambunctious Nashe and his tribe), one can and must surely say it is necessary for its integrity and excellence. And not just moral purpose, but a plenitude of purposes: the merely rational, the moral-rational, and the suprarational, whether one sees this as geared to the Church Militant and Triumphant (as Erasmus so frequently sees it), or to the transcendent life of the individual spirit. In Erasmus' satires this interplay of many and varied standards ennobles the instructiveness and makes it worthy of the author's effort of literary enrichment. Even from the standpoint of human interest, his satire has the more interest and vitality for being Christian-humanist, rather than mere humanist, for he can slide suggestion under suggestion, and in the final vision leave time for dogs and apes, since man has his forever.

This double pulse of satire, intellectual and emotional, should be kept in mind as we turn to the consideration of the individual satires, and see in them the interplay of reason and charity. The satirist is himself made up of constantly held loyalties that are both of mind and of heart, and his perception of the vice and folly that violate these loyalties is both reasoned and beyond reason. Erasmus was writing during a time of disunity, when old sanctions and reverences were disintegrating or dying of inanition, when rituals and ceremonies were empty signs because the 'thing,' the substance of faith, was at low ebb. It was a time that called for satiric outcry; a few years earlier there might have been less cause, for faith was warmer; a few years later, when issues had come to ignition point, excitement and anxiety would not admit of being disciplined into the rational moulds of satire.

Erasmus was the man for the time. With convictions felt in the mind and reasoned in the heart, he was yet more humanist than zealot, and was able to convey them with finesse and charm and so to alert a great new reading public to a richer understanding of truth and goodness.

TWO

❦ The Praise of Folly ❦

ONLY THREE FULL-LENGTH WORKS of Erasmus are satiric: *Encomium Moriae* (which I shall continue to call *The Praise of Folly*); *Julius secundus exclusus*, and *Ciceronianus*. Some of the colloquies are satirical, but not all; satire is incidental in the adages, but not continuous; the Lucianic translations though germinal to much of the satire, are Erasmian by adoption rather than birth, and have proportionately small place in this work (but see pages 22, 23, 117–19); *Querela pacis*, or *The Complaint of Peace*, though it is censorious from start to finish, makes no use at all of the ridiculing devices and allows the figures which might have been surrogate for ridicule to dissolve before the work has proceeded far. Of the three properly satirical works, the *Praise* is the best and the earliest.

The date of its composition is uncertain. The first edition was published in 1511; that much it is safe to say. But Erasmus makes bewildering statements about the writing of this declamation, and of how he intended it to be read. In a letter to Martin Dorp he says he wrote it in one week, while visiting Thomas More on his return from Italy.[1] But the preface which he claims to have written at the same time is dated 1508, though the visit to More was in 1509.[2] In any case, the *Praise* is one of the early works, probably written in 1509, and certainly before 1511.

1 P.S. Allen (ed) *Erasmi Epistolae* II 94
2 *Ex rure, quinto Idus Iunias, An.* M.D.VIII: so runs the mooted date line at the end of the preface. The late Professor H.H. Hudson, whose edition and translation of the *Praise* I am using for this chapter, comments that

The debonair comments he makes about the worth of the 'little declamation'[3] composed with such dispatch are another source of bewilderment, though Dorp's censure may have moved him to disparage the seriousness of the work. He may indeed have written the book in short order during the scant leisure of his visit to More, but it is no trifle, as Erasmus, never one to underestimate his own worth, knew well. Nor is he quite serious when he says that his end is 'pleasure rather than censure,' and that he nowhere rakes into any Juvenalian 'cesspool of vice.'

A third source of confusion occurs in the foreword, for, in spite of the haste with which Erasmus claims to have written the *Praise*, he took time to write a preface and thereby to catalogue it. Let no one be astonished, he begs, at the triviality of his subject: let them but remember those eminent men who have previously written in such vein; and an imposing list follows – imposing but heterogeneous. Homer, he remembers, once sported with a battle of frogs and mice, Virgil with a gnat and a salad, Ovid with a nut; Polycrates, Isocrates, Favorinus, and even Seneca have falsely praised the unworthies of history; Lucian

1508 cannot be accepted, nor even 1509, unless 'June' is wrong. He thinks the writing was probably in the late summer or autumn of 1509, but offers no suggestion about the impossible dating. Walter Kaiser, in his *Praisers of Folly* (Cambridge, Mass. 1963, p 32), proffers the idea that the whole dating, together with the cavalier shrugging off of the worth of the book and of the time used in writing it, is just part of Erasmus' 'scholarly disclaimer, used to remove his book from the battleground of scholarship on which it could more easily be attacked.' Christopher Hollis, in his *Erasmus* (Milwaukee 1933, p 128), conjectures that the confusion of dates stems from Erasmus' apprehension lest the two translations of Sebastian Brant's *Narrenschiff* appearing in 1509 leave him open to the charge of plagiarism. There is, however, little similarity between the Brant verses with their simpler and more single-minded criticism and the veering, cross-currented wisdom of the *Praise*. Perhaps Johann Huizinga (*Erasmus of Rotterdam*, London, 1952, p 5) provides the simplest and most viable explanation when he comments that Erasmus' 'sense of chronology was always remarkably ill-developed.'

3 Erasmus *The Praise of Folly* Hudson translation, p 2. Subsequent references will be to this edition, the title shortened to 'the *Praise*,' and the page references, when feasible, bracketed into the text. The Latin text in which the *Praise* is called a *declamatiuncula* is LB IV 401, line 5.

and Apuleius have eulogized the fly and the ass; certain other reputable ancients have praised baldness, fever, and even injustice (p 2).

If Erasmus was himself casual in his classifying, it is not surprising that others, critics of his own time and later, were equally so. *The Praise of Folly* has been called learned parody, paradox, mock panegyric, an adoxigraphical essay;[4] and rightly so, for it is indeed all that. But it is primarily satire, and the parody, eulogy, and paradox are geared to a serious moral purpose. It is no trifle, surely, to be shouldered easily into the group which Erasmus himself reviews, nor reduced to the level of its imitators.

Erasmus' list includes no work so complex as his own. Parody is not always panegyric, nor mock panegyric always parody; neither is necessarily satiric. Homer's *Battle* is parody but not mock praise; nor is there mock praise in Virgil's tale of the gnat; of the mock eulogies listed, only Lucian's two are parodies of rhetorical declamations; and of the fifteen works listed only five are satirical.[5]

The *Praise* is unique in that it comprises all the qualities of all the works Erasmus lists. It is surely parody with the mocking Moria delivering such an oration as never before had followed the rules of rhetorical declamation. It is also an incisive and serious moral indictment of European society in all its aspects, an indictment that is sometimes eulogy, sometimes direct censure. It is, moreover, an oration that attempts, though awkwardly enough, to point in the end to that heavenly Jerusalem which sixteenth-century writers knew to be the end of any work of exhortation. Finally, and especially in comparison with contemporary works, it is a thoroughly human dramatic monologue,

4 See, for instance, E.N.S. Thompson *The Seventeenth-Century Essay* (University of Iowa Studies III 3, 95); Arthur Pease 'Things without Honour,' *Classical Philology* XXI (1926) 41; Warner G. Rice 'The *Paradossi* of Ortensio Lando' (*University of Michigan Publications* VIII [1932] 59–75); Hudson's introduction to his translation of the *Praise* xx–xxi; and Charles Lenient *La Satire en France* (Paris 1966) 14–16.

5 Kaiser points out, however, that the list of analogous paradoxes does serve to warn the reader that he should 'look below the surface' (*Praisers of Folly* 29).

having as its satirical and allegorical device a woman. She is christened Moria because, like Europe, she is foolish, or perhaps because, like Thomas More, she is wise. Nonetheless she is no mere abstraction: she is a woman with a woman's varying moods, now confidential, now aloof, sometimes amused, often furious, ready to break her ironic vein to coax or plead, or to pursue some tangential thought; and she grows in folly or in wisdom as we listen to her diatribes and rhapsodies.

Although it is unlikely that Erasmus, who was not modest about his achievements, underestimated the worth of his work, it is surprising to find his Renaissance admirers failing to recognize its difference from other paradoxes. To some the *Praise* seems little more than a merry commendation of folly; others consider it a Jeremiad attacking immorality and ecclesiastical abuse. Sir John Harington, for instance, in *The Metamorphosis of Ajax*, mentions the *Praise* as one of many such pieces, serious treatments of light subjects, of which he cites seven. The *Praise* heads the list, although the other six are no more of its kind than is the *Metamorphosis* itself: 'an encomium on the Pox, a defense of usury, a commendation of Nero,' and so forth. John Grange, writing in 1577, does recognize that the *Praise* hides many profound reflections beneath a 'cloke of mery conceyte,' yet he couples Erasmus very easily with Skelton, whose good place in English letters is surely not in the Erasmian neighbourhood. Not long afterwards, Sir Philip Sidney points out that 'Agrippa will be as merry in shewing the vanitie of Science as Erasmus was in commending of follie'; and although Sidney's final comment (that both had 'another foundation than the superficiall part would promise') is sound, the casual juxtaposing of the mercurial Moria and Agrippa's sturdy denunciations is surprising.[6]

6 John Harington *The Metamorphosis of Ajax* (1596) Peter Warlock and Jack Lindsay (eds) (London 1927), 8; John Grange *The Golden Aphrodite* (New York: Scholars' Facsimiles and Reprints 1939) sig. N_{iii}; Philip Sidney *An Apologie for Poetrie* E.S. Shuckburgh (ed) (Cambridge 1891), 35. It is interesting to note that Thomas Nashe makes no mention of the *Praise* in his exhaustive lists of works similar to his 'light friskin' of wit, *The Prayse of Red Herring*, although he opens the second of these lists with a sentence reminiscent surely of Erasmus. Nashe

In all these paradoxes there is, of course, some common denominator by which we recognize them as cognate to one another; but an examination of the paradoxes and false praises current in sixteenth-century England should, one thinks, justify the contention that Erasmus' *Praise of Folly* is not only superior to them, but, with one or two possible exceptions, quite different in scope and purpose.[7] Its complexity is such that it seems to father two kinds of essay distinct from each other and germane only through this Erasmian progeniture. As mock eulogy and parody the *Praise* inspires some paradoxical essays delighting in clever urbane dialectic, little more than *jeux d'esprit*; as satire it is godmother to seriously didactic writing. Few of the works that follow in its train are similarly compounded of both toothless and biting wit.[8]

Yet all the elements of form found in the 'trifles' he lists in his preface, mock rhetoric, parody, irony, and so on, Erasmus uses in the *Praise*; and the real achievement – a paradoxical one in another sense – is that he combines these forms and fuses them not only with each other, but with his critical purpose, so that they become satire. The mockery of his panegyric reduces the

begins: 'Homer of rats and frogs hath heroiqu't it ...' (*Works* R.B. McKerrow [ed] III 176); Erasmus' citation of other false praises and paradoxes begins: 'Homer, all those ages ago, made sport with a battle of frogs and mice ...' (2).

7 Caspar Dornavius, in an anthology of some 1130 large folio pages, *Amphitheatri sapientiae Socraticae loco-Seriae ... syllabus* (Hanover 1619), has gathered together over a thousand items. He has been generous in his inclusions, canvassing from Homer to the writers of his own day, and including some verses and essays having in them little of *sapientia* and nothing at all of *ioco-seriae*: lines to a rose, for example, or to a violet, are lyrical rather than paradoxical; praises of the rustic life by Thomas More and by Henry Stephen are true praises, not false ones. The items, all in Latin or Greek, are grouped according to subject matter, but no biographical or bibliographical help is given to the reader.

8 Two exceptions one might mention: Erasmus' friend, Willibald Pirckheimer, wrote a *Prayse of the Gout* (*Apologia seu podagra laus*), which does, to some extent, fuse the techniques of paradox with the serious purpose of satire; as does Robert Turner's praise of being intoxicated, *De laude ebrietatis*.

pomposity of serious rhetoric to absurdity, so the panegyric is parody, and the pretended seriousness is ironic; the subject of the eulogy is something about which the writer cares immensely, and the total effect is satirically ironic. The irony becomes doubly inverted, made both dramatic and satiric, because everything that Erasmus says he says through the person of a woman whom he calls a fool but who can grow to Christian wisdom and spirituality.

Perhaps there is more in a name than the poets think. If Sir Thomas' name had been other than 'More' – if it had been, say, Jones or Hopkins, and Erasmus had not been a learned philologist easily beguiled by puns, this praise might too have been a 'praise of injustice' (it is often that), or a 'praise of madness' (it is that too), or of cowardice or bravery or deception or love – for Folly is all of these and more. If so, the mood and tone and drive of the *Praise* would have been simple and single, as were the learned eulogies which were to follow. But folly is all things because wisdom is deeper than definition; and as wisdom shifts to new and richer levels, folly must be constantly reborn too, like the very cock Erasmus loves to mention, or the Silenus box with one self for the casual observer, and another for the percipient. Folly is madness and pleasure and sloth; it is pedantry, solemnity, greed; it is puritan and libertine; it is hatred and love; it is misfortune, unavoidable and innocent, and sin, humanly willed and active; it is temporal happiness; it is the pearl of great price for which man can foolishly sell all tangible pleasure. Folly has individual life and social; there is moral folly and spiritual. And a woman who calls herself Folly[9] can adopt every kind of foolishness, seeing aright and choosing wrong, or thinking foolishly and choosing according to the foolish reasoning, praising the folly that is her own, or praising that of her fools, and in the end becoming so foolish as to forget altogether that she is Folly and to opt for Wisdom.

The subject matter of the *Praise* has three broad divisions:

9 To avoid confusion, I shall refer to her as Moria, Erasmus' latinized Greek form for 'folly,' and to the topic of her eulogy as 'folly.'

the first part (roughly a third of the work) deals with the folly that is the natural concomitant of life, excusable, perhaps even unavoidable; the long middle section shows folly that is closer to vice, selfish, wilful, and deceitful; and the last part, less than a third, praises the folly of the cross. This division, of course, greatly oversimplifies the author's manipulation of complex moods and ironies, and is valuable only for surveying the substance of the work.[10] But substance is important enough to warrant a few paragraphs of expansion.

Actually the *Praise* does begin as a mock declamation in the old classical style, a fairly simple affair, full of sound and fury and mock pomposity, finding absurdity in an inevitable condition and capitalizing on it in an oratorical style. There is nothing in the first few pages to suggest that vast intention of cataloguing all human folly, of finding fresher viewpoints and stronger wisdoms from which to view the frailties of men.

The tone of the mockery is light and graceful in this part, and it is interesting to remark that Moria will try to recapture this railing tone from time to time in the later parts of the declamation when she finds her gaiety becoming bitter and her irony turning to invective. She begins, then, by introducing herself, justifying her claim to speak by reason of her glorious birth, breeding, state, her usefulness in the economy of the world and the happiness of her devotees. As she states her case, we see that the folly she represents here is a constant of man's estate, a part

---

10 There are, of course, other ways of dividing and analyzing the *Praise*. It can, for instance, be shown to have all the parts of a classical oration, as Quintilian had outlined them: *exordium, narratio, partitio, confirmatio*, and at least the recognition of a *peroratio*. Professor Hudson does so analyze it in the introduction to his edition. Kaiser, however, thinks the Quintilian schema less than satisfying unless it is set beside other paradigms for *encomia*, in particular those established by T.C. Burgess in his *Epideictic Literature* (University of Chicago Studies in Classical Philology III 1902, 89–261), Professor Kaiser singles out the Aphthonian categories of *praxeis, synkrisis*, and *epilogos* as offering a reorganizing of the Quintilian *confirmatio*. Since I am using a much simpler structuring, it seems unwise to detail Kaiser's arguments, convincing as they are; and in any case, I shall be referring to them in another connection below.

of his nature, and not really folly at all, certainly not something crying out for rebuke or remedy. It is love's folly, she says, that effects procreation and so stands at the very fountainhead of life; the folly of innocence that makes childhood happy and lovable; the folly of forgetfulness that makes old age bearable; the folly of pleasant recreation and of the social give-and-take that makes life liveable. Folly promotes the arts too, and spurs man to build cities and defend them.

All of this is surely in the vein of the traditional paradox praise. This folly has in it no more of human choice than has quartan fever, or baldness, or the state of being a louse, and much less of obloquy. There are few overtones here and little irony. But it is more excellent than most of the paradoxes by reason of its vitality: Moria is even here a lively figure, and the emerging character of the speaker gives warmth and charm. Sometimes she is remote here, however, and the man she talks of remote too, for he tends to be natural man in a natural world (she herself speaks of the 'golden age'), and never has there been such a man really. In this slightly unreal world she could hardly come to asking, as later, puzzled beyond measure, she is to ask: 'What is the nature of man?'

She moves closer to reality when she begins to treat of man in his relation to others, first in friendship and marriage, then in the larger relations of society, where emulation, self-esteem, ambition become part of folly's composition and bring it closer to iniquity. Of the many images in this first round of Moria's oration, none is more significant for our understanding of its structure than that of the theatre (35–8). Moria has been reflecting, half-ironically, on the relation of prudence to wisdom. Prudence, she thinks, depends on experience of affairs; and it is the fool, unfettered by the wise man's restraint, that has tasted life to the full.[11] In the theatre image that follows prudence and wis-

11 The irony here is plain enough when one thinks of Erasmus' insistence, especially in De pueris ... instituendis, that exercitatio (in its broad sense a form of experience) is an inept teacher if it precedes the normal process of learning: 'exercitatio nisi ratione gubernetur multis periculis

dom are again contrasted. On a stage the parts are often miscast, and Moria tries to picture what havoc would be wrought by a person who sees the miscasting and tries to interrupt the scene and strip the disguises from the players. But life, she goes on, presents an analogue; and 'suppose some wise man from the sky' should drop into the theatre of life and try to wrest from the characters the roles for which they are not suited. In this broader sense of theatre, the implication seems to be that the players are not miscast merely as a result of the producer's miscasting, but have connived and fought for position. Thus the intruder is not simply denouncing what cannot be helped, but the wilful folly of the masquers.

The significance of this passage (quoted below, p 65) touches many aspects of this analysis and will be given more detailed study later; the character of Moria, for instance, becomes more complex here as she recognizes two faces to folly – or to wisdom; and the irony slithers between poles, now seeing right and choosing wrong, now seeing asquint but choosing well. In the second place, it is structurally important because, with the introduction of a more wilful and heinous folly, the new movement is heralded, though the lady moves back into her *jeu d'esprit* manner for a time. And the passage has a third importance: pattern is now beginning to emerge; we do not recognize it as such here, of course, and will not, until it begins to repeat itself in the later parts of the work. We do recognize, I think, that Moria is playing now with two kinds of folly, praising and damning both, for the 'wisdom' opposing the obvious folly is not entirely sound, and the succeeding pages show that Erasmus does not think it so, whatever Moria thinks; and in the next phase this pseudo-wisdom is to become the folly that is prime object of her praise. Against the new folly, Moria will oppose another wisdom, and this in turn, will become the folly of her predilection in the last part of her

atque erroribus est obnoxia' (LB I 497A). The *ratio* that must precede had been identified in an earlier passage as 'doctrina quae monitis constat ac praeceptis.'

speech. Finally the human element is amplified in this theatre scene too, as fools, near-fools, wise men, and a woman orator gather before the reader.

The first movement ends with a crescendo of scorn as man's absurd preoccupations and pastimes are derided, in fulsome praise. For the first ones, hunting, building, gaming, boasting, and mere worldliness, Moria's inverted censure is not very trenchant;[12] but she comes then to the recounting of unlikely stories, a folly surely not very heinous in itself, but having affinity to one that delights Moria and exasperates Erasmus: that of too-credulous exchanging of old wives' tales concerning unlikely miracles. For superstition Erasmus had never had any sympathy: it is a betrayal of right thinking, a sin against reason itself, and so against man's humanness. In Augustinian terms, it is flagrant confusion of things and signs. And Moria's words are harsh:

> But why should I launch out upon this ocean of superstition? 'For if I had a hundred tongues, a hundred mouths, a voice of brass, I could not set forth all the shapes of fools or run over all the names of folly.' Yet the whole life of Christian folk everywhere is full of fanaticisms of this kind. Our priests allow them, without regret, and even foster them, being aware of how much money is wont to accrue from this source. [58]

And here again Moria supposes some 'wise man' brash enough to intrude into the play of life. The last sentence of the passage quoted is, however, the crux of the matter: 'our priests allow it ... aware of how much money ...'

The long middle portion of the oration presents for our admiration the follies and vices of men and women in all walks of life: kings, statesmen, churchmen, scholars, and merchants. But there is no mistaking where the great interest lies. For the folly or iniquity of churchmen, prelates and priests, monks, theologians, and friars, even the Pope, only a veneer of praise covers the cor-

---

12 These pastimes do not bulk large as objects of Erasmus' satire. See, however, *Colloquies* 307–8, and *Adages* 281. The editor's note prefacing the colloquy 'Hunting' speaks of both Erasmus and More as disliking this sport.

roding censure. Theologians, for instance, are likened to the herb *anagyra foetida* and called marvellously supercilious, and we note the trickery of the fancy botanical name and the damning adjective, even as we note the new intensity. Moria presently becomes conscious herself of having lapsed from her original role and for a moment tries to recapture it, building up another paradoxical defence of herself, which forms a sort of transition to the last movement.

Mankind has not only wedded Folly, Moria tells her audience, but has written in her honour. With hoydenish indecorum, and at times an almost offensive disregard for proper reverence, she cites and quotes from the most authoritative writings to show that folly has been praised by men of letters, of wit, and of religion. She begins with the classics and proverbial sayings, but she cannot ignore the sacred writings, she declares, and on she goes to the scriptures. We, with our orderly wisdom, know well that this folly lauded by the evangelists is of another colour altogether, and at first we are repulsed by the unseemliness. But indeed there is a sort of cyclic logic to her procedure. Her early follies had not been execrable: in some of them there had been an innocence that, set in a Christian framework, might easily have developed into a praise of Christian folly. In any case, once we have passed through the indecorous transitional part into the last movement of the *Praise*, we forget the indecorum.

For all its teeming subject matter and rocketing moods, a structural pattern does emerge, cyclic rather than straightforward, but obvious enough. The first cycle begins with a survey of natural folly and swells into a picture of man in the golden age, happy in his natural world; as the movement comes to completion we have the man-fool elevated, foregathering with the gods whence he had emanated, and leaving Moria to eulogize herself. But somewhere in this part a counter-movement had been set up, a growing preoccupation with the wise man who had been contrasted with the fool; and as the cycle of natural folly closes in, this counter-movement arches up to become a new cycle. Here the man who had been the wise man on the first pages has become the fool, the target of Moria's praise: in a particular and real civilization, far from the Arcady of the early part, he is deluded by Folly into thinking himself wise – and happy, though he is neither. The temporal sequence of the first part (one man from childhood to old age) has been discarded now for a spatial one (many men in various positions in life). The upswing of this cycle brings in tones of harsh and bitter reproach for man's worldly-wise ways, but as the movement rounds off, Moria tries once more to recapture the initial high-hearted tone and the earlier association with myths and gods.

But still another cycle had been in preparation: just as, in the first part, the wordly-wise man who was to be anatomized later had been faintly discernible in the shadows as foil to the natural fool, so throughout this long middle section, the truly wise man, the *philosophus Christi*, has been present by implication as the opposite to the pseudo-wise man. And this true wisdom now becomes the subject matter of Moria's third and last part. Thus the wisdom of one part is repeatedly made the folly of the next – or, if we use Moria's inversions, the follies of each part become the wisdoms of the next. In the last third of the book, the folly of the cross is to resolve the contradictions arraigned in the preceding cycles. Once again too, Moria, in a sudden, whirling recollection of her original role, reaches for the old manner, tosses aside the need for a peroration, and as Folly, waves goodbye to her foolish audience.

It has been said that satire is not ageless, as is great literature, because its figures are unreal, that 'Gulliver cannot reach a happy hunting ground together with Robinson Crusoe, nor Pope's dunces hope to dance with Congreve's Millemant.'[13] But Moria, we think, might aspire to flirting with Mirabell, and she does indeed wedge herself into a species of happy hunting ground. A complex figure, she rarely quite deviates into sense, yet never quite sinks to absurdity either. Because she is a woman, she can change her mood and tactics, can be now knowing, now unaware, can recognize folly and choose it, or fail to recognize it and so

13 Humbert Wolfe *Notes on English Verse Satire* (London 1929) 27

reject it, thinking it wisdom; she can even be wise at times and then pretend to an ignorance that is an obvious mask. Thus her irony can shift and turn and sometimes disappear, changing not only in intensity but in character.

Her simpliest irony, the one to which she keeps returning, after vehemence has led her to abandon it, is to recognize folly for what it is and yet to choose it for very love. This is not the usual kind of dramatic irony, for the ordinary satirist speaks through a dunce who lauds the folly because he thinks it wise.[14] In the simple ironies of the early part of the oration, and intermittently throughout it, Moria's irony lies in choice, not recognition.

But Moria is rarely simple. Often she begins with a simple lauding of a folly, only to wriggle into an irony less characteristic of this kind of double-talk. For the most part she simply says: 'The combination of senility and sensuality is folly supreme' (seeing rightly); then 'In this folly is my delight' (choosing wrong). But now and then she dallies with some folk-sayings, and in them we find some provocative half-truth, and are seduced into thinking out the proposition for ourselves.

Moria's perception becomes flawed towards the end of this first part, in anticipation perhaps of the next section where percipience is often faulty; and in the passage on prudence she uses the tricks of witty paradox to set up a false syllogism. She has been speaking of folly as the mainspring of great exploits. The active life, she has said, depends on folly; and now it is a simple step to begin proving that folly is very like prudence:

> And now, since I have made good my title to renown for courage and resourcefulness, suppose I should lay claim also to prudence? 'But,' someone will say, 'with no more effort you might mix fire and water.' Perhaps so; still I shall have good success in this, I

14 Chaucer, for instance, in his role as fictional pilgrim, does not recognize, or pretends not to recognize, the unseemliness of the prioress's affectations, or the worldliness of the monk. In Donne's *Ignatius his Conclave*, on the other hand, the irony is much like Moria's. Ignatius knows all the answers and certainly can distinguish between virtue and vice, but chooses falsely – or falsely according to Donne's way of thinking. Thus the irony is not in false perception but in false choice.

am convinced, if only you will lend me ... your ears and minds. And first, if prudence depends upon experience of affairs, to whom does the honour of this attribute belong? To the wise man who, by reason partly of modesty ... will attempt no action? Or to the fool, who is not deterred from any enterprise by modesty, of which he is innocent, or by peril, which he never pauses to weigh? The wise man runs to books of the ancients and learns from them a merely verbal shrewdness. The fool arrives at true prudence ... by addressing himself at once to the business and taking his chances. Homer seems to have seen this, for all that he was blind, when he said, 'Even a fool is wise after a thing is done.' There are two great obstacles to developing a knowledge of affairs – shame, which throws a smoke over the understanding, and fear, which, once danger has been sighted, dissuades from going through with an exploit. Folly, with a grand gesture, frees us from both. Never to feel shame, to dare anything – few mortals know to what further blessings these will carry us.[15] [35–6]

The argument here depends obviously on a syllogism wherein a debatable first premise leads into a quite untenable second premise:

1 / The prudent person is one who is successful in the experience of affairs;
2 / It is not the wise man, modest and faint-hearted, but the fool, unfettered by shame or fear, who acquires this experience of affairs;
3 / Therefore it is the fool who is prudent.

Stripped of their rhetoric and the lively intimacies of Moria, the statements look pretty silly; but this is paradox procedure and

15 Erasmus says this non-ironically in the opening paragraphs of *Dulce bellum inexpertis* where he speaks of pastimes 'fine and splendid' in youth but undesirable as age and experience come. 'In the same way,' he says, 'this idea can be applied to any enterprise carrying with it great risks and many evils, such as no one would undertake unless he were young and without experience. Indeed, Aristotle in his *Rhetoric* says this is the reason why youth tends to be bold and age to be diffident, because the former is given confidence by inexperience, and the latter acquires diffidence and hesitancy from familiar knowledge of many ills' (*Adages* 309).

quite in keeping with the airy persiflage of this section. Even here, however – and this is the point I want to make – Erasmus is alerting the reader to profounder meanings, not very clear ones, and never to be wholly clear, but provocative surely. The false dichotomies set up between prudence and wisdom and between wisdom and folly seem to question all the attitudes suggested. So too the underlying implication that shame and fear are the panoply of the wise man makes one wonder what this wise man is – really wise, or worldly wise, or Stoic-wise, and what place is to be given that 'verbal shrewdness' the wise man learns from ancient lore; and whether shame and fear, restricting elements as they are, are not yet a part of man's mature nature, for all that.

The vexed question of prudence leads Moria into the imagery of the theatre and here the irony deepens considerably and becomes more complex. Long as it is, this passage warrants full quotation:

> If a person were to try stripping the disguises from actors while they play a scene upon the stage, showing to the audience their real looks and the faces they were born with, would not such a one spoil the whole play? And would not the spectators think he deserved to be driven out of the theatre with brickbats, as a drunken disturber? For at once a new order of things would be apparent. The actor who played a woman would now be seen a man; he who a moment ago appeared young is old; he who but now was a king, is suddenly a sorry little scrub. Destroy the illusion and any play is ruined. ... Now what else is the whole life of mortals but a sort of comedy, in which the various actors, disguised by various costumes and masks walk on and play each one his part, until the manager waves them off ...[16]

Up to this point the folly has had about it some inevitability, the praise has been simply false praise, and the irony hardly more

16 In the adage 'Simia in purpura' (not translated in full in Mrs Phillips' *Adages*, but quoted on p 111) Erasmus makes a similar comment: 'How many people in princes' palaces, if they were to be shorn of their purple, their chains and their jewels, would be found to be no better than labourers!'; again, in the adage 'Sileni Alcibiadis' he speaks of one 'born to the oar' being lifted 'to sovereign power by the whim of fortune,' an allusion, no doubt, to Julius II (p 292).

than recognition of the irony inherent in life. But as Moria goes on and makes of the theatre an analogue to life and its miscastings, new complexities arise:

> But suppose some wise man who has dropped down from the sky should suddenly confront me and cry out that the person whom the world has accepted as a god and master is not even a man, because he is driven sheeplike by his passions ... or again, suppose the visitor should command someone mourning his father's death to laugh, because now his father has really begun to live – for in a sense our earthly life is but a kind of death. ... Suppose ... Suppose ... As nothing is more foolish than wisdom out of place, so nothing is more imprudent than unseasonable prudence. And he is unseasonable who does not accommodate himself to things as they are, who is 'unwilling to follow the market,' who does not keep in mind at least that rule of conviviality 'Either drink or get out,' who demands in short, that the play should no longer be a play. The part of a truly prudent man ... is not to aspire to wisdom beyond his station, and either, along with the rest of the crowd, pretend not to notice anything, or affably and companionably be deceived. But that, they tell us, is folly ... [37–8]

In assessing the irony of these paragraphs, surely we pause at the sentences beginning 'As nothing is more foolish ...' Here Moria seems to have dropped her ironic tone and to be speaking soberly, even as Erasmus would speak.[17] And although the mocking tone has returned by the end of the paragraph, so that we are less than sure about the place and wisdom of moral intrusion, those perceptive sentences about unseasonable wisdom have pre-

---

17 There are other instances throughout the work of this emergence of the sober non-ironic voice of Erasmus. A tone of sympathy, for instance, invades the passages on vanity in the early part (pp 28, 30, 62, 64) – sympathy for man's real need for a crumb of self-deception to bolster his flagging confidence; and Moria can comment that when man is too dissatisfied with himself and his poor endowments, 'every grace and elegance of life suffers taint and is lost.' At such a time, she thinks, he may with some justice woo the Lady Philautia, so that, in life as in art, there may be grace and seemliness. There are other instances.

pared the reader for a new kind of folly to make its appearance, a folly masquerading as wisdom.

The transition is made through a shift in the irony, a shift that becomes more obvious if we oversimplify for a moment. Moria has been saying 'This is folly: and I love it,' with percipience right and choice wrong. Now she is going to present a pseudo-wisdom, and (except for that one revealing sentence) she is going to say 'This is wisdom: and such wisdom is not to be borne, 'with recognition wrong (for the wisdoms she proceeds now to detail have small part with true wisdom), but judgement or choice right, for she wisely rejects this counterfeit wisdom. And this shift in ironic position allows Moria (or Erasmus) to use a more trenchant satire.[18] Not that there are any hard and fast divisions: throughout this long middle portion the irony shifts from judgement to percipience and back again, as Moria now scorns the wise man and rejects him, and now takes his wisdom for folly and loves him.

Before we leave the theatre image, it might be well to notice that here the human and dramatic elements of the irony are enriched, for it gives us three sets of people all judging and choosing. The players on the stage have chosen not to see; this is folly of the intellect, though the will is hardly uninvolved: outwardly noble, inwardly inept, these players strut and fret their time upon the stage, quite unfit for their responsibilities. But Moria is hardly concerned with them (though she does come back to them later in the oration); she is preoccupied with the man of insight, whom she calls a 'wise man from the sky,' recognizing in

18 George Faludy (*Erasmus* [London 1970] 130) speaks of an 'imperceptible change' at about this point from playful ridicule of the human comedy to a note of violent abuse and arrogance. I find the change quite perceptible and pin-pointable, though the sporadic excursions into the older tone are confusing. It is pertinent to note here that Kaiser, in his re-ordering the structure of the oration, suggests that one result of the Aphthonian subdividing is the de-emphasizing of the attacks on the clergy, the princes, the papacy, and other estates, which are seen to occupy smaller proportions of space in the speech than some other topics and to negate the popular opinion that the whole book is an attack on church and state.

him some illumination beyond that of the rest. He is a Lucianic figure, who might have graced the Dialogues of the Dead or the Menippean satires. He is similar too to More's Philosopher-councillor ironically proposed by Hythlodaye and repudiated in some measure by More. Moria's wise man has a difficult choice to make: he must either interrupt the play and so let loose the furies, perhaps doing more harm than good, or must compromise with injustice. Thirdly there is Moria herself, by now a human being caught in the web of her own argument, made to ponder and judge between two follies.

Still another variation in the ironic technique appears when at times the orator seems to forget by what standard she is judging the wise man wise and the fool foolish, and this within the space of a couple of paragraphs. In one single orgy of condemnation, for instance, she lauds the court fools first because they provide jests and laughter and not the rasping truths uttered by the wise man, and then (in the very next paragraph) because they tell their monarch some good home truths very frankly indeed, and do not have, as the wise man has, 'two tongues ... one used for speaking truths, the other for speaking what [they] judge most opportune at the moment' (p 49). So Moria must know two kinds of wise man, one outspoken and without diplomacy, the other an opportunist and with a neat duplicity. Neither is really wise, for the first lacks courtesy and so can effect no good, and the second lacks honesty, and so does not care to try. Moria condemns both and loves the fool (who also has two selves). One suspects the lady here of having dusted off two kinds of pseudo-wisdom and a couple of follies with one gesture.

But Moria undergoes a kind of conversion as the oration proceeds, first moral and then spiritual, and as she does so, her hold on the original line of inverted praise becomes tenuous. For instance, the scoring of certain professional men holds almost no irony at all, only angry invective. For these fools whose folly is quite wilful, growing out of ambition and greed, she has only token commendation, whereas she had had effusive sympathy for the naturals. A veneer of praise covers the folly of merchants, grammarians, poets, scientists, and scholars, but no praise, however wry, can she find for the theologians and clerics. Sometimes too she appears to have broken with her old friends and to be ashamed of having nurtured fools. She even 'takes a seat alongside the gods of the poets' and laughs unsympathetically at them, as if she thought she were Wisdom instead of Folly; indeed she shows anxiety lest she herself be considered *stultissima* and worthy of the laughter of Democritus. Again, speaking of the grammarians, whom she calls her devotees, and should therefore praise, she is disparaging and shows exasperation. And why exasperation? What business has Moria being exasperated with the members of her own entourage?

This kind of irony, imbued with a certain awareness, and thus more satiric than dramatic, becomes almost continuous when Moria speaks of theologians and religious, of officials of Church and State. In place of Lucianic detachment there is envenomed bitterness. She has forgotten now her promise not to 'rake into the occult cesspool' of Juvenal. But in fact the passages here are no more Juvenalian than Lucianic. More reminiscent, perhaps, of Jerome are these sentences with their holy scorn for the supposedly elect who are more devoted to the letter than the spirit of their calling. This is characteristic of Erasmus. One critic, H.A. Mason, speaking of the special contribution made to Renaissance letters by translations of such writers as Lucian (see above, p 22) can comment that it is 'surprising to find Erasmus so little dependent on the Classics for what he really has to say. ... The feeling he evokes seem to me to come from genuine participation in the life of the times and in the living tradition.'[19]

Forthright exhortation is frequent enough through the long middle section, and sometimes the rational life is given a boost into the life of the spirit as Moria prepares to move into this realm in the last section. In this final part, except for the strange irony that it is a woman called Folly and wearing cap and bells who makes this speech, there is no irony. Up to this point there has always been some satiric spirit in the *Praise*, and a recurrent irony – dramatic because Moria was nearly always unaware of

19 H.A. Mason *Humanism and Poetry in the Early Tudor Period* 82

the total meaning of what she said, and satiric, because through her twisted insights, Erasmus censured prevailing vice with ridicule. But there is no irony at all about such a passage as this:

> Hence those who are permitted to have a foretaste of this (what eye hath not seen, etc.) suffer something very like to madness. ... When presently they return to themselves, they say that they do not know where they have been, whether in the body or out of it, waking or sleeping; they do not remember what they have heard, seen, spoken, or done; and yet through a cloud, or as in a dream, they know one thing, that they were at their happiest while ... thus out of their wits. ... And this is a tiny taste of that future happiness. [124]

So might Juliana of Norwich have written, or Richard Rolle; such is the experience offered in the *Cloud of Unknowing*. One cannot rationalize the supernatural quality of this kind of experience. Moria does not try.[20]

Knowledge, however, does precede both charity and charity's activity; and knowledge does lie within the province of reason. In a later work *Julius exclusus*, Erasmus hints that the key of knowledge might have opened the gates of heaven to the errant Julius; and satire is not incapable of augmenting knowledge and awareness. Even faith, the *quid credas* of the exegetes' couplet, when it is facing bankruptcy and selling out to charlatans, can be persuaded to survey itself; and this too is sometimes the province of satire. Or so Erasmus thought when he wrote the *Praise*.

Techniques other than irony also enrich the *Praise*, of course. The character of Moria gives body and dramatic rightness to the work; without her esprit the piece would never be so lively. Analogues and metaphors abound too, many of them bringing a new field of reference from classical writings; the Platonic image

20 Not many of Erasmus' biographers and critics have made much of his occasional excursions into the realms of the mystical, a journey that sorts badly, one supposes, with veneration of Lucian and Quintilian. One long study of him, however, *Erasme et l'Espagne*, by M. Marcel Bataillon (Paris 1937), sees the influence of Erasmus in Spain as being one of increasing the spirit of devoutness, and Bataillon at least sees him as one always and honestly seeking experiential knowledge of Christ (pp 210–12).

of the cave and its simulacra points up the darkness of self-delusion, and the double face of Janus and the Silenus box of Alcibiades[21] do a like service for wilful deception; superstition is an ocean, and the theologians a Lake Camarina, a race apart, a field of noxious herbs, *anagyra foetida*. Sometimes metaphors are prolonged to make little scenes and so enrich the tapestry: the curtain goes up on some theatre folk, natural man foregathers with the gods in some heavenly bleachers to laugh at the human vaudeville act, Juvenal rakes into his 'occult cesspool,' scholars squint into their books by stingy candlelight, and the monarch listens to his court and his jester.

We have already noted too that the structural modes of classical oratory are followed, and thus the work becomes parody; and that the title is the best of literary jokes, with Moria doubling as two genitives, objective and subjective, and doubling too in allusion, as European folly and a wise Englishman.

Although the ironic inversions drop away from the *Praise*, and the satire fails to sustain the work to the end, it is not in any sense a failure. Indeed the sustaining of its satire might have been less satisfying. As an instrument of persuasion, satire is often unable to bring the work to completion; it is the expedient of a man aware of life's anomalies but unsure of how to resolve them. In many ways it is as tragic as comic, furtively concealing its tragic direction in a web of comic devices. Sometimes perhaps the perplexities find their resolution as the satirist's exasperation works itself out; and he is then ready to turn to his auditory with words of sweeter persuasion.[22] The reader or listener may also respond to this catharsis – and the writer assumes he does, of

---

21 The Silenus box of Alcibiades is one of Erasmus' favourite images, the time-honoured symbol of the disparity between seeming and being; it is the subject of one of his longest adages, wherein through this symbol he works his way into his favourite topic, the abuse of religion and its practices by those who should honour them most.

22 John Donne, Erasmian in so many ways, would have disagreed with Erasmus here. He came in his later days to think satire an inefficient tool for persuasion, and in a sermon in 1627 pointed out that the satiric mood, once established, cannot be dissolved to make way for the milder tones of exhortation (*The Sermons of John Donne*, George Potter and E.M. Simpson (eds) Berkeley, Cal. 1953–61; VIII 66).

course. Hence the satire, if it has prepared both speaker and listener for the exhortation, has been effective. The satiric parts of the *Praise* do just that. In the end, Moria's audience is readier to listen to her penultimate sober words than they would have been earlier, their minds prepared by the speaker's adroit tricks and tropes; they have been dislocated from accepted attitudes and made to see truth in new guises.

If the *Praise*, as a piece of cunning literature, is of high complexity, this is still more the case when it is considered on the level of instruction. For it is not assertive of a simple sustained rationale, but is rather a study in speculation about the nature of man. We can, of course, find and isolate certain of Erasmus' known preoccupations: monastic abuses, the prevalence of greed in high places and of superstition in low, worldly ambition among rulers and simony among ecclesiastics, the quarrelling, brawling, and fighting that destroys peace. But in this supposedly frivolous work, whether we concentrate on its survey of behaviour or its sometime excursions into the realm of the spirit, we are constantly aware of Erasmus prodding Moria to ask, 'What is the nature of man?' And if one is going to ask 'What is man?' instead of simply saying 'Don't be greedy, and don't talk in church,' one cannot expect to arrive at neat conclusions. As one commentator says, Moria 'undercuts and undermines her whole argument herself, to leave each reader alone with the unpleasant realization that Folly has been consistent to the last ... she has abandoned the reader to make his own decisions about value.'[23]

Erasmus' preoccupation with life's anomalies was well served by the genre of paradox, and he is ingenious in his use of *double entendre*. *Sapientia*, for instance, he interprets in a variety of ways, and the reader must be wary. The truly wise man is, for Erasmus, one supposes, the humanist devoted to the *philosophia Christi*, with all that title implies. But Moria, not quite percipient, though capable of choosing well, knows another wisdom, the proud perquisite of the Stoic, and wisely she rejects it. Here, as

23 Rosalie L. Colie *Paradoxia epidemica* (Princeton 1966) 20

in many other instances, much that seems purely paradoxical and specious on first reading is worth a second. Moria, as we have seen (above p 64), can use a tricky logic to lay claim to prudence, to show that prudence and wisdom are ambivalent terms, hardly laudable and mutually repellent, that shame and fear are not the qualities of the fool but of the man of experience. But this is more than clever dialectic, for Erasmus the moralist is very much behind Moria the wag as she advances her faulty syllogisms: *prudentia* and *sapientia* are just abstract terms to cover the ways in which silly man behaves and misbehaves. And if Erasmus hints that certain kinds of wise men are best left to scratch out their eyes in bramble bushes, he is in good company – with Horace, for instance, and Thomas More. And if the active life begets, with prudence, some modicum of shame and fear, are these not the brakes and disciplines of sober maturity? Whatever the answer, Moria turns soon to the man of thought, somewhat apart from the game of life.

After the reader has been led to conjecture that there is one prudence that is wise and one not wise but only expedient, Moria worms into the subject from another angle, obliquely, through the apparent examination of a problem in seeming and being. Removing her cap and bells, and speaking without any irony at all, she says:

> All human affairs, like the Sileni of Alcibiades, have two aspects, each quite different from the other: even to the point that, what at first blush ... seems to be death may prove, if you look further into it, to be life. [36]

A moment or so later she is illustrating this theme with a picture of a king seemingly rich yet impoverished in the goods of the spirit, given over to vice so that he is a 'vile slave.' But the king's folly is only a threshing ground for a more provocative one: the king hardly concerns Moria here – though she is to turn on him in fury later. Now she is rather concerned with the prudence and wisdom of the percipient beholder. What is the prudent procedure – and what the wise – for the man who sees all too well? Moria hardly knows; perhaps Erasmus hardly knows. But in the theatre image that follows she tries to show the havoc interference would work. The likening of life itself to a stage (quoted above, p 65) follows this. Household jargon since Shakespeare made it so, the analogy was fresher, no doubt, to Moria's hearers.

Here again folly is a complex thing. There are two kinds: the wilful folly of the unworthies on the stage – though some may be merely apathetic – and the folly of the intellect which the discerning spectator must consider. The players' choice had been simple – a choice between truth and falsity, between obvious good and obvious wrong; and the flunkey king had chosen the wrong. It is the spectator's problem that is more arresting, forcing a choice between two goods. And however he opts – for acquiescence and peace or for remonstrance and truth, there is some folly in the election: Moria says so.

In the end it is only a half-truth she provides, yielding her voice in favour of non-interference. We see in this the peace-loving, tolerant Erasmus, but we see too that he is less than sure of his position, that he is trying out his solution. Moria's half-truth says that 'nothing is so foolish as wisdom out of place,' and begs the question of real wisdom's capacity for dislocation. For certain urbanities, however, Moria has only damning praise: man should be 'affably deceived,' and should 'accommodate himself.' Deception and accommodation are shabby terms, though the latter had not yet acquired the bad odor Shakespeare was later to give it.[24] Some seven years later Erasmus' friend Thomas More was to discuss the role of the wise and forthright counsellor in *Utopia*, and we wonder if Moria's reflections were then in his thoughts. It seems not unlikely, for, although More, or rather Hythlodaye, is talking of a king's counsellor, here, as in the *Praise*, the theatre image is introduced. More optimism and faith rests in More's solution: he concedes to Hythlodaye that remonstrance would be unseemly during the performance, and futile in

---

24 To speak of the implications of an English word in this Erasmian context may seem fatuous; yet actually the Latin word is the same: *accommodet se.*

any case, but he would justify apparent acquiescence, for a time at least, in the hope of gradual persuasion.[25]

Reflections about prudence and wisdom lead Moria into some cognate profundities. About to concern herself with knowledge and virtue, and preparing for this consideration, she generalizes again: 'Nothing can be called unhappy if it fulfils its own nature.'

But what is the nature of man? In one of his educational works, under the direct influence of Quintilian and classical educational theory, Erasmus was to define it quite simply: it is the nature of man to be inclined towards 'honest things,' or again 'honest actions,' and 'philosophy'; man needs only proper direction and knowledge to fulfil his being (De pueris, LB I 496F–497A). But in the Enchiridion, which, he told Martin Dorp, was the companion piece of the Praise, saying directly what the Praise said inversely (Allen II 93), he grants that man's nature knows conflicting elements. 'Man,' he says here, 'is ... composed of two or three vastly unlike parts: a soul that is like something divine and a body like that of a dumb brute' (p 63). Although in mind he may excel the brute world and even aspire to rise above the angelic, in many ways he is no more than beast. To explain these contradictory elements in man, Erasmus here resorts to first causes: the Creator had meant the body to live in harmony with the soul, but the serpent had put them asunder so that now they can live neither together nor apart.

The Praise, however, raises questions and sees perplexities that the easy resolutions of the Enchiridion do not seem to cover. It may be true that 'nothing is unhappy if it fulfils its own nature'; but it may be man's nature to 'surmount ... the nature of the angels,' or, as the Praise itself admits, to strive 'to go beyond the bounds proper to his station' (47). If man can desire eternal life, hankering after 'the life of the immortal gods,' leaving the now for dogs and apes, is 'nature' as slippery a term as 'wisdom'? And

---

25 *Utopia* E. Surtz and J.H. Hexter (eds), in Yale edition of the *Complete Works* (New Haven 1965) IV 99. Subsequent references will be to this edition and bracketed into the text.

if man can long to be like those mighty giants who 'with arts and sciences as their engines ... wage war on nature,' knowledge of the arts and sciences must help to fulfil his nature. But Moria will not have it so. It is the fool who is happy, she says, and only the logic-choppers who say that man is made for knowledge.[26] To cap her point, she thinks again of man in the golden age, the innocent 'natural man' of the early part of the oration. He had had no need for sciences, and free of conscience, of shame and fear and envy, he is of course, free also of sin, though here Moria's eschatology leads us to Elysian fields, not a Christian heaven. Again, as in the larger pattern, the first few illustrations of delightful not-knowing are innocent enough, but soon become a kind of self-delusion that is a far cry from *honestae res*, and perhaps closer to not-thinking than to not-knowing.

The child of nature surveyed at the beginning of the book and glanced at again in this part may be free from sin and shame and assured of immortal happiness, but, of course, he is not real; and one cannot but think again of the *Enchiridion* with its insistence that man's goodness (and so his final destiny) depends on two things: knowledge (acquired through effort) and prayer.[27] Better to have less of knowledge and more of love, Erasmus grants here, than more of knowledge and less love, but the point is academic, for knowledge of God and the scriptures precedes both faith and love. The Erasmian Donne was to say it succinctly when he said 'Faith lies not on this side knowledge, but beyond it' (*Sermons* V 102).

Eternity with its lasting weal or woe is not much considered in the second part of the book where the not-knowing is either

26 The irony here involves, of course, Erasmus' own logic-chopping (so-called). Among many texts of this colour the following from the *De Pueris* is sufficient to bespeak the Erasmian attitude: 'Quemadmodum autem canis nascitur ad venatum, avis ad volatum ... ita homo nascitur ad Philosophiam et honestas actiones; atque ut unumquodque animantium facillime discit id ad quod natum est, ita homo quam minimo negocio percipit virtutis et honesti disciplinam, ad quam semina quaedam vehementia naturae vis insevit, modo ad naturae propensionem accedat formatoris industria' (LB I 496D–E).
27 *Enchiridion* chapters 3, 5, and 6, esp. pp 47ff, 70, 85ff

delusion or madness, but natural delight in ignorance is reduced to absurdity on even the natural level when Gryllus is made to stand as symbol for happy unreason and Moria asks who would not rather be Gryllus, happy, than Odysseus in his griefs. And in the last section of the oration the wise fool pursues eternal union with God not because he is too witless to reckon its price, but because, having full knowledge of earth's pleasures, he yet chooses to heed the rumble of a distant drum.

There is still a problem, and I do not think Erasmus solves it; perhaps no one ever does. For in the end, choice may depend on knowledge, or intelligence, or vision; and such vision as that wise fool has may compel his choice. What it is that makes one man seek integrity or holiness and another care nothing for it, one cannot perhaps say. In *The Education of a Christian Prince* Erasmus attributes the germ of all goodness or badness to the 'idea,'[28] and so perhaps relieves man of much of his responsibility. For the teacher would teach according to his own idea, and the one taught would act on ideas partly his own and partly ingrafted by the teacher. Years later, when the Lutheran controversy forced Erasmus to take sides and formulate his principles, he was strongly on the side of man's freedom of will. In the *Praise*, where he has Moria's freedom of speech, he assumes man is responsible for the kind of vision he has and the kind of choice thereby compelled. And Moria does consider the question of vision and choice in the last few paragraphs of the book. One dominant image in this part is that of the cave of Plato's myth; and this time the shadows and substance do not concern indifferent things as they had done before – pictures, pearls, and kippered herrings had then been the mooted goods – but the things of eternal worth. Again, as before, those within think those outside are mad, while those outside (and they are few) know those inside to be deluded. It does seem here to be a question of vision, and so of the intellect (and grace) rather than the will. But the following paragraph

28 *The Education of a Christian Prince* trans. Lester K. Born (W.W. Norton and Company, New York 1968; by arrangement with Columbia University Press, who first published this translation in 1936) 146ff

throws the responsibility for holding one vision or another squarely on man's will to see.

> On particular points there are great degrees of difference between those two sorts of persons. In the first place, although all the senses have alliance with the body, certain of them are grosser, such as touch, hearing, sight, smell, taste, while certain ones are less closely tied up with the body, as the memory, intellect, and will. *To whichever one the soul applies itself, that one grows strong.* For as much as every energy of the devout soul strives towards objects which are at farthest remove from the grosser senses, these grow numb, as it were, and stupefy; whence it comes that we hear about saints who have chanced to drink oil in place of wine. Among the passions and impulses of the mind, again, some have more connection with the physical body, as lust, love of food and sleep, anger, pride, envy. With these the pious are irreconcilably at war, while the multitude, on the other hand, consider that without them life does not exist. Then there are some feelings of the middle sort, merely natural, so to speak, such as love of one's father, affection for one's children, relatives, and friends; to these feelings the multitude pays considerable respect, but *the pious endeavour to pluck them too out of their minds*, except so far as, rising to the highest spiritual place, they love a parent not as a parent – for what did he beget but the body, and even that is owed to God as Father – but rather as a good man, one in whom is manifest the impress of that Supreme Mind, which they call the *summum bonum*, and beyond which, they assert, nothing is to be loved or sought for. [p 121; italics mine]

The satire in the *Praise* is not always so speculative and interrogatory. Many of the attacks strike at quite obvious wrongs. But we never get entirely away from Erasmus' interest in the part played by the well-informed intellect in the pursuit of virtue or vice. The Silenus box, for instance, shouldered aside just now for other interests, has great significance. It is one of Erasmus' favourite symbols, and stands for one of his constant preoccupations: the gap between what is and what should be, or (what is worse) between what is and what pretends to be. Sometimes this denotes simple deceit or hypocrisy, but more often it involves self-delusion, something in which intellect and will are interactive. One might say that self-delusion bespeaks defective knowledge, but self-imposed by a faulty will. Erasmus himself offers some explanation in the *Christiani matrimonii institutio,* where he speaks of *exercitatio* or *usus* making what has been taught become habit (LB V 710D); it could do a like service for what has been self-induced, so that the mind's ability to distinguish between good and less good is dulled, and habituated to its faulty judgement; and here one could hardly exonerate the will.

Within this area of self-delusion are many follies which might be channelled under two headings: 1 / good things (or indifferent) pushed to extremes; and 2 / confusion in distinguishing between signs and things.

Erasmus' love of moderation is well-known. His peculiar list of Seven Deadlies (p 68) is simply a series of violations of the golden mean, the reasonable. With the desirable middle way unexpressed but quite implicit, Moria scores monks who stay at home all the time and monks who never stay at home, miserly merchants and extravagant spendthrifts, reckless adventurers who hazard life needlessly, and men who vegetate for very caution, the over-prudent and the utterly indiscreet, the Stoics who care nothing for men's esteem, and the worldly who care too much.

The second channelling of folly is more interesting. If the foregoing is redolent of Aristotle and St Thomas, we come now to St Augustine. Of Erasmus' respect for Augustine we have already had occasion to speak (p 38). Augustine's *De doctrina* begins with a declaration that all teaching is concerned with things and signs. And it is thus that Erasmus too begins his *De ratione studii* (1513), written when his enthusiasm for Augustine was perhaps at its height. All knowledge, he says in this treatise, is concerned with things and words (LB I 521A); and as late as 1518 he was still using these Augustinian distinctions and even phrasings in the *Enchiridion,* though in that same year, in a letter to Johann Eck, he admits that he rates Augustine below certain other Fathers, notably Jerome. It is not unlikely then that during the writing of the *Praise*, he was aware of Augustine's thought patterns.[29]

A thing, Augustine had said, was a simple thing when it was not used to signify something else; a sign had as its sole usefulness the quality of signifying. But a thing might indeed be a thing and yet have its major importance as a sign or symbol. Words are signs, trees are things, but a tree might be both sign and thing: and Augustine points to the tree that Moses casts into bitter waters.[30]

In the *Praise* one can find three kinds of thing-sign confusion: That the word, the indisputable sign, is too often treated as a thing Erasmus is well aware; but it is rather in the *Ciceronianus* that he develops his arguments against this absurdity, the rhetoricians' folly. In the *Praise* there is only mild censure for those who pay too great homage to dialectic and grammar and oratory, so that, dissociated from their true meaning and purpose, these things become things in themselves. There is some scorn, but not much, for the things that are both things and signs but whose sign-value has been lost; the superstitious people of Erasmus' day were too prone to see signs where there were none. One example does come to mind, however: the candle burnt at noon before the Virgin Mother – at noon, says Moria, when it is unnecessary to have light (p 66). But the irony here doubles in on itself in a strange way: Moria thinks the candle is 'thing' only and useless in the circumstances; the people lighting it think it a sign, and are using it as such. But Moria is right in a sense, for the sign-value of the candle has slipped for these people, it *is* just a candle, its light then *is* wasted in the noonday sun. One might say too that ceremonies and the minutiae of tradition have replaced the one thing necessary, charity, both in court and monastery, and thus have become things in themselves instead of the signs originally intended. And this whole theme is made

29 Allen III 330–8: 'Imo Augustinum primum omnium legi, et relego cotidie, quoties res postulat. Et quo magis lego, hoc magis mihi placet meum de utroque judicium' (335).

30 In *Fathers of the Church* chapter 3, section 4, no. 29

explicit when Moria sets the princely and priestly vesture beside the unworthy prince and prelate and weighs the symbolic aspect against the empty thing (pp 86 and 95).

With things perfectly indifferent in themselves but given unwarranted significance as signs Moria frequently concerns herself. She pours her praise on monks, for instance, who will not handle money, since money, a simple medium of barter, has become for them the sign of their poverty – a poverty that does not shrink from enjoying what the money will procure. The monk cares too much too for the material in his girdle, the knots in his shoe-string, the shape of his cowl.

In the consideration of things as things, Erasmus may have remembered too that Augustine had reflected that some things were to be enjoyed – they were ends in themselves; and some to be used – they were means only:

> But if we ... strive to enjoy the things we are supposed to use, we find our progress impeded and even now and then turned aside. as a result, fettered by affection for lesser things, we are either retarded from gaining those things which we are to enjoy or we are even drawn entirely from them.
>
> To enjoy anything means to cling to it with affection for its own sake. To use a thing is to employ what we have received for our use to obtain what we want, provided that it is right for us to want it. [*De doctrina* 13]

Among Moria's worldly followers almost all tend to make ends of means, enjoying what should be only used – merchants, scholars, preachers, schoolteachers, monks, and prelates, all are bemused. If 'wisdom were to descend on them' even the members of the papal court would soon come to distinguish between using and enjoying their honours. The sacraments too might be instanced. Too often they are esteemed as ends, as indeed the evidence of holiness, rather than the means to attain it. And of course, so too with fasting and pilgrimages. Distress for this confusion becomes more articulate as the end of the oration is reached: and the clearer vision of the *philosophus Christi* becomes the norm:

By the same rule they also measure all others of life's duties, and in general they either scorn that which is visible or make much less of it than of things invisible. They say also that both body and spirit enter into the sacraments and into the very offices of piety; as in fasting they do not account it of much worth if a person abstain from meats or from a meal, that which the vulgar esteem an absolute fast, unless at the same time he in some measure frees himself from passions, yielding less than he is wont to anger, less to pride; and then the spirit, weighed down less by the burden of the body, may climb upward even to the partaking and enjoying of celestial bounties. In like manner too with the Eucharist ... of itself it is either of little profit or indeed harmful except so far as that which is spiritual is added to it – in a word, that which is represented under the visible symbols. For the death of Christ is so represented, and this it behooves mortal man to translate into the taming, extinguishing and, as it were, burying, of their carnal affections ... [122]

The final wisdom is, for Erasmus, the 'philosophy of Christ.' All morality and theology are to him a return to the Gospels; and the interpretation of their message is far more to him than the writing of a satire. The exegete's penchant for finding in a text, or providing for it, a multiple interpretation was very familiar to him; it is a skill he uses in some of the colloquies. The *Praise*, it is true, does not provide any one passage that is capable of yielding a multiple interpretation. But in its totality it does provide sustenance for man's several appetites. It is in man's nature to delight in the human comedy, in wit and literary allusion; and Moria has provided an abundance of this. It is his nature to be a reasoning being and a moral one; and the great central portion of the oration concerns the behaviour of man. Even in this part, Moria hints that it is proper to man's nature to strive to go beyond its bounds. In the final and climactic part of Moria's oration, she reaches for what Erasmus the exegete might have called the anagogical level.

A place among Folly's protegés is given to this wise-fool at the end because indeed some of his senses are 'stupefied,' deliberately so, with the vision of earthly things blotted out with the glare of the eternal. This final folly brings to its victim a delight even in this world of temporal joy, as natural pleasures had delighted the first of Moria's devotees, and vain delusion the second. For the good man whom Moria has finally described is more than merely a good man – he is a man in love with God, filled with the delights of anticipation of the Beatific Vision. In a sense this joy makes him kin to the other fools: each has been made happy according to his capacity for being so.

Many of the seeming contradictions are resolved perhaps in this area of degrees of vision. Wisdom and prudence, for instance, at first two separate qualities and mutually repellent since one holds back through shame and fear and the other cares nothing for appearances, are resolved; for the shame and fear which the one is too witless to know is a half-way vision of good, centred on worldly prudence and social consciousness; and acting, just acting, is an indifferent thing, its good or bad determined by the end to which it tends. Social consciousness can be absorbed in God-consciousness, and acting can be determined to a good end.

Again, the natural man loves life and the Stoic wise man hates it. The philosopher of Christ both loves and hates it. He 'dearly prefers death,' not because it is liquidation from a tiresome living, but because it is the door to life's fullness. The value of opinion is another point. The first fool cares little about it, and is happy in his indifference to, or ignorance of, his fellow man's attitude. The second fool rests his happiness on vanity, and his fellow's approbation matters mightily. The scholar is close to the man of God and does not think it shame to live 'neglected, inglorious, disliked.' The man of holiness is 'wholly rapt away in contemplation'; his indifference to opinion does not come from a Stoic pride in his own competence but from his absorption in charity.

Moria has asked other questions as she proceeds. The answers, which she did not know then, are implicit in the last sections, or if they are not answered, they have come to rest in the repository of faith. Truth, we noted, was sometimes the property of the naturals, sometimes of the wise man; it was sometimes to be tempered with discretion, sometimes to be spoken frankly; scholars who concerned themselves with the least abstract studies, medicine and law, were beloved of folly, dearer than those who studied metaphysics and theology; yet the students of abstract knowledge had seemed to merit the greater scorn in the end; and the answer is obvious: they have made an end of a means, and turned the *optimus* to *pessimus*.

One could wish, however, that the conclusion of the *Praise* gave a glimpse of some great good wise man who is not an ecstatic. The perplexing tangles of the strongly satirical centre of the oration are hardly unravelled on their own rational level. It is right, of course, that all should be resolved in the life of faith and charity which the last part suggests. But one feels that Erasmus is making an awkward transition from the life of reason to that of faith in more than an artistic sense, that his answer to the problems that beset the stage of life is to retreat from them – a wise man returning to the skies.[31]

Nevertheless the life of faith and hope and charity is warmly acclaimed in this last section, and we do find there a tranquillity that lifts the work to a transcendent level rarely found in Erasmian writing, and rarely found in satire. Erasmus was not a philosopher, nor even a theologian, if we take philosophy and

---

31 For an opinion about this last part of the *Praise* that is both like and unlike the one I have expressed, see H.A. Mason *Humanism and Poetry in the Early Tudor Period* (London 1959) 83–5. Professor Mason finds this section disturbing, and thinks that Moria does not identify herself with this supreme folly, but only 'treats it from a point of view at bottom hostile.' To substantiate his point Mason quotes from a letter Allen II 105) in which Erasmus admits having in this work feared to offend and 'come short of the dignity of the theme and the demands of piety,' and so having preferred to 'break the rules of art and injure the dramatic credibility of the book.' The book, then, Mason reasons, is not primarily 'an affirmation of the spontaneous instinctive and anti-intellectual element in life'; and with this I would, of course, agree. But I do not find the section so mined with the rejection of the life of the intelligence as to be unacceptable, nor do I find Moria either indifferent or hostile to it.

theology to be speculative sciences. And we might look a long time to find his own definition of true wisdom. All thinking is behaviour to him; he is interested in ethical and practical wisdom primarily. But the converse is true too: if all thinking is behaviour, so too all behaviour is thinking in his estimation. The man who thinks well behaves well; and man can be taught to think.

THREE

❧ Colloquy and Declamation ❧

NO OTHER WORK OF ERASMUS' shows his capacity to handle all man's responses as does the *Praise*, and no other work is capable, therefore, of the manifold interpretation attempted in the previous chapter. Folly is, after all, a far-ranging subject, and Moria an expansive character, fictitious and yet actual, abstract and yet particular. Since the *Praise* is an indictment of all folly, it does not concentrate exclusively on any one evil and so provide a definitive key to preoccupations uniquely Erasmian. Many critics have fastened on its excoriation of monasticism and superstition; but such a singling out is hardly warranted. So too the theme of dissension – private quarrelling or warfare – is hardly given more importance in the *Praise* than in a host of other iniquities. This was, however, one of Erasmus' greatest distresses; and three works, *Julius secundus exclusus*, *Querela pacis*, and the lengthy adage 'Dulce Bellum Inexpertis,' all written within the decade following the *Praise*, bring us sharply to an awareness of Erasmus' hatred of the peculiar evil of discord.

Julius secundus exclusus was written within a year or so after Julius' death in 1513, probably in the quiet of Erasmus' study at Cambridge, and with the memory of his disillusionment in Italy still vivid enough. Huizinga, in his *Erasmus of Rotterdam*, speaks of its being written 'in the deepest secrecy, between the work on the New Testament and Jerome' (p 94). Certainly Erasmus must have considered the work perilously imprudent, for he circulated it only in manuscript at the time, and when in 1517 it did appear in print and begin to create a small furore, he disclaimed responsibility at least for having published it, 'resorting when necessary,' as one editor says, 'to every form of equivocation short of literal mendacity.'[1]

Leo x was Pope by this time, and Erasmus had high hopes for the peace of Christendom now that the warlike Julius, exclusus or inclusus, had gone to his reward. The hopes were hardly justified, as we know, but it is likely that Erasmus had something of positive didactic purpose in the writing of an attack on war and a militant papacy at this time when there seemed to be hope for peace and for greater probity in the high places of the Church.[2]

1 W.K. Ferguson *Erasmi opuscula* (The Hague 1933) 42. I am assuming the work is by Erasmus. Thomas More's letter, if there were nothing else, seems to me conclusive evidence: 'Lupsetus [More writes to Erasmus] restituit mihi aliquot quaterniones tuas quas olim apud se tenuerat. In his est Julii Genius, et declamationes duae, alter de pueris ... tua manu omnia, sed prima tantum scriptio, neque quicquam satis integrum (Allen II 420). Allen's own comments prefacing the letter show that he has no doubt that Erasmus is the author, and he advances the argument (both here and in his *Age of Erasmus* [London 1914] 184–9) that, although he was too canny to proclaim himself the author, Erasmus never explicitly denied having written it, but only having published it. Most of the critics agree: Drummond (*Erasmus* [London 1873] 24) neither claims nor disclaims it, nor do Huizinga, Margaret Mann Phillips, or Bataillon; but Jortin (*Life of Erasmus* [London 1808] II 596), Renaudet (*Etudes erasmiennes, 1521–9* [Paris 1939] 85), Preserved Smith (*Erasmus* [New York 1923] 213), Mangan (*Life, Character, and Influence of Erasmus* [New York 1927] II 67–70), Froude (*Life and Letters of Erasmus* [New York 1894] 147), Bainton (p 109), and W.K. Ferguson himself all consider the dialogue unquestionably Erasmus'. Professor Ferguson gathers together all the evidence and attitudes and lists many names not included here (pp 42–7). See too J.K. Sowards' introduction (pp 7–14) to the Pascal translation of the dialogue documented below, and also his 'Thomas More, Erasmus, and Julius II: A Case of Advocacy,' in *Moreana* 24 (November 1969) 25–8. The case against Erasmus' authorship is presented by James D. Tracy in *Renaissance Quarterly* XXI (1968) especially p 286. Tracy does not find the letter from More conclusive, and refers the reader to another letter (Allen I 483) wherein Erasmus gives reasons for disliking Julius, reasons other than the ones advanced in the dialogue.

2 There was an interval of comparative peace during the reign of Leo x, but it was short-lived. Although Erasmus died before the worst of the mid-century distresses, he must have foreseen them as inevitable. In 1526, a decade or so after the writing of Julius, he listed some of the evils of the time in 'The New Mother' (*Colloquies* 269–70).

The similarity between this work and Lucian's *Dialogues of the Dead* is not to be denied, though it is largely in the form. Lucian liked to see human foibles from an other-worldly perspective; Erasmus presents Julius at the gate of heaven with Peter confronting him – aghast at his wrong-headedness. Lucian is credited with having originated the comic or satiric dialogue,[3] and Erasmus, who had translated and imitated Lucian's work, was, of all people, best able to bring the lively colloquy to perfection. But *Julius exclusus* has more dramatic irony than most of Lucian's dialogues, and perhaps less conscious irony; for most of the Lucianic dramas have only one important character, a wise fellow who is spokesman for the author's satiric views, and ready to enlighten his less percipient companion; but the companion (who might so easily have supplied the element of ridicule) is hardly more than a listener, whereas in *Julius exclusus*, as in most of the colloquies, at least one character is naive and impercipient and ready to chatter fatuously about his folly. Compared with Lucian's dialogues, perhaps *Julius exclusus* comes off fairly well; and one can imagine that, for the sixteenth-century reader as fluent in Latin as in his own tongue, it must have been lively reading.[4] Julius himself is one of those culpable unintelligent people that are peculiarly Erasmian creations.

---

3 See the introduction to Fowler's edition of Lucian's *Works* I xii.

4 Huizinga, a Dutchman himself, thinks longingly of how charming the colloquies would have been if Erasmus had written them in 'racy Dutch' (*Erasmus of Rotterdam* 43). And H.A. Mason might be sympathetic with such a wish. It is of the *Praise* he speaks, not the colloquies, it is true, but what he says easily applies to the colloquies as well. After saying that 'the brilliance of the book as a piece of Latin is something separate from the intrinsic interest [of its substance],' he asks himself the unanswerable question whether it would have been a better book 'in one of the vernaculars, if the vernaculars could have been made to embody it.' It is better in the Latin, he thinks, than in any of the English translations, having a 'genuine raciness and a variety of tone that have not been reproduced by the translators.' In the end Mason hesitantly advances the critical opinion that the impact of the book would have been greater if it had been written in, say, the old French of Rabelais' day. (I have quoted more of this passage in chapter two, p 69.) Professor Roland Bainton, in his *Erasmus of Christendom*, gives a lively translation of part of the dialogue (pp 106–8). Until 1968 Erasmian scholars

The dialogue, on its literal (and literary) level, has three avenues of approach: 1 / its effectiveness as drama; 2 / the quality of its irony; 3 / the limits of its characterization.

Obviously, the form of *Julius exclusus* is dramatic, since it is not declamation but colloquy – and might perhaps have been included with the other colloquies had its subject been less palpably real and its author less apprehensive of its reception. The setting is outside the gate of heaven, where Julius, recently deceased, demands entry, St Peter questions his credentials, and a familiar spirit (whom Erasmus tends to forget) acts as a sort of chorus character. Julius is exasperated that the doors are locked and will not yield to his key; the 'genius' or spirit suggests that, since the key of power is obviously useless, perhaps the key of knowledge would fit better, but Julius protests that 'this is the only one I ever had'; and so the motif is established. Peter appears but does not recognize Julius' spurious claims, the key, the triple crown, and the pallium. All of them, Peter says, show signs of 'that most wicked huckster and imposter, who has my first name, to be sure, but not my calling – Simon [Magus].' Julius then produces his card, but the difficult doorkeeper is not impressed with the Pontifex Maximus motif, and when the infuriated Julius advances his splendid titles, *sanctissimus Dominus, Sanctitas* ... , Holiness itself, Peter is strangely indifferent. 'But do you honestly believe,' he asks, 'there is no difference between being called holy and being holy?'[5]

Expostulatory and acid, the dialogue is still not quite brilliant, though again the Latin (even to untrained ears) has a certain staccato smartness, verging even on the stichomythic, that the English misses. Here, for instance, is Peter putting deceptively innocent questions to the insensitive Julius:

were dependent on, and appreciative of, the translation made by J.A. Froude and included in his *Life and Letters of Erasmus* (New York 1894) 149–68.

5 *Julius secundus exclusus* (1513), translated by Paul Pascal as *The Julius Exclusus of Erasmus* with introduction and notes by J. Kelley Sowards (Bloomington, Ind. 1968) 46, 47

PETER: Ni merita narras, inquam, nihil agis.

JULIUS: Quae merita?

PETER: Dicam. Excelluisti doctrina sacra?

JULIUS: Minime; nec hoc vacabat, tot occupato bellis. Verum abunde satis est fratrum, si quid hoc ad rem pertinet.

PETER: Ergo vitae sanctimonia multos Christo lucrifecisti?

GENIUS: Tartaro quam plurimos.

PETER: Claruisti miraculis?

JULIUS: Obsoleta loqueris.

PETER: Pure orasti et assidue?

JULIUS: Quas nugas hic gannit.

PETER: Jejuniis quoque vigiliisque corpus emacerasti?

GENIUS: Desine quaeso: frustra haec; apud hunc ne ludas operam.[6]

The dialogue has dramatic liveliness at times, but little activity; once St Peter has appeared everything is static, for neither Peter nor Julius budges an inch either physically or in mind and judgement. Nor does the conversation narrate much imaginable action, since the wars are, for the most part, generalized and very pluperfect: we do not vicariously feel the alarms and excursions. Donne was to do much better indeed with the releasing of dramatic energy in his *Ignatius his Conclave*, in many ways so similar to *Julius exclusus*.

The irony that emerges, as Julius presents his credentials, is very different from that of the *Praise*; formally different, of course, because of the dialogue form, but different in total effect too. In the *Praise* all the irony was in Moria herself; the reader had to be continually alert to her changing tone to discover what the author intended; he had to make his own judgements, guided by Moria sometimes, but sometimes tricked by her. In *Julius exclusus* Peter is always present, thinking and judging aright and without irony, rebuking and contradicting Julius, so that the reader need only recognize Peter's right reason, then relax and be lectured – and Peter's lectures are often banal. All this gives

6 *Erasmi opuscula* 70, 71

the reader a more immediate recognition of corruption, but a less interesting one. The didactic Peter never points a finger at the reader's sins, of course, but only at Julius', and so the response is slightly deflected from the purely directive.

When the man who is the butt of a satire has already encountered St Peter, he is surely beyond the pale of instruction, and one might think the didactic element in the satire rather negligible. But Erasmus must have known he could depend on his audience's including a large segment of the continuing Church, and in it some of those who would be the electors of future popes. However he might attack its abuses, it was not the dissolution of the Church he wanted; nor did he expect it. He hoped rather to modify or even re-create the climate of opinion and judgement among those ecclesiastical nobles who had the power to put a man like Julius into office. That Erasmus could reach these men there is little doubt. For all his disclaimer of responsibility, *Julius exclusus* seems to have been well known as his work, and this, coupled with the daring character of the skit, would have assured its being read by prelate, cleric, and layman in this early sixteenth century. W.K. Ferguson lists thirteen editions published almost certainly during Erasmus' lifetime, and references to it, some oblique, some explicit, appear in much high correspondence.[7]

Further, one cannot but remember that when Erasmus was writing the *Praise* just a few years before this, it was not grossly sinning villains who claimed his primary interest, but the spectator of folly or iniquity. In that work the spectator, not quite of earth, nor yet of heaven, had speculated about the prudent or wise response to folly, though his recognition of the right or wrong of it had been secure enough. For Erasmus percipience and good judgement constituted more than two-thirds of integrity,

---

7 It is frequently referred to in the letters of the period, as Professor Ferguson's impressive lists and quotations show (*Opuscula* 42–4), and by 1519 we find Erasmus writing to two cardinals, Campeggio and Wolsey, disclaiming responsibility for it, a fact that argues for its having penetrated into ecclesiastical high places (Allen III 961, 967, and IV 995). Ferguson conjectures that the ferment following the appearance of Erasmus' Greek New Testament would have assured any writing of his a hearing among highly placed ecclesiastics.

and for the advancement of this awareness he was prepared to labour and take risks. *Julius exclusus* may be well directed to this end.

We are always aware of Julius as a historical figure: all too real had been this warlike pope, all too real his ambitions. He had been Julian della Rovere, nephew to Pope Sixtus, and as such he had held a rich plurality of bishoprics – four, to be exact, none of which he had occupied. His election had not been without chicanery, and his ten years of papal reign had seen a succession of unnecessary wars. Fate must have laughed ironically at his election; for surely this was the very time when the Christian world needed a pope strong and holy, one who could have concentrated on purging the abuses threatening the life of Christendom, on the revitalizing of the Church's theology and the spiritual life of its members, on the prevention of inner strife or political attack; and finally on the repelling of victorious Islam. Julius was the antithesis of this kind of vicar, interested only in enlarging his principate and worldly power by arms, in strengthening Italy against invasion. In the League of Cambrai he made an alliance with France and Castile against Venice, which was then threatening the borders of his own state. Venice subdued, he provoked wars with the very princes and statesmen who had helped him subdue it. He challenged the French at Milan, fought with them at Bologna, and suppressed the council they had been exasperated into calling at Pisa against his outrageous policies. On the whole, the rulers of France, Spain, Italy, and the Papal States seemed to be dancing some macabre Paul Jones, partnering and re-partnering easily and casually until all combinations had been tried. And the central figure, Erasmus would have had to tell himself, was a prince of the Church, earthly vicar of Christ, and an old man at that, who might better have been preparing for death. He is one of the badly cast players of Moria's theatre scene.[8]

8 In the adage 'The Sileni of Alcibiades' a stormy paragraph on the true and false dignities of ecclesiastics ends with an explicit reference to Julius: 'I want to see the Pontiff ride in triumph, not in the bloodthirsty triumphs of a wicked Marius or a conscienceless Julius, so empty as to

But not all Renaissance thinkers thought as Erasmus did. A serious and significant factor in the kind of humanism now emerging was the new outlook which proposed as hero a man indifferent to divine sanctions, wanting to assume full custody of his life and the security of the state without recognition of divine omnipotence or of the need to pay to it the usual homage of ordinary moral integrity. Machiavelli could urge the prince that 'he who abandons what is done for what ought to be done will rather learn to bring about his own ruin than his preservation'; he could, moreover, rely on a sympathetic hearing as he lauded the merits of Julius for his 'successful enterprises' to increase the power of the Church; he could point out that griefs brought to the Italian people after the French victories had not been occasioned by any divine rebuke for transgressions against God's law, but rather by the natural course of events – political ineptitude resulting in carnage and sorrow.[9]

England was embroiled too – and Erasmus was in England throughout most of the year 1513 when perhaps *Julius exclusus* was taking shape in his mind.[10] Ferdinand of Spain had been the

be the butt of the Satirists (if old Democritus were to see them I think he would die of laughing), but truly magnificent and Apostolic, such as Paul (a warrior himself and a much finer general than Alexander the Great) describes with a great flourish, as it were blowing his own trumpet: "in labours more abundant ..." ' (*Adages* 285)

9 Niccolo Machiavelli *The Prince and the Discourses* (Modern Library edition, New York 1950) 43, 35, and 56

10 It is, however, from the letters dated October 1511, and especially those to and from Erasmus' friend Ammonio, that we get the greatest evidence of his exasperation with and distaste for Julius and his politics. For the most part, it is Ammonio who reports (from London) the news of fracas and triumphs, and Erasmus who comments with sardonic irony and sometimes sorrow. He hears 'the mighty Julius is dead,' but Julius was not dead, and Ammonio tells of further troubles and of the pope's going to the shrine at Loretto 'to give thanks for his recovery.' 'What piety!' Erasmus scoffs, 'As to the war ... I'm afraid now at last the Greek proverb the *singed moth's doom* may come to pass. For if anything happens to the Roman church then who, I ask you, could more properly be blamed for it than the all-too-mighty *Julius*?' In an earlier letter he had wanted to vent his annoyance on 'that circumcised physician of the Pontiff's who either is surely a poor workman, or else the sources of hellebore are quite exhausted.' Still, he has some lingering

Pope's ally throughout, both against Venice and against France. In 1512 he had persuaded his son-in-law, Henry VIII of England, to declare war against France also. For his help in driving the French out of Italy, Julius had promised Henry the title of 'Most Christian King,' hitherto the title of Louis XII, but forfeited by him after his unfortunate attempt to call the council at Pisa. Actually England had not benefitted by Henry's participation in the unsavoury strategies and wars: the empty title did not materialize and heavy taxes did.

The historical reality of the protagonist and subject matter is an important factor in estimating the readers' response to a work.[11] In our discussion of the *Praise* we had to consider and appraise the quantity and quality of fiction standing between the denunciation and the reader. The *Praise* was not a complete fiction, for although Moria and her rostrum were fabrications, the ills she ridiculed were real. Except for the situation, everything about *Julius exclusus* is real – characters, dispositional traits, follies narrated. And the confrontation, the only fiction, is a prosy piece of business. The tone of it and the mood hardly rise above the sordid particulars; and we cannot but remember with nostalgia the good times we had with Moria, who flicked us in and out of caves, showed us wonderful birds, took us to the theatre, and in the end ran us almost into Paradise. Julius cannot get even himself into Heaven, much less his readers.

Moreover, when Moria talked of folly, she spoke lovingly at times to the very fools about whom she was declaiming, for they made up her audience. Erasmus was stretching two ways there, as artist and humanist to the understanding wise people who

hope that 'the fates themselves will find a way'! See the translation of D.F.S. Thomson in *Erasmus and Cambridge* with introduction and notes by H.C. Porter (University of Toronto Press 1963) 112–37.

11 One remembers, for instance, the strong indignation aroused a few years ago by Hochhuth's *The Deputy*. Professor Bainton, in explaining Erasmus' reluctance to claim authorship of *Julius exclusus*, points out that it was not merely 'a photographic portrait of Pope Julius, but rather a conflation of the Renaissance popes,' and that the new pope (Leo X) might well feel that he too 'would not emerge unscathed from a dialogue with St Peter' (p 109).

were as percipient as he, and as preacher and pastor to the victims of his oratory. But in *Julius exclusus* the victim is already
four days in the grave: Erasmus cannot hope to save him.

Furthermore, although we may recognize Erasmus' awareness
of the papal court, the electors and counsellors, and the wise and
percipient onlookers, the moral aspect of *Julius exclusus* is less
interesting than that of the *Praise*. It is not entirely negative and
denunciatory; St Peter does painstakingly point out the good life
(and in the early parts with some éclat); but he never achieves
the heights of exaltation: what he says is solidly true, obviously
true, but never inspired.

Julius is arraigned for private sins of sensuality and luxury,
for vainglory about hereditary titles and acquired ones, for glory-
ing in being a self-made man; for simony and bribery and all
sorts of political chicanery; for issuing bulls and granting dis-
pensations at a price – he had indeed granted one to Erasmus
himself, at a price. False and unchristian had been his ideas of
culture, of barbarism, and of nationalism; and above all, he had
engaged the whole world in war, not to drive the Turk from the
holy places, but to enrich the earthly territories of a church whose
glory lay not in earthly kingdoms.

All the foolish thinking we had found underlying particular
ills in the *Praise* are to be found here, though with a difference:
there are discrepancies between what seems and what is (for
Julius is glad to remain in the shadows of Plato's cave), and between the enjoyment and the use of material goods (with Julius
using his grace of state and his power over the Christian world
not to promote the good life but to further the temporalities);
symbol and ceremony, voided of all spiritual meaning, remain
merely signs and are invalid as things. But Julius' faults are
largely of the will: he is in cavernous darkness because he chooses
to be, he boasts of having no learning, and when Peter speaks
of wicked popes and virtually includes him in the grouping, he
does not protest. The reader has no more perplexities than has
Julius: to him it is obvious that thinking as Julius thinks and
acting as Julius acts are bad ways to think and act. In the *Praise*
Erasmus had recognized that there were problems too complex

to be ticked off with easy judgements. Julius hardly glances at the complexities, though the curious reader may conjecture about what kind of *natura* so easily sidesteps its potential *ratio* – as perhaps the readers of More's *Utopia* may ponder what first cause or geographical accident made the Utopians so good and the nearby Anemolians so foolish.

On the positive side we have some emphasis on faith, and strangely enough, on hope, though in the human rather than the theological sense. The Council seems to be composed of good men appalled at Julius' grossness and greed and trying as far as possible to hold it in check. These men are able men too, 'with a conscience, who will speak their minds.' One Rothomagensis, Cardinal of Rouen, must also have integrity, for Julius makes withering remarks about his *nescio qua sanctimonia*, and says he was always crying for Church reform. Another, the Cardinal of Santa Croce, is a man *vitae inculpatae*, though a 'rigid old theologian,' epithets not so damning as Julius thinks. This man had had the courage to say openly that the Church was disordered and in need of a council, and to remind Julius that he had promised there would be a council in two years. Then too the monks, often enough the butt of Erasmus' irony, have preserved, as Julius has not, some modicum of respect for doctrine; the world itself, says St Peter, has some good in it: faith and the desire for good leadership. If Julius were holy, learned, charitable, virtuous, the world itself would esteem him more, not less (88); yet there must be good in the world, he goes on, when such a 'filthy sewer' can be honoured merely because he bears the name of pope.

Julius himself is not wholly without virtue, as Ferguson points out. Erasmus, as befits a satirist, attacks him relentlessly, exaggerating his insensitivity and his greed. But in one place he allows him a sentence or two showing misguided good-will, and a smack of loyalty to the body he governed so badly:

But I always wanted the Church to be adorned with all good things. They say that Aristotle established three categories of goods, of which some come from fortune, some from the body, and some from the mind. So I did not want to reverse the order of goods; I began with the goods of fortune. Perhaps I would gradually have reached the goods of the mind if a premature death had not snatched me from the earth.[12]

In the early passages of the dialogue, knowledge had been suggested as the key to heaven. In Peter's final adjudication it seems to be the life of faith, the contempt of the world, and the teaching of Christ and his doctrine (and *'purissime,'* says this *philosophus Christi,* Peter). Many there are, he says, who wear the livery of the Church's ministers – an old story this[13] – but who are unaware that the service should be marked by the cross, not by the pleasures of life. Churchmen should be fewer and the few well-chosen,[14] if the Church is to fulfill her mission.

Beyond the moral sense, there is little of interest. If there is allegory, it is very slight. This is no *Inferno* where a questing Dante is Everyman and the journey is life itself. It is only Julius and Peter, a Peter neither terrible nor lovable, arguing about Julius' particular sins and the general state of the world. There may be moments when the reader might say 'Ah, well-a-day, for this indeed is I'; but such moments are rare.

In one sense, of course, the whole episode is anagogy, for we do stand beyond life and at the door of eternity; and this is the *quo tendimus* of behaviour. But the door never opens and we never do see into the glory within; nor does the comic aspect lend itself to sober reflection on the last things. All in all, of the ultimate wisdom compounded of charity and faith there is no glimpse.

The limpness of the dialogue's spiritual impact is not unrelated to the quality and quantity of irony and of character. Moria's

12 The order 'kept,' according to Aristotle's division, refers to the *Moralia* I (See *Adages* 278, where Erasmus lists these 'good things' as riches, noble birth, bodily health, and grace.)
13 See the *Praise* 98, for similar denunciation of splendid apparel; also the *Adages* 265, 276, 277; and *Colloquies* 206, 210–13 ('Well-to-do Beggars'), and pp 366ff ('The Funeral'). The last two rather outline a philosophy of clothes, however, than simply denounce empty ceremonial dress.
14 For a comparable opinion see Thomas More's *Utopia* (Yale edition) 227.

folly had not been primarily of the will – indeed it was rarely other than wrong thinking; and when one presents the mind in wrong choice one has scope for (a) telling irony, as the unwitting speaker betrays his poor judgement, and (b) dramatic progression, for the unwise can be lessoned and so attain to some wisdom. Moria had had all this potential; but Julius is too knowing, and his vices are largely of the will. True, there is gross stupidity in his threat to Peter: 'If you make me angry ...' and again 'watch out what you're saying.' But he speaks from habit. In any event, a moment later he is a sinner having full knowledge and advertence. Peter has been appalled at the flimsy excuses for war, and Julius blusters:

> Don't talk like that! I would prefer hundreds of wars to a council. What if they had removed me from the Pontificate as simoniac and a Pontifical trafficker, not a Pope? What if they had investigated my whole life and revealed their findings to the people? [80]

When John Donne, a century later, came to write his *Ignatius his Conclave*, although the narrative is peopled by souls who know all too well the import of what they say and do, and who cannot grow in wisdom or cognizance or charity, he wisely included a 'little sportive soul' who is not of eternity but of time. He gave himself thereby opportunity for irony and for a movement on to a level of charity. How well he used his opportunity is another matter.

Two years later Erasmus wrote several new attacks on war, to be incorporated into the new edition of the adages published in 1515. The best known of these is the long essay developing a theme whose title at least is ironic, 'Dulce bellum inexpertis,' or 'Sweet is War to Those who Know it Not.' It is a convincing and compact argument against the unreason of war, more coherent and less diffuse than *The Complaint of Peace*, published in 1516. In Erasmus' own day it must have been very popular. But since, except for its title, it is not satiric and not even incidentally ironic, it has no place in this discussion.

Querela pacis, or *The Complaint of Peace*, is complementary, in a sense, to *Julius exclusus*: it is everything that *Julius* is not; it lacks what *Julius* has. And it is as such that it has place here, for it is hardly more satiric than the 'Dulce bellum.'

The Lady Peace, who makes the complaint, is, like Moria, a woman, one who laments that nowhere in all the civilized world can she find shelter. She is moved, however, to grief rather than scorn, grieving over the coldness afforded her even by those whose business it should be to assure her hospitality: churchmen, statesmen, and kings. The recurrent lament is that war is a defiance of Christian ethics and an outrage against man's greatest attribute, his reason. But, unlike Moria, Peace is an honest woman and respectable, saying exactly what she means and meaning exactly what she says, with no ironic indirection or naiveté. Her declamation follows more loosely than Moria's the accepted rules of oratory; and rightly so, for whereas the *Praise* had used rhetorical eloquence for purposes of parody, the *Complaint* is too sober to lend itself to such comic devices. Contrasting the two, we see the enormous literary twist given to exhortation when it is ironic. Peace laments:

> If I were hated of dumb beasts I could forgive their ignorance, because that strength of the mind is denied them, the which only can perceive my gifts. O unworthy thing, and more than prodigious! – nature hath created man indued with reason and that receiveth the will and mind of God, benevolence and concord; and yet do I sooner obtain a place among wild beasts, how wild and how brutish soever ... than among men.[15]

Moria had not lamented at all: she had exulted. It was she, she bragged, who prompted her friends to go to war, the 'seed plot and fountain of renowned actions,' and the glory of its exploits must go to her clients. Indeed, she goes on:

> when armoured ranks engage each other and bugles bray with harsh accord, of what use are those wise men who, exhausted

15 *Querela pacis* (1516) translated by T. Paynell as *The Complaint of Peace* (New York 1946) 7

by studies, scarce maintain any life in their thin cold blood? The
day belongs to stout gross fellows: the littler wit they have, the
bolder they are ... [30]

We find ourselves wondering just how the *Complaint* might have
read if it had been an *Exultatio belli*, and War, like Folly, had
rejoiced in the world-wide hospitality offered her. For indeed
Erasmus seems in this long-winded oration to be more preachy
than inspired.

As literature the *Complaint* is thin. Even the slight allegory
of the orator's being a condition as well as a woman falters after
the first few pages; there is no dramatic change of personality
or mood, and little intensity. Peace is one of the woodenly allegorical figures considered in the first chapter, and perhaps the
kind of 'ornament' Augustine would have thought not quite consonant with high persuasive purpose.

The Lady Peace is all moral earnestness. Distressed and dis-
heartened, she pleads and reasons with the contentious inhabi-
tants of earth. Christian and religious reasons for peace are not
ignored, and so one might say there is a spiritual level; but one
feels at times that Christ is here a kind of trump card in the
crusade for moral regeneration and peace, not a personal Re-
deemer – not a person at all. If man but followed the way pointed
out by Christ, the Lady Peace says in effect, the world would
not now be the chaotic, fretful place it is; his precepts would
make the world a paradise, especially a paradise for writers and
scholars. This is the moralist's plea, and a long way from that
fullness of vision found in Dante or Teresa of Avila, or even, one
might conjecture, in John Donne. That is why one keeps remembering Moria: she had gone beyond the limited view of the
moralist, because her creator had had it in him to go beyond it,
and she was, it seems, his most completely human, and so his
most completely superhuman, figure.

Erasmus was approaching fifty in the summer of 1516 when
the *Complaint* was being written. Perhaps his attitudes tended,
with the passage of years, to undergo, if not actual change, at
least a shift in stress and emphasis. He himself, in a letter to Al-

phonso Fernandez, who was translating the *Enchiridion*, urged him to translate only those works which were of profit for the bettering of morals and manners. He would have been pleased, no doubt, that Paynell rendered the *Complaint* into English as a counterblast to those who 'notwithstanding that I am alive and do command otherwise,' persisted in publishing the foolish trifles of his restless youth (Allen v 356–7). The tone of the *Complaint* is sober enough.

Perhaps if the two pieces, *Julius exclusus* and the *Complaint*, could be blended, the emulsion might be better flavoured. *Julius Exclusus* has its virtue as a piece of literature and a moral directive, for the dialogue has elements of both dramatic and satiric wit and a certain energy. Its moral sense was not entirely negative, though what was positive in it was hardly more than the corrective for Julius' wrong-headed arrogance. The *Complaint*, on the other hand, has only a false front of fiction and what little it has is enfeebled by being woodenly allegorical and neither witty nor dramatic. It is heavily moral, loudly lamenting the moral turpitude of man, but giving more attention to the exposition of the good life than did *Julius exclusus*. The direction of the moral preoccupations show a change too; for Erasmus seems to have muted some of his old exasperations: with monks undisciplined and monasteries unholy, with clerical abuse and sterile sophistry, with injustice in high places and ignorance everywhere. All these do get some peppering, but the denunciation has become less sarcastic and sweeping, and the denouncer less self-righteous. The anagogical level is present in both satires if we do not demand too much of it: it is not inspiring.

The purpose of the *Complaint* is one that derives from a Christian rational standard: the creation of public feeling against war. Whether Erasmus' detestation of war results from rational perception of its unreason, or from his cultural craving for conditions conducive to scholarship, or merely from his desire to see a new society built on Neo-classical Christian principles of reason, or even from a genuine Christian hatred of unchrist-like discord, it is hard to say. All kinds of motives can be found in his argument. His strongest point perhaps is that war prevents the reign of Christ on earth, but the emphasis is rather more on earth than on Christ. The Lady Peace is concerned to promote a peaceful earth, with true Christianity as guarantee of its endurance, rather than to offer peace as guarantee for the pursuit of the Christ-life in the individual man. There was much more of the exemplum about *Julius exclusus*, and much less of the social document; and the near-heavenly setting made even the literary worth of the piece more secure. Perhaps, in the end, it is all a question of the human symbol. Moria had enough of the universal to keep the symbol quality; Julius was solidly individual, but a representative of his class too. Lady Peace hardly needs cry out for a place to lay her head: she really has no head.

Although Erasmus wrote a fair amount of fiction and even of poetry, on his roster of priorities that of pleasing or delighting the reader would surely have come second to instructing him. Fiction was means to that end. Even the tightly organized fiction of the *Praise* he thought of only as a device through which to make more palatable the same advice as that given in the *Enchiridon*. Instruction is the prime purpose of the colloquies too, a twofold instruction, since they were initially planned to teach young boys the Latin they would have to use through their subsequent student days and in their later careers. The later colloquies came to include a meed of instruction on the moral and Christian life for both the boys and their elders. To the 1526 edition he subjoined an address to the reader concerning the 'profitableness of Colloquies,' in which he lamented the more or less pirated edition which had appeared the previous year, and asserted his purpose in consenting now to publish:

> As physicians do not always prescribe the most efficacious remedies for patients but make some allowance for their cravings, so likewise I thought it well to allure the young – who respond more readily to pleasing than to strict or harsh treatment – with this kind of bait. Accordingly I revised what was published, then added what might help to develop manners also; stealing into the minds of young folk, who, as Aristotle

truly wrote, are unsuitable hearers of moral philosophy, at least of the sort that is taught by formal rules.

Now, if someone protests that it is undignified for an old man to play in this childish fashion, my answer is: 'I don't care how childish, if only it's useful' ...

Well, if I had only been joking in their affair, my critics would apparently have put up with it. But now, since in addition to dealing with refinement of language I have added here and there some passages to direct the mind toward religion, they slander me; and they probe the syllables solemnly spelled out in these pages![16]

Classical scholars admire in the colloquies the 'lively and smooth elegancy of the language,' and certainly the sixteenth-century reader must have delighted in the thinly veiled presentation of his contemporaries and his own times. Charles Reade, in *The Cloister and the Hearth*, calls Erasmus the 'heaven-born dramatist of his generation,'[17] and if he has any claim at all to such a title, it is by reason of the colloquies. In spite of their doubly didactic purpose, they have literary value – crisp dialogue, clever word-play, and good repartee, figurative and allusive language, and sometimes a structural nicety.

Since, as Erasmus says, the purpose of the colloquies is to direct the mind, it may be useful to remember that his own blueprint for education has three focal points: *natura, ratio,* and *exercitatio* or *usus*. The educator, whether he presides in a school-room or writes colloquies, is concerned with the last two; and the colloquies do supply full measure of that ordering of right reason implied in the word *ratio*; and, somewhat vicariously, something of practice or experience that makes reasoned thinking operative. Thinking of the coloquies as emphasizing one or other of the two educative channels, one might say some of them are discur-

16 *The Colloquies of Erasmus* trans. Craig R. Thompson (Chicago 1965) 625. (Subsequent references to the colloquies will be to this edition and the page number bracketed into the text.)
17 Charles Reade *The Cloister and the Hearth* (London 1961) 664

sive (and wholly didactic and directed to the *ratio*), and others are illustrative, providing a proxied experience of living.

In most of the dialogues, some wrong-headed opinion is tabled and given either ironic or straightforward consideration until its absurdity or inequity is obvious – obvious to the gull if there is a gull, to the reader in any case. Other colloquies, no less directed to the correction of wrong thinking, introduce an episode, some-times presented, or represented, with immediacy, but usually through the medium of some onlooker who remembers and talks. In the latter kind there is a plot of sorts and a progress. Many colloquies are partially dramatic: 'The Godly Feast,' for instance, has an elaborate setting, and a suggestion of being moulded to act and scene: we begin with a street scene, move to the pre-prandial walk in Eusebius' garden, and then to a table-setting within the home, and finally to the leave-taking. But all the action is in the conversation.

To most readers – and surely to the boys using these colloquies to learn their Latin – the episodic kind of colloquy is more in-teresting, especially if its episode is represented and not merely narrated. In a few colloquies the two techniques, instruction and plot sequence, are carefully interwoven. These are, of course, the best of all.[18]

One of the early colloquies is of this kind, presenting a quality of drama finer than in most of the others, and being as well sufficiently satiric to warrant our interest. I propose to examine 'The Well-to-do-Beggars' in some detail before passing on to more general discussion.

The 'Beggars' (1524) has, for one thing, a setting and a situa-tion: the first scene plunges us *in medias res* with two Franciscans pleading with a country parson, at the rectory, we suppose, for hospitality. The testy old pastor will have none of them, however, and we see them next trudging towards an inn with night closing

---

18 In this category are 'The Shipwreck,' 'The Well-to-do Beggars,' 'The Unequal Match,' 'The Seraphic Funeral,' and the so-called marriage group.

in on them. They plan to burst into the stove room, and to beg St Francis to prosper this questionable strategy. As the scene changes to a room in the inn, we fear their patron saint must have turned a deaf ear, for the friars are having a hard time of it. But that is the delight of this little colloquy: we feel the suspense, we witness the action, and do not have to depend on an eye-witness's account of it. Contrast in character deepens here, for the inn-keeper is a burly fellow, not very bright at all, though not un-teachable, and ready to interpret everything the monks say according to the letter of the speech – even to challenging their claim to being sons of St Francis, since 'you're always telling us he's a virgin, and has he so many sons?' He has a one-track mind too, and keeps hammering away at his one good question: why the fancy dress? But indeed the question serves Erasmus' purpose well, for in trying to answer it simply enough for the hard-witted innkeeper to understand, the scholarly friars present many aspects of the dress philosophy. The thrust and parry of the dialogue carry us on quickly, but the beggars make little dint in the innkeeper's reluctance to provide table and bed, until at length his wife comes in to swell the *dramatis personae*. With a woman's adroitness, she coaxes her hard-bitten husband into yielding to the friars' request, and although he calls her an 'inter-cessor woman' and 'madam preacher,' the servants are presently setting the table, and the innkeeper, who had been very much *en déshabillé* when the friars burst in, is soon struggling into his shirt. When it is then discovered that the monks have in their knapsack victuals to share with the taverner and his household, the supper gets pleasantly under way. If the colloquy were really a drama, it should, of course, end here happily. But Erasmus' idea of the perfectly satisfactory ending is one of a conversion of mind, a convincing by one of another; and so we sit in at the supper table while the innkeeper and his guests dine on some strongly argumentative conversation as well as on chicken and wine.

This is a rare example of rich characterization and a variety of characters. Most of the colloquies classified as satiric have two speakers only, some have a third, and a few are in the nature of a symposium or panel discussion, with speakers only slightly differentiated, or differing only as rational – irrational.[19] In these there is little clash of opinion and so no need of any petticoat preacher to intervene in behalf of peace and charity. There is movement in the 'Beggars' too, and suspense, with the activity both material and intellectual. Not only do the friars achieve their purpose and get their night's lodging, but the innkeeper is brought to a new way of thinking on the subject of monks, their dress, and their institutions.

The irony of the piece is not sustained, nor is it very sharp, vested, as it usually is, in the heavy scoffing of the innkeeper – at the monks and their dress, at his neighbours and their revels, and especially at his pastor. The colloquy opens with a somewhat double-edged irony, however, as the pastor justifies his lack of hospitality on the strength of his past experience, scoring off what he considers to be monkish ways, but inadvertently revealing too his own weakness:

> It's because if you saw a hen or chicks in my house, you'd abuse me before the people in a sermon tomorrow. That's the thanks you generally return for the hospitality shown you. [204]

But these friars are of a truer colour, and with some of Erasmus' own love of moderation, are ready to counter the pastor's (and later the innkeeper's) harsh judgements, or at least to temper them. This may not be good satire, but it is very good teaching, and the reader is well lessoned, made to see the modicum of truth in the popular criticism of many monks and friars, but to see as well the strength of the ideal so ardently conceived and so indifferently practised. The quotation that follows, for instance, is part of a long disquisition on dress, as it accords with need, use, and decorum, and as it is moulded by custom and tradition:

19 The best known (and probably the best) of these symposium-colloquies is the non-satiric 'Godly Feast,' discussed in chapter one. In this dialogue some nine characters, all of them literate, cultured, and religious-minded, give excellent expression to opinions which, although they do not clash, are sufficiently divergent as to broaden and supplement one another's.

Conrad, the talkative friar, has conceded that convention has been responsible for the many forms of monkish dress:

CONRAD: And so when you see this outfit you see the relics of an age long passed.

KEEPER: Therefore your dress has no other sanctity?

CONRAD: Absolutely none ...

KEEPER: But there's less variety in birds' feathers than in your dress.

CONRAD: Well, isn't it a fine thing to imitate Nature? But finer to surpass her?

KEEPER: Would that you surpassed her in variety of beaks too!

CONRAD: But come, I'll defend variety also, if you permit. Don't the Spaniard, Italian, Frenchman, German, Greek, Turk, Saracen dress differently? ... And in the same land how much variation of dress is there even among persons of the same sex, age, and rank! How much do Venetian, Florentine, Roman differ in appearance, and within Italy alone! ... Hence our variation came about. Dominic took his habit from the honest farmers of his native part of Spain; Benedict from the peasants in his native part of Italy; Francis from farmers in various parts ... [215]

Not without reservation could one commend the dramatic form and structure of the 'Beggars.' Its dialogue overruns its plot and the three scenes make no pretence of being proportioned: the first two are fleeting, the last one heavy with too much talk; and that talk, during the latter half of the colloquy, is confined to Conrad and the Innkeeper, for Conrad's companion and the innkeeper's wife seem to have been forgotten. Still, the colloquy has some claim to unity, and at least three devices for binding up the sprawling structure can be discerned: 1/at the beginning of the episode and again at the end, we have the question of the friars' preaching on the following day: the pastor at the beginning is afraid of it; the innkeeper at the end looks forward to it with pleasure; 2/the mooted philosophy of dress is never far from the reader's (or spectator's) horizon: the monks' dress and the innkeeper's undress are visible and component parts of the scene, and the conversation returns again and again to the validity and use of special dress, because this is an *idée fixe* in the innkeeper's one-track mind; and 3/there is a strange accompaniment of animal imagery running through the dialogue: the pastor calls the friars wolves, and the wolf motif continues, the word (or its plural) occurring no fewer than eight times, usually standing as hieroglyph for greedy, selfish man; the sign swinging outside the inn shows dog and wolf, and another such emblem is seen in a print on an inside wall, where three clerics are pictured as fox, ape, and wolf; the town is to hold a feast for St Anthony, who is the protector of herds, and is therefore adored[20] here where swine abound, and the implication follows that they are themselves swinish; the long trains of women's robes and cardinals' are likened to tails, and variation in monastic dress to the variety in birds' feathers.

One may be too facile in reading arcane meanings into recurrent imagery, and after all, there is nothing unusual about any of the images used in the colloquy: they were commonplace comparisons. At most perhaps Erasmus is suggesting that, although these two sons of St Francis are worthy men, often enough wolves do appear in sheep's or shepherd's clothing. And, since the innkeeper does comment that 'the lid fits the pan' and the people have the priest they deserve, he may well be hinting that a swineherd would do nicely for these people. Again the innkeeper's undress and its yielding to suitable clothes may make comment on his ignorance yielding to reasonable thought. But all this is merest conjecture: the dialogues were written for boys.

Three main lines of thought run through the colloquy, and several collateral ideas. Prominent, of course, is the idea of dress, and we cannot but see in it the old Erasmian preoccupation with signs and things. Conrad tells the querulous innkeeper that 'as clothes don't make a man better, so they don't make a man worse. It's wrong, therefore, to judge anyone by his dress.' The three purposes for dress he first enumerates and then amplifies.[21] It is

---

20 The Latin here is *colunt*, which implies a special cult or devotion certainly, but 'adore' seems to me to stretch the silliness even farther than Erasmus would (LB I 1740F–741A).

21 In 'The Soldier and the Carthusian' Erasmus speaks of a double (rather

hard to say how the first two, need and use, differ from each other in practical terms, and Conrad wisely treats them together; as for the third, decorum, it arises, Conrad says, from two sources: 'sometimes from the very nature of things, sometimes from human custom and opinion.' Often Erasmus inveighs against custom and opinion, but here he puts the case for observing it to some extent, countering the host's question 'Why don't you discard your cowls?' with another: 'Why didn't the apostles, from the first, eat whatever they pleased?' and then proffering the answer:

> Because inviolable custom stood in the way. What's deeply imbedded in men's minds, has been confirmed by long and general usage, and has become second nature, so to speak, cannot be abolished at a stroke without grave danger to human composure, but must be removed gradually, as the man plucked the hairs of the horse's tail. [215]

Charity is less overtly the subject of the piece, but it has its place too. One cannot but contrast the pastor and his intransigent denial of charity with the man and wife, who do yield to the beggars' plea. That was charity of action. Charity of word is present by default in the pastor's experience of those who accepted his hospitality and then spoke against him, and the friars' comment later on about such unsavoury words; and Conrad has a word for charity of judgement too: because of their dress, the monks are judged by some to be rascals and by others to be holier than they are: 'Both are wrong,' Conrad says, 'but those who think well of us ... err more generously than those who think ill.'

Likewise linked with the idea of dress is the idea of responsibility. When the innkeeper, beginning at long last to grasp the friar's point, says, 'then, you're no holier than we, unless you live holier lives,' Conrad quickly caps the point: 'Worse than you, in fact, for our wicked lives would shock simple souls more

than three-fold) purpose for clothing: 'warding off the weather and covering what shame bids us conceal'; but the 'Seraphic Funeral' treats dress as the sign of one's way of life – and with much caustic comment thereon.

deeply.' The parish priest has already provided illustration of how to be indifferent to the responsibilities of one's state. He too wears a dress that makes his behaviour doubly shocking.

Some other subjects also get brief attention. Miracles, needed perhaps in apostolic times, are no longer needed,[22] and cannot now be considered the touchstone of holiness; vagabondage has an ancient sanction and is not an epithet of shame if applied to Franciscan beggars; a feast day, supposedly honouring a Christian saint, should not be made the occasion of 'carousing, dances, games, quarrels, and fights,' worthier of Bacchus than of Antony. For one rather provocative opinion the innkeeper is chorus character: fool's dress has been mentioned in Conrad's amplifying of decorum; it is reasonable, Conrad thinks, for fools to have a special dress 'to keep them out of harm's way if they do or say something rash.' But the innkeeper thinks otherwise:

> I'll refrain from observing that this very thing is a provocation to outrage – so much so that often they turn from fools into madmen. And I don't see why, when an ox that gores a man to death or a dog or a sow that kills a baby is punished, a fool who commits worse crimes is permitted to live under the protection of folly. [212]

It seems strange that, in all Moria's praise of the fool and his privileges, she had never advanced this idea. But there are many good opinions for all life's problems, and Erasmus would not gainsay the grain of truth in even the innkeeper's reflections.

Few of the episodic colloquies have the liveliness and immediacy of 'The Well-to-do Beggars,' and of the few, still fewer are satiric either totally or in part. In the edition of 1523 we do find action and interest in the five dialogues that make up a sort of 'marriage group.'[23] Although there is only a sprinkling of satire

---

22 Strangely enough, a decade earlier Erasmus had had his St Peter query Julius about his miracles, as if they might indeed have been considered a mark of grace (p 50).
23 Professor Thompson lists eight dialogues as constituting this marriage group: 'Courtship,' 'The Girl with no Interest in Marriage,' 'The Repentant Girl,' 'Marriage,' 'The Young Man and the Harlot,' 'The New Mother,' 'A Marriage in Name Only,' and 'The Lower House.'

in them, there is movement and immediacy and a dénouement. We see and hear the principal actors and witness a modification in their opinions and sensibilities – we even witness a change in one character's manner of life. In the first, 'Courtship,' Pamphilus' ardent wooing elicits from Maria a less warm response than he may have expected. She puts the case well for deliberation in choice, and even for virginity – a virginity lived in the world, one imagines, since the aspirant to conventual life appears in another colloquy. Pamphilus is not too lovelorn, however, to argue well in defence of chaste marriage, and, though by the end of the conversation Maria has not capitulated, neither has she utterly rejected Pamphilus. The girl with no interest in marriage, in the colloquy of that name, is likewise possessed of an affectionate suitor, whom she does reject outright because of her determination to enter religious life; and the dénouement of this bit of drama comes in a later colloquy, 'The Repentant Girl.' Unfitted for life in a cloister, Catherine has returned to her home. In this colloquy, although the dialogue is between the principal actors in the episode, there is not much action: Catherine has already leaped over the wall and the story of her trial of convent life is only narrated. A spate of drama must have spiced that off-stage fortnight of postulancy, but it comes to us only in retrospect and from the anticipated security of Papa's home and the ever-constant Eubulus. 'Marriage' comes closer to the satiric spirit, as a shrewish and discontented wife is taught by her wise neighbour how to live with her husband. The slight activity within the dialogue causes us to envision livelier stuff in the past and perhaps in the future, and we do see the movement of persuasion. More irony is evident in this than in the others of this group, for the termagant is loud in her wrong-headed lamentations, and we have to think through them to find the truth, though, of course, the virtuous Eulalia helps us to find it.[24]

In many of the colloquies carrying an exemplum there is this

24 The interest in this colloquy is enhanced, however, when Eulalia recounts the story of the wife of a 'certain nobleman, a learned and remarkably clever man,' recognizable surely to the contemporaries of Erasmus as Thomas More's first (and beloved) wife, Jane Colt. See *Colloquies* 115 (for editor's note) and 120, 121.

much immediacy: that experiences told or ideas offered are those of the speakers, and not just hearsay. 'Penny-pinching' and 'Inns' are of this kind. Although there is no action in them, physical or mental, one character is still emaciated as a result of his experience of meagre dining. So too with each of 'Rash Vows' and 'A Pilgrimage for Religion's Sake.' One character in each has just returned from a pilgrimage more absurd and superstition-ridden than devout, and gives his friend first-hand information and criticism about it.

'The Shipwreck' (1523) is an example of a very good colloquy which holds the reader's interest although it has only partial immediacy. In it a tale of shipwreck and superstition is narrated by the man who actually experienced the storm and witnessed the superstition, and the liveliness of the narration compensates for the remoteness. It is satiric too and not without irony, though both speakers are right-thinking. Adolph tells the story so well that Preserved Smith can suggest that Shakespeare borrowed from its details in the recounting of the storm in *The Tempest*; Professor Thompson too thinks Shakespeare may have had 'The Shipwreck' in mind, and notes that it is perhaps also the source of a chapter in Charles Reade's *The Cloister and the Hearth*, some of Thomas Heywood's verses, parts of Rabelais' *Gargantua and Pantagruel*, and possibly some of Defoe's scenes. Antony, at the end of the story, is sure he would rather hear such stories than experience them. Shakespeare ventured to give his audience a more imme-diate (though still vicarious) experience of the excitement of a storm.

The satire in this comedy, against rash promises, false piety, and superstition, is effective, and made the more so by being accompanied by the excitement at sea. Whatever of dramatic irony there might be is remote, of course, for being filtered through the knowing narrator, but the satiric irony is in the story itself even as it is told, and is effective. A sample of the dialogue will make this clear:

ADOLPH: There you'd have seen what a wretched plight we were in: the sailors singing *Salve Regina*, praying to the Virgin Mother, calling her Star of the Sea, Queen of Heaven, Mistress of the World, Port of Salvation, flattering her with many other titles the Sacred Scriptures nowhere assign to her.

ANTONY: What has she to do with the Sea, who, as I believe, never went a voyage in her life?

ADOLPH: Formerly Venus was protectress of sailors, because she was believed to have been born of the sea. Since she gave up guarding them, the Virgin Mother has succeeded this mother who was not a virgin.

ANTONY: You're joking.

ADOLPH: Prostrating themselves on the deck, some worshipped the sea, pouring whatever oil they had on the waves, flattering it no differently from the way we do a wrathful sovereign.

ANTONY: What did they say?

ADOLPH: 'O most merciful sea, O most kind sea, O most splendid sea, O most lovely sea, have pity on us! Save us!' Many songs of this kind they sang to the sea – which was deaf.

ANTONY: Absurd superstition! What did the rest do?

ADOLPH: Some did nothing but get sick. Many made vows. There was an Englishman who promised heaps of gold to the Virgin of Walsingham if he reached the shore alive. Some promised many things to the wood of the Cross at such and such a place; others, again, to that in some other place. The same with respect to the Virgin Mary, who reigns in many places; and they think the vow worthless unless you specify the place.

ANTONY: Ridiculous! As if the saints don't dwell in heaven. ... Did nobody remember Christopher?

ADOLPH: I couldn't help laughing as I listened to one chap, who in a loud voice (for fear he wouldn't be heard) promised a wax taper as big as himself to the Christopher in the tallest church in Paris – a mountain rather than a statue. While insisting on it again and again, an acquaintance who chanced to be standing by nudged him with his elbow and cautioned: 'Be careful what you promise. Even if you sold all your goods at auction, you couldn't pay for it.' Then the other, lowering his voice – so Christopher wouldn't overhear him, of course! – said, 'Shut up, you fool. Do you suppose I'm serious? If I once touch land, I won't give him a tallow candle.' [141–2]

Adolphe tells the story well, but his presence, safe, sensible, and right-reasoning, puts not only the drama but also the irony at one remove from the reader. Even the obvious parallel of pagan immanentism and Christian superstition he overworks with careful explanations. All in all, nevertheless, this is one of the best of the satiric and episodic colloquies, with the excitement of the storm and the recitation of absurdities kept close to each other, so that excitement pulses in the scorn, and ridicule keeps the storm from being melodramatic.

If the journey from time to eternity is activity, 'The Seraphic Funeral' (1531) is within this category. Whatever action (or passion) there is in the colloquy is distanced, as is so often the case, since the event is narrated by one who has only witnessed it; but the dialogue has irony enough, with its narrator, Theotimus, fairly well convinced of the rightness of what is foolish. Thus, once more, the thing-sign motif. The listener, Philecous, pretends to be impressed too, so this dialogue is enriched by a more dramatic and satiric irony than most. There is also the slight drama of the convincing of Theotimus that dying in religious dress does not guarantee immediate entry into heaven. Once convinced, he and Philecous join forces in a Socratic dialogue about the validity of religious dress and of religious life in general. This dialogue is characteristic of Erasmus in more than one way: not only is it filled with the usual preoccupations – empty symbols, pious hypocrisy, woolly reasoning – but the drama of the piece, slight as we may think it, is of the utmost importance to him. This is the drama of a mind being turned from wrong thinking to right, a tremendous activity and a neatly satisfactory ending. Again and again this is the activity – and the only activity – plot, progress, dénouement – of these colloquies. To the reader of our day, fed on more sophisticated fare, used to subtler forms of counselling, it is sometimes tiresome; to the little boys who went 'unwillingly to school' in Erasmus' day it must have been deadly; but to Erasmus himself the bright radiance of education's activity was theatre enough.

If we too can consider this change of mind or heart as dramatic action, the merely argumentative or discursive colloquies are little dramas often enough. One of the best-known of the discursive kind is 'The Abbot and the Learned Lady' (1524). Scholars have made learned conjectures about the identity of, or model for, the Abbot, Antronius; but one can be fairly sure that Magdalia was drawn from Meg Roper, Thomas More's eldest daughter, though indeed she inclines to being less genial and kind than her father and rather more like her father's caustic friend Erasmus. The 'Abbot' is an interesting colloquy because of its ideas (it was paradoxical enough in that age for a woman to be represented as being more learned than a monkish man), and because of its fictionalizing of real persons; but for all that I should not rank it among the best colloquies. Magdalia just misses being witty or charming, and the abbot is, of course, made to be dull; there is no irony, and not even the movement of total conversion. The colloquies that are purely discursive or conversational do sometimes tend to become rather contentious and wearisome. Most of the colloquies, however, are at least initiated by an episode or experience related by one of the speakers.

The irony in the colloquies is less satisfying than in the *Praise*, largely because the characters are too knowing. Sometimes one of the speakers is a gull and does provide some irony, but his reasonable friend is too ubiquitous, present in every colloquy to purvey the good Erasmian right reason, and the reader rarely has to flex a cerebral muscle of his own. Thus, although the abbot is a stupid fellow, the learned lady has wisdom in her answers; Theotimus, just home from the 'seraphic funeral,' and Ogygius, returning from a pilgrimage that fulfilled his mother-in-law's vow, are forced to see the absurdity of their superstition almost as soon as their recital of events begins. More often the gull is not present at all, but is a remote third person, a 'voice without,' and two wiser characters not only detail his unseemly or irrational behaviour, but pronounce judgement on the spot, as is the case in 'Merdardus,' 'Inns,' 'The Shipwreck,' and many others.

Charon, however, in the colloquy of that name, is drawn with a different kind of irony. A citizen of a world beyond this, he has a kind of knowledge mortals do not have. He knows there is a European war, knows that war brings death and that it corrupts a people. But his relation with truth is only factual; his preferences are wrong, and thus the irony lies in distortion of desire. News of carnage and violent death delights him, and he hopes for a 'splendid slaughter' soon; he looks lovingly at the friars promoting war and thus 'helping our cause.' (p 391). His interlocutor, Alastor, is of like disposition, though occasionally less well-informed.

Erasmus must have had Lucian's *Charon* in mind in writing this colloquy, and there are notable similarities: both use the device of looking at familiar activity from an unfamiliar stance; both remark on the levelling effect of death and the uselessness of either prestige or wealth to buy eventual happiness, and both see greed and pride as the great world-wide evils; strangely enough, both have a note of hope, for Erasmus' Charon thinks it is only the few who prolong the war and fears some persuasive wise man may yet interfere, and Lucian's world-viewers focus for a time on Solon, the good and wise man. In one sense there is no activity in either colloquy; but this is not wholly true, for Lucian gives us some little dramas at one remove.

The differences, nevertheless, are just as significant. The setting is different, for one thing. Erasmus' Charon seems to be on the shores of the Styx where he chats with Alastor about his projected purchase of a new river-boat to accommodate the ever-increasing number of shades, while Lucian's boat-man has come to earth to see what kind of life these passengers of his have been having.[25] Erasmus has particularity in the situation: his Charon is excited about a tremendous transfer of souls caused by a particular war[26] in Europe in the sixteenth century; Lucian's two

25 The ability of Charon and Hermes to pile mountain on mountain in Homeric fashion, and according to the magic of his verses, argues, of course, that this is not quite the earth we know (*Lucian* with an English translation by A.M. Harmon [London 1960] II 403–7).
26 The three rulers of the world mentioned by Charon are the Emperor Charles V, Francis I of France, and Henry VIII of England. In his introduction to the colloquy, Professor Thompson points out that 'Francis had been captured at the battle of Pavia, 1525. When released by the Spanish after the signing of the Treaty of Madrid, he joined with Milan,

characters speak of a universal situation of life-in-death, a constant. War indeed is a particular evil (caused, so Hermes thinks, by too much attention to boundary lines and money), but not any particular war. Erasmus' colloquy betrays a true Christian's distress at the sight of fellow-Christians' infidelity and stupidity – greedy Christian kings and pandering Christian friars gulling the people into believing this is 'God's war' and that those who die in a just war 'fly straight to heaven.' Lucian's objections are those of a humanist.

But the great difference is in the manipulation of irony. Lucian's dialogue is a work of greater length and complexity than Erasmus'. His Charon and Hermes are both right-thinking and their right thoughts extend to their judgements and desires; they know evil for evil and reject it or lament its prevalence. Where Erasmus' Charon had worried lest some god turn up and stop the war before he has made his boat pay for itself, Lucian's applauds Clotho who tries to show the great ones, the arrogant, that they are human. Lucian's pair have some pity for man, and after they have built themselves a Homeric verse-montain and adjusted their lenses, they see five vignettes of life – life at the threshold of death. The first two viewings are dramatically ironic, not satiric: a man invited to dinner accepts with alacrity and promises to be there; and Charon smiles ruefully, knowing the man is a few minutes away from sudden death; a victorious bull-fighter exults in his strength, unaware that soon he will be without the strength of life, unable to 'lift a mosquito' (p 415). The remaining three episodes add satiric irony to the dramatic, for in them we see men arrogant and ruthless towards their fellow-men, building their wealth on the ruins of others. Yet among the earthlings there is also Solon, the wise lawgiver and the good man, against

Venice, Florence, and the Papacy in a league against Charles. England supported the league unofficially. In the Italian campaigns that followed, the fighting mostly favoured the Imperial forces. It culminated in the famous sack of Rome by undisciplined Imperial soldiers in May, 1527. By this time Henry VIII had joined Francis and gave the war his active assistance. A new Italian campaign opened, but after six months the Pope began efforts to make peace. Charles rejected the terms and war continued until August, 1529. By that date the Empire had won control of Italy' (p 389).

whom the others can be measured. And above all of them is Clotho spinning inexorably, and one supposes the other sisters are beside her. Thus Lucian presents a full stage and a various irony.

In Erasmus' *Charon* there is no such variety or complexity. Perhaps in compensation it has an immediacy that Lucian's drama has not, for neither Hermes nor Charon (Lucian's) are much disturbed at man's ignorance and malice, whereas at least one of Erasmus' couple is in danger of becoming property-poor, and the reader catches the energy of even this facetious excitement and inverts the direction of the anxiety. It is Christian culture and the life of the spirit that are in danger of becoming poor.

In any case, Erasmus' *Charon* is one of the important colloquies, though it is dramatic only in its situation and character presentation, and provides no action. Its excellence is in its blending of classical pattern with very topical subject matter, of right vision and wrong desire. Europe had more than a few of Charon's colour.

In a letter of 1526 to the Bishop of Lincoln, Erasmus says of the colloquies that 'entertainment was thrown in as a bait, to entice an age sooner captivated by what is agreeable than by what is good for it.'[27] To achieve this enjoyment quotient, he uses many devices other than irony and good talk. The traditional dream-vision is used in the 'Apotheosis' to give a semi-supernatural prognosis of the learned Reuchlin's entry to heaven; a genial group of 'fabulous' dinner guests regale one another with anecdotes of *fabliau* nature; 'Exorcism' and 'Alchemy' are themselves *fabliaux* in dialogue form; the garden, so dear to the sixteenth-century writer, is setting for many of the discussions, as is the dinner table, so that we are reminded often of Erasmus' boast that Socrates had brought philosophy from heaven to earth, but Erasmus had brought it 'even into games, informal conversations, and drinking parties.'[28] An exciting storm acts as stimulant to interest while superstition is ridiculed in 'The Shipwreck'; a Stygian boatman gives an opinion on war which is, if

27 Allen III 333 ; and C.R. Thompson's translation, 624
28 *Colloquies* 'Of the Usefulness of Colloquies' 630

not quite heavenly, at least *sub specie aeternitatis*; specific gravity is used to measure the weight of sin and thus initiate the moral teaching of 'A Problem.' Although characterization in the colloquies is neither subtle nor profound, Erasmus likes to surprise the reader in his castings: thus a fishmonger is able to talk intelligently on the theology of fasting and penance in 'The Fish Diet,' and a fine lady is found to be more learned than an abbot. On the other hand, Erasmus also likes to let his characters use a speech idiom befitting their calling and station in life: the two scholars who have survived two kinds of hotel-living lard their disparaging talk with the classical allusions such scholars would naturally use, saying, for instance, that a woman is so lovely she would cheer Cato himself, that Lyonnaise sirens might have tempted Ulysses and his men, and so on; but the doughty Adolph, in 'The Shipwreck,' (probably drawn from a certain Flemish admiral) uses the nautical terms of an old sea-salt; and the innkeeper's images are of field and barnyard.

Each of two colloquies uses an ingenious device to filter ironic comment into its comedy. 'Non-Sequiturs' presents two characters in conversation. Both are either deaf or so preoccupied with their own topic as to be oblivious of the other. Leucius talks of a shipwreck he has experienced, while Annius speaks of a wedding he has attended, and, as their comments dovetail (and with more relevance than either of them suspects) the auditor listens in on what might be called 'theatre of the absurd':

LEUCIUS: Then – presto! Another danger.
ANNIUS: Why did they entrust an innocent girl to such a brute?
LEUCIUS: A pirate ship came into view.
ANNIUS: That's the way it goes: in many a man villainy makes up for age.
LEUCIUS: There we had a double fight on our hands ... [423]

In 'The Echo' it is the insentient, whispering air itself that sends back variations on the youth's playful shouts. This colloquy must have presented its translator with a test of wit and imagination, and the Thompson translations are a delight in themselves. With very slight mutations of the literal meaning, the English echo is made as clever as the Latin. Indeed, from the many witty replacements, it is hard to select a small excerpt to give the flavour. Here, for instance:

> JUVENIS: *Censes igitur terendos auctores, qui conducunt ad bonas literas?* / So you believe those authors who lead us to polite learning should be read?
>
> ECHO: *Teras.* / Readily.
>
> JUVENIS: *Quam igitur mentem habent isti qui haec studia linguis traducunt suis?* / Then what shall we call persons who traduce such disciplines by their discourse?
>
> ECHO: *Suis.* / Coarse.
>
> JUVENIS: *Sed utinam harum cultores similiter essent et pietatis studiosi.* / But would that devotees of these studies were zealous after virtue as well!
>
> ECHO: *O si!* / Well would it be!
>
> JUVENIS: *Et multis hominum, pecatum confertur in nomen eruditionis.* / And with many men learning passes for a sin.
>
> ECHO: *"Ονοιs.* / Asinine men!
>
> JUVENIS: *Quid facere censes eos qui terunt aetatem in sophistico doctrinae genere?* / What do you think of those who waste a lifetime on the logic of Duns?
>
> ECHO: *Nere!* (LB I 817C–D). / Dunces!　　　　　　　　　　[374]

Beguiled thus by sound and meaning, Erasmus is sometimes tempted too into punning, and here again his translator's ingenuity matches his own. In the 'Apotheosis' the two friends who have been eulogizing Reuchlin part jovially, Brassicanus saying 'Vale,' and Pompilius answering 'Vale tu quoque,' whereupon Brassicanus quips: 'Valebo, sed non coquus!' The English equivalents, 'also' and 'cock,' are not pun material, but Professor Thompson translates:

> – Farewell.
> – Farewell to you, too.
> –I'll fare well, but I'm one, not two! [LB I 692E; *Colloquies* 86][29]

29 About this pun on *quoque* and *coque* D.F.S. Thomson notes that it 'comes from Cicero by way of Quintilian' (chapter entitled 'The Latinity of Erasmus' in *Erasmus* T.A. Dorey (ed) [London 1970] 127).

As for those figures of speech which provide a differential for meaning, in the colloquies Erasmus is content to work with simple similes and rather obvious metaphors. In the satirical colloquies, at any rate, there is no allegorical level, either in the theological or the market-place sense, but many of the characters who talk their way to conclusions are symbolic personifications of the attitudes and aspirations and absurdities of man as he is generally found in the society of Erasmus' day, qualities imprecisely realized in actual people, more fully realized and recognized in the exaggeration. That Erasmus thought of character and incident in story and fable as the great symbolic devices is clear (though not explicitly stated) from 'The Usefulness of Colloquies' with its reiterated 'in this I have depicted the folly of. ... here is depicted the characer of. ... here is ample demonstration of the lack of wisdom in ...' Not all the characters are thus expandible: surely the burly innkeeper in the 'Beggars' is just himself; and the commentators who do not partake in the action but merely narrate it are not symbolic. But the good monks and the bad, soldiers, harlots, good wives and termagants, the scholars and villains of the pieces are, if not symbols in the full sense of the word, symbolic in function as they strut and posture the lively lessons the colloquies aim to teach. At least they carry to the reader the concrete figures of truth. And significant names are often given to these characters: names that bespeak the quality isolated in each one, as Hedonius, Pamphagus, Misoponus, Eusebius, Theodidactic; or names encrusted with literary significances: Iphigenia, Hanno, Cyclops.[30]

But the symbolic quality of the figure or its name extends to circumstance or incident in only the most obvious way.[31] No

30 Pamphagus, in the colloquy 'In Pursuit of Benefices,' is a good illustration of Erasmus' conditioning the educated reader's response to character and situation. The name means 'eater of everything,' but as well as that, it is the name of a dog in Ovid's *Metamorphoses* (Book III). Thus the reader is primed in advance to see the unreason in his seemingly plausible arguments.
31 The colloquy 'The Apotheosis of Reuchlin' might be cited as an exception. The name 'Reuchlin,' Professor Thompson notes, is cognate to the German word for 'smoky': *rauchig*, and Reuchlin himself in a letter to

activity is made to represent some other activity, no journey symbolizes life, no sleep is to be read as death, though indeed Erasmus may refer to such symbolism in a didactic way. In 'The New Mother,' for instance, Eutrapelus, talking about a mother's care for her child, uses many parallels from nature's self-nourishment and from the ancient classical writings, but uses them as a teacher does, not as an artist:

> Wheat [he says] sown in alien soil degenerates into wild oats or winter wheat; a vine transferred to a different hill changes its character; a young plant torn from its parent earth droops and dies, as it were; for that reason it is transplanted with native earth if possible. [273]

This is symbol in its matter but not in its form, for the parallels are used as straightforward analogies. Eutrapelus is himself much aware of the symbols provided by nature and literature, and comes very close sometimes to using them as symbols. When he speaks of the human soul's dependence on a human body, he thinks of Apuleius' ass who, 'when he wanted to call out to Caesar could ... scarcely sound an "O",' for want of a properly formed human mouth; Christ's seamless coat, he says later, is torn to shreds by the wars that split Christendom, and the vineyard of the Lord is prey to more boars than one.

But the simple comparison or simile is usually Erasmus' way. This is persuasive work primarily, not fiction or poetry, and boys in a schoolroom – and they are never far from Erasmus' vision – are notably impervious to subtle effects. Perhaps too, it is, as Bainton suggests, that Erasmus 'had no itch to become a creative writer. ... His role was not to create but to transmit the wisdom of the seers and the grace of the Gospel.'[32] To Erasmus – and indeed to most sixteenth-century writers – it was the highest kind of creation to so write as to increase the being of a man through

Erasmus had played on the idea. In the colloquy Erasmus 'utilizes the symbolic connection between smoke and death, for example, by his reference to Reuchlin as a phoenix.' This is the colloquy in which he also makes 'camels' of Carmelites (*Colloquies* 81).

32 *Erasmus of Christendom* 38

increase of his understanding. In any case, the ornament here is used as Augustine had advised it should be used by one preaching or teaching, and not as by one aiming only to delight. In these colloquies, as in the adages, Erasmus does teach his readers to see the symbolic in life, teaches them by creating for their admiration men and women who recognize and talk about the symbols surrounding them.

Although he was no Wordsworth recollecting in tranquillity an exultation once experienced in nature, Erasmus has given the colloquies a generous sprinkling of nature images. He is not at all unaware of the literary function of the *locus amoenus*, the garden, field, and forest as setting, nor of the birds and animals in them. But the reader hardly needs much perspicacity to note that (a) the flowers that appear (occasionally) and the birds and animals (more often) are used as emblems only; they give no evidence of the naturalist's tenderness or even of any particular power of observation; and (b) as with all Erasmus' images, they are used with careful decorum.

The animal imagery is most often used to epitomize some quality in man. We have already noted the references to wolf, fox, and sheep that run through the 'Beggars,' and fix it in the tradition of the pastoral exemplum. In 'Cyclops' there is explicit mention of the transferable quality of some animal traits: 'You can meet many men,' says Polyphemus, 'who are fiercer than lions, greedier than wolves, more lecherous than sparrows, more snappish than dogs, more venemous than vipers'; and Polyphemus knows too that a man can have a sheep's head and a fox's heart. A toad is used as symbol for the devil in 'Pilgrimage,' and a goose, in the 'Abbot,' stands for a fatuous clergyman; an organ in a pretentious building 'whinnies' and neighs. As one would expect from a man who had canvassed all literature for proverbs, Erasmus often uses adages in which beast stands for man: 'Pack-saddles don't fit an ox,' and 'You can't catch a fox with a noose.'

Not all the images are measuring rods for human villainy. Reuchlin, for instance, is called a phoenix, and in the 'New Mother' Eutrapelus cites as examples for imitation the animals' care for their young. Sometimes too the animal provides a simple parallel, with no associations of morality: a sleepy boy crawls out of bed 'like a cuckoo from a warm nest,' an hostler leans out a window 'like a turtle from its shell'; the liar is no more ashamed of his lies than 'a cuckoo of her song.'

Occasionally too nature images are used to buttress Erasmus' strongest convictions, as we noted in the 'New Mother': 'Kites don't come from doves,' he says, clearing the way for his insistence that it is the good and intelligent parents that bear and rear good and intelligent children; again, man, made for reason and virtue, is unfulfilled and thus unhappy in the guise (literal or metaphorical) of a hog or horse, as even the learned lady's unlearned abbot had to concede.

As for decorum, it is a lover, we note, who, speaking to his lady-love of strong influences, uses the lingering scent of roses to provide illustration; but a seasoned old traveller (Ogygius, of the proxied pilgrimage) says rather that the stench of an adder remains after its life has gone. A learned lady proposes to her hunt-loving abbot a problem in metamorphosis: monks into hogs or horses; but Eutrapelus, not one to offend a new mother's ears with such monster-imagery, uses for *his* imagined metamorphosis an ass duly refined by legend and cast in gold.

Before we move away from the literary character of Erasmus' colloquies into their moral content, we might allow ourselves some little fault-finding with the fault-finder. He is sometimes untidy in his progress towards a quite flawless conclusion. His truth and his logic are practical, and true enough in the practical order; his logical progress towards this truth is not always so secure. This indifference is especially noticeable in the later colloquies. In 'The Sober Feast,' for instance, Jerome comments that:

> the thirst for glory has tremendous power and is an emotion that leads many men astray. One of these once asked Socrates how he could find a short cut to the most honourable reputation. 'By showing yourself to be what you long to be thought,' was the answer ... [457]

Certainly this is a truth, but so obvious a one that one thinks Socrates' own 'honourable reputation' hardly rested on such banalities; yet James is full of admiration at this saying, and says: 'Indeed I don't see what could be spoken more briefly and more perfectly'; and then goes on to emphasize and paraphrase what any school-boy-moralist might have said. James goes on to tell of a maid being auctioned off. Asked by a purchaser if she would be honest if he bought her, she answered: 'even if you don't ...' Children staging a make-believe market-day might be capable surely of this. Yet Lawrence commends it as a 'manly saying from a girl, truly.' Perhaps the niceties of the *sententia* and the authority of Socrates would have recommended such repartee, however, to the sixteenth-century reader.

Trite these phrases are, but at least they are true. Not quite so sound is the tale Charles tells in the same colloquy of Socrates' being insulted as he walked the highway, and of his saying, when urged to bring action against the offender: 'Nonsense. ... If a donkey had kicked me should I have had the law on him, with you for witness?' That was Socrates' irony, surely; and it is understandable that a man so insulted should rate his insultor as less than human and unworthy of human punishment. But it is Socrates' patience, not his percipience, that Charles (and later Denis) commend in fulsome praise. All through this colloquy Socrates is compared to Christ, with his Christian virtue substantiated by references to most unchrist-like self-esteem.[33]

'The Epicurean' gives further illustration of a questionable logic. Hedonius, declaring to Spudaeus that Christians are the true Epicureans, since they persistently pursue happiness, asks him to grant, with Plautus, that 'nothing is more wretched than a bad conscience.' When Spudaeus concedes this, Hedonius continues: 'If nothing be more wretched than a bad conscience, it follows that nothing is happier than a good one,' a conclusion

---

33 Yet the self-righteousness of Cato is pinpointed in the 'Godly Feast' when Chrysoglottus cites him as an example of pagan nobility worthy of Christian imitation, but then puts limits to his admiration for him, saying that one might object to the self-confidence of his speech, as 'expressive of a pride that ought to be very far from a Christian.' None of this complacency does he find, however, in Socrates, but rather he finds him 'diffident ... about his own deed' (p 67).

perhaps true in the practical order, but not emerging logically from this reasoning. One might as well say that since nothing is lamer than a shortened leg, nothing is sprier than a lengthened one, which would be nonsense. The best we can say of Hedonius' good conscience is that it is less wretched than the bad one. But Spudaeus commends this very 'correct' inference, and is greatly impressed by the logic of the preachy Hedonius, who celebrates at length the pleasures of the mind over those of the body, with hardly an arresting sentence from start to finish, nor one calculated to convert any but the thoroughly two-dimensional Spudaeus.

The moral lessons taught in these openly didactic colloquies must be abundantly clear by now. Over and above all the particular distresses, we find the old familiar preoccupation with the sign that is emptied of meaning because the thing it stood for has festered or died. That is why the evils of superstition (among the laity) and ambition, greed, and indifference (among clerics) loom so large in the dialogues. In some of them moral and intellectual content is interesting and thought-provoking; but most are simpler than the *Praise*, partly because each colloquy is limited to one phase of behaviour, and partly because of the realistic tone.

Although the chronology of the editions spans some dozen years and the writing covers an even longer period, there is no very great change in either the techniques or attitudes as the years go by, except that the last two colloquies, 'A Problem' and 'The Epicurean,' are more general in their counsel. One expects to find heavy scorn for superstition and false values, and one is not disappointed. 'The Profane Feast,' for instance, an early colloquy, disposes sharply of making an end rather than a means of fasting; 'Rash Vows' cries down making a fetish of pilgrimages; 'In Pursuit of Benefices' exposes greed and ambition among clerics; and the same concern with lost significance runs through the later colloquies: 'Exorcism' shows a parish easily gulled by the deceit of a pseudo-exorcist; 'Shipwreck' has a similar theme, ridiculing prayers without meaning or devotion; 'Pilgrimage' attacks the same abuse as had the earlier 'Rash Vows' – with greater ridicule, for it is not even in fulfilment of his own vow that the silly Ogygius has made his journey, but to redeem his mother-in-law's. (One can but marvel at her persuasive power, used first on the Almighty, then on the son-in-law.) In the 1531 edition 'The Seraphic Funeral' deflates the idea that to die in religious dress is to go surely to heaven. In all these, although the episodes and characters and even the faults are various, the basic exasperation is the same.

This concern with signs and things, with things indifferent and things good or bad, is implicit in all the colloquies which score superstition and show the confusion between ends and means: the pilgrimage that was simply a bargain, the meaningless promise of a candle to St Christopher whose appreciation of the candle is assumed to be as stupid as that of the giver, to whom it is surely a 'thing'; the call to shepherding souls regarded as a mere money-making affair, and so on. But this relation between things and their signs is explicitly the subject of one of the colloquies, 'Things and Names' (1527), which begins very simply by distinguishing between seeming and being, between being thought to be honest and really being so. Boniface thinks the difference would be very evident if everyone realized that:

> a king is one who by law and justice looks out for the welfare of his people, not of himself ... a bishop is one who devotes himself entirely to watching over his master's flock ... a magistrate is one who wholeheartedly serves the public good ... and a philosopher is one who, disregarding Fortune's gifts, strives only to attain a good conscience. [384]

and Beatus continues after a bit, using some of Erasmus' rare symbols:

> Wouldn't one be a fool if he fished with a golden hook, preferred glass to jewels, loved horses more than wife and children? ... Aren't men fools who rush off and enlist in the army in the hope of booty – not very much booty at that – at risk to body and soul? Who toil to amass wealth when they have a soul in need of every good? Who wear fancy clothes and live in fine houses when their souls lie sloven and neglected? [385]

This colloquy, pretending to be innocently speculative, has a strongly satiric bite. The two friends come to discussing those who are really miscreants and yet are reputed fine fellows, even leaders, capitalists, politicians; Beatus thinks 'it makes very little difference what they're called by men if they're thieves in God's sight,' and he goes on to note the impunity covering the sins of the great – a theme that has provoked many a satiric pen since Erasmus' day. The colloquy concludes with Beatus summing up in another figurative phrase: 'Knights fit for a hobbyhorse, you mean. But Gelderland has more than a few such knights.'

Erasmus' distress over the failure of significance is made explicit in other places too. We have already noted the good Franciscan's choric comment, in the 'Beggars,' that the man wearing monastic dress might be wolf, or fox, or goose, but by the same token, he might be a good man. This for the wearer of habits, but Erasmus rarely forgets the spectator:

> As clothes don't make a man better, so they don't make a man worse. It's wrong, therefore, to judge anyone by his dress. Otherwise the dress *you* sometimes use must be abhorred because it covers many thieves, murderers, poisoners, and adulterers. [206]

The innkeeper here was not too dull to be taught; yet the Almighty himself is expected to be less than discerning by the falsely pious who would make (in the 'Seraphic Funeral') a Franciscan of the worldling on his death bed.

'The Soldier and the Carthusian' carries on the idea of the significance of clothes. The Carthusian gives two uses for clothes (Conrad had given three): 'Our garments serve the double purpose of warding off the weather and covering what shame bids us conceal'; but the third purpose, that which denotes the sign quality, he implies in what follows:

> What colour is more appropriate to all Christians than the one given to them in Baptism? And you are told, 'Receive a white garment.' So this garment serves to remind me of what I promised in baptism, namely an unremitting zeal for purity of heart. [130]

Other Erasmian views can, of course, be noted too. A rather
sympathetic attitude to women shows in several of the pieces.
The colloquies sometimes called the 'marriage group' present
the woman as the hub of the family; and in the 'Beggars' it is
the innkeeper's wife who has put heart into the family business
too. 'The Repentant Girl' tables a young woman's prerogative of
free choice in following a vocation and incidentally pleads too
for greater sympathy on the part of parents; the 'Abbot and the
Learned Woman' extols woman's ability to grapple with deep
thoughts and neat distinctions and her right to do so. A harlot,
in another colloquy, is easily persuaded by good counselling, to
adopt a sounder means of livelihood, and one senses the author's
feeling that such women are more sinned against than sinning.
In the 'New Mother,' although Eutrapelus thinks men stronger
and better than women, Fabulla is created with charm and fineness and is allowed to give some excellent points in the debate
that follows; nor is it ever implied that her role in life is trivial;
on the contrary, she is the responsible agent in the child's education and development. Erasmus' appreciation of woman's capacity for learning and wisdom had been nourished by his own
experience: his friend Thomas More had a daughter able to speak
Latin fluently, and to write it with polish; and another friend,
Willibald Pirckheimer, had sisters who at least rated a remem-
brance in one of Erasmus' letters to him.[34]

A peculiarly Erasmian lesson runs through the 'Apotheosis.'
This is one of the discursive colloquies, though the telling of a
dream provides some distanced activity. Pompilius and Brassi-

34 'Saluta sorores tuas [Erasmus writes to Pirckheimer] et si qui sunt qui
diligant Evangelicam doctrinam' (Allen v 17); and in an editorial note
introducing Ep 318 (II 40) Allen speaks of Pirckheimer's having 'five
young daughters whom he educated carefully, and who afterwards
became as famous for learning as the daughters of Sir Thomas More.'
In Bainton's *Erasmus of Christendom* there is mention too of Erasmus'
respect for Mary of Hungary, sister of Charles and Ferdinand, a woman
who delighted in Latin codices; and one Margaret Peutinger, 'famous
among other things for having published an ancient road map of the
Roman Empire,' and learned enough to be able to compare German,
Latin, and Greek commentaries and so to argue with Erasmus about
a scriptural text 'quite on his own level' (pp 232, 233).

canus discuss the death of Johann Reuchlin, a renowned Hebrew scholar. Brassicanus tells of how a 'Franciscan of singular holiness' (identified by both Preserved Smith and C.R. Thompson as Conrad Pelican, one-time Franciscan, later Lutheran) had dreamed he saw Reuchlin passing over a little bridge to a delightful meadow. A flock of harpies (Dominican inquisitors) pursuing him were put to flight by Reuchlin's making the sign of the Cross before them. Reuchlin is met by St Jerome, not rejuvenated, but wearing his years in dignity and joy, and clothed in a robe on which are embroidered three tongues in various colours, signifying the three languages he professed; angels hover over the meeting and escort the two into the radiance beyond. The two friends agree that Reuchlin is a saint and, *mirabile dictu*, would have him wrought in gold or even in diamonds and set in a chapel for veneration, a wish not quite consonant with Erasmus' usual scoffing at such ostentatious piety. Later, when Pompilius scruples at anticipating the Church's pronouncements on Reuchlin's sanctity, Brassicanus voices the usual Erasmian distate for officialdom:

> Who canonized (as they term it) St Jerome? or Paul? or the Virgin Mother? Whose memory is more sacred among all the devout: that of persons whose extraordinary holiness and the record of their character and life recommend them to the hearts of everyone, or of Catherine of Siena, whom Pius II is said to have canonized to please an order and a city? [85]

The adulation proceeds until Reuchlin seems to be becoming the patron of languages as St Christopher is of travellers, and one wonders why the hard-headed Erasmus allows Brassicanus such enthusiasms.

The colloquy seems, in any case, to be a singular emulsion of reverence for holiness and respect for erudition, of dependence on the Church's forms (the liturgical collect, for instance) and rejection of those who narrowly interpret her sanctions, of rational argument and wholesale enthusiasm such as Erasmus would have scorned in other contexts. Nevertheless, the principle behind the dialogue is sound, the execration of rash judgement and the right relation between honest scholarship and sanctity.

The 'tyrant custom' comes in for some passing scorn in 'The New Mother.' Eutrapelus, visiting Fabulla, finds that she is allowing a paid nurse to suckle her infant son and justifying this on the score of its being the custom, the 'common custom.' 'Alas,' says Eutrapelus, '... you name the worst authority on good behaviour, Fabulla. Sinning is common, gambling is common, visiting brothels is common; cheating, boozing, folly are common.' (p 272)

Into the same colloquy Erasmus pours many of his favourite theories about the care and teaching of the child and the close relation between the mind and body. He touches too on the nature of the mind and of the soul; and Eutrapelus seems, like Erasmus, to have just finished editing Aristotle. After he has expounded the Aristotelian definition of the soul, Fabulla thinks the same definition could be applied to the soul of an ass or ox. Eutrapelus makes his own distinctions here between man's soul and animal's; but – and this is the significant point here – he avoids the question of the destiny or end of the soul of man. One rather expects here that the sound piety of this visitor might reach out to man's ability to know and love God, and to live the life of grace as well as that of nature; but this is Aristotle's doctrine of soul and Erasmus will not push it into probing the nature of man's super-rational self. In much the same way he cozened the expectations of the reader in his *De ratione studii*, stopping short of identifying the ending end of all knowledge as virtue engraced by faith and hope. Here indeed he seems to say it is in the amount of knowledge rather than in the nature of it that man differs from beast. Even the beetle, he says, has a soul, not quite the same as man's, but having a common faculty up to a certain point, and being to the beetle body what man's soul is to the human body. Fabulla would go on to apply the principle to angels, but angels have no bodies to relate to their souls, and this seems to scuttle the argument effectively. The inexorable woman would go further, however, and conjectures that 'with regard to its essential nature, therefore, a fool's soul is equal to

Solomon's ... [and that] consequently angels are equal too since they have no substance (which you say is the source of inequality).' But Eutrapelus comes back to the safer problems of caring for the child.

Erasmus is well represented in Eutrapelus. Too finely geared to be indifferent to the purely speculative in so far as it determines the activity of man, he is, nevertheless, either unwilling to push his speculation to a precise conclusion, or considers (as Dryden was later to do) that 'nice speculation' was unsuited to a lady's preferences. One would have liked to see some expansion of the notion of the fool's soul and the wise man's. The whole question of knowing and willing is in it; but it is left standing. And the cognate question of the angelic equality, with all its provocative implications about grace and predestination is also left unprobed.

Eutrapelus never seems to find Fabulla's endless questions too tiresome or too trifling for reply. On two other occasions his solicited opinion is worth consideration: Fabulla is surely less than a serious mature woman when she queries why souls are sometimes painted as infants with wings, similar to angels. To humour her, Eutrapelus refers to the Socratean fable of wings broken in the fall from heaven. But Fabulla counters: 'Then how can they be said to fly up to heaven?' Eutrapelus answers:

> Because faith and charity cause their wings to sprout again. These wings he sought who, wearied of this habitation of his body, cried, 'O that I had wings like a dove! for then would I fly away and be at rest.' For the soul has no other wings, since it is incorporeal, nor has it any shape visible to bodily eyes; but what we see by our minds we perceive with the greater certitude. [278]

Strange mixture of fable and Christian symbol! We remember that one of the speakers in 'The Sober Feast' had encouraged using the myths and fables of the pagan writers as symbols of the Christian belief; and that the *De conscribendis epistolis* was to protest theology's reluctance to encourage poetry: 'Theologians ought not to be listened to when they urge that poets should not be read because they so vehemently entice the reader by the splendour of their words,' for such delight [he goes on] may not be merely free from evil but contributive to much good (LB I 408E). This is an illustration perhaps of such a use. But the emphasis on faith and charity is significant too, in that it is almost the only explicit reference to high spirtuality in this dialogue which, for all that, brushes close to the anagogical from start to finish.

The other noteworthy passage in Eutrapelus' sober answer to Fabulla's arch insinuation that the Almighty could have no worthier occupation than looking after her and her new baby: 'What could he better do ... than preserve by propagation what he created?' But Eutrapelus can think of things he could better do. His long reply summarizes the distresses of the time (1526):

> What could he do, my good woman? ... if he weren't God I don't think he could get through so much business. King Christian of Denmark ... is in exile. Francis, King of France, is a 'guest' of the Spaniards ... Charles is preparing to extend the boundaries of his realm. Ferdinand has his hands full in Germany. Bankruptcy threatens every court. The peasants raise dangerous riots and are not swayed from their purpose, despite so many massacres. The commons are bent on anarchy; the Church is shaken to its very foundations by menacing factions; on every side the seamless coat of Jesus is torn to shreds. The vineyard of the Lord is now laid waste not by a single boar but at one and the same time the authority of priests (together with their tithes), the dignity of theologians, the splendour of monks is imperilled; confession totters; vows reel; pontifical ordinances crumble; the Eucharist is called in question ... [269]

That this spokesman for Erasmus – he is that, surely – should show concern for the retention of such things as confession and vows seems significant. For these things Erasmus had formerly expressed small reverence, or at best a reverence modified by his awareness of their tendency to become ends instead of means. Perhaps the change in tone is attributable to the decorum of the colloquy, hortative and expository as it is. But one might point too to two other factors that are possibly modifying agents: the author has by now been dispensed from his vows and the threat of being recalled to his monastery has been removed; when there is no goad to kick against, there is relaxation in the nervous attacking; and secondly, Luther's voice is strong by now, and the once secure church is perilously close to disaster. Erasmus had no wish to help in its destruction. Professor Craig Thompson notes Erasmus' mention of the 'vineyard of the Lord,' and links it to the opening lines of the papal bull condemning Luther, commenting that the passage (quoted above) is 'an effective comment on the progress of Lutheranism by 1526.'

Erasmus himself, of course, would say that in none of the colloquies did he intend to attack the institutions or practices of the Church, but only their abuses. In his answer to the divines of Louvain who had taken exception to his satire, he says 1 / that he did not aim to give a full exposition of Christian life, but only to insinuate into exercises primarily linguistic a modicum of moral and religious instruction; 2 / that one must regard the sort of person to whom each speech is ascribed in the colloquy; not all of them are Erasmus' mouthpieces; and 3 / that it is not the institutions or practices themselves but the abuses of them that he attacks, aiming always only to redress a balance.

Nevertheless, one can hardly believe, in reading, for instance, 'The Repentant Girl,' that it was merely the abuse of conventual life that is attacked, though indeed it is a man in love who protests against the enclosed life, and a shallow little piece much in need of good guidance who had offered herself as postulant. Nor can one agree that the man who writes the 'Pilgrimage for Religion's Sake' has much regard for any veneration of saints, or any pilgrimage, however sincere. In any case, it is too simple to say that the early colloquies are biting and the later ones more tolerant. The traditional assumptions are sometimes treated with sympathy in the early pieces: 'Beggars' (1524) puts forth a strong argument that a good man may wear a religious habit and be a member of the very order that in other places Erasmus seems to abominate; the Carthusian who talks to the soldier is contrasted favourably with him, and this in 1523. In 'Military Affairs'

(1522), although there is censure, even calumny, of the Dominicans, there is also the solid assumption that the sacraments and
sacred vessels have their own validity and that irreverence to
them is deplorable. Looking at each colloquy as a unit, one is
sometimes aghast at the ruthless indictments and obvious pre-
judices so openly expressed, but looking at the whole collection,
one can in part accept Erasmus' *apologia*: he is looking to redress
a balance, to restore the traditions, not those accruing from the
middle ages but the still older ones, by purging them of the accre-
tions of superstition and by restating their significance, the symbol or sign value equated with the thing signified, the thing
quality and sign quality redefined.

One cannot say that the colloquies have any one particular
abuse to castigate. Almost any villainy, wilful or ignorant, can
be found punctured in the dialogues; wisely so, for they are designed for the schoolboy whose moral temptations are neither
subtle nor select. But special emphases may be noted: it has been
clear from the start that Erasmus is concerned most often with
the sins of the mind rather than of the will, with ignorance and
shallow thinking and prejudice. These non-thinkers have false
values, do not recognize the discrepancies between seeming and
being, and make much ado about things indifferent in themselves
and only truly estimable in their related significance. But,
although Erasmus' concern is with thought, it is with such
thought as governs behaviour and not with its speculative
attenuations.

This supreme emphasis on the moral and intellectual life does
not quite cancel Erasmus' recognition of faith and charity as the
impetus and end of good living. We must remember too that the
students who learned their Latin from this text would not be
limiting their study to the satiric dialogues, but would be always
balancing the positive lessons of the non-satiric ones against the
corrosive quality of the satiric. In the former we look for and
often find a gracious recognition of man's dependence on prayer
and the theological virtues, and a warmer reverence for the
things of God. St John of the Cross talks of a 'purgative' and an
'illuminative' way: we might, in the satiric colloquies find the

purgative well presented; in the hortative pieces we are more likely to find the illuminative. The ladder does not end there, of course. When we have urged the purgation of unseemly behaviour, and have expounded the good, first the merely rational good, then the morally, socially good, then the good leavened with Christian faith, we have perhaps finished with the exigencies of human choice and activity. But there is still the life of grace that overflows its normal channels in some rare souls so that they are immersed in awareness of the divine, seeing it in all the events of life, in all the neighbours who are its proxies, in the anxieties of life and in its moments of joy. But the person thus divinely orbited is not so because of a rational choice (which satire might perhaps effect) but through faith and hope and charity and through some exceptional grace: and this is not the province of satire.

Strangely enough, however, satire may act as a remote pre-evangelizing agent, a ground clearance before the approach to such envisioning. In the last moments of Moria's oration, Erasmus allows her to nose into an area that is very close to the ecstatic; in a lesser way, the *Ciceronianus* pays tribute to the life of grace. Neither *Julius exclusus* nor the *Complaint* has quite enough *esprit* to allow for much of this, but in a couple of the colloquies we again come close to the area of grace. 'The New Mother' and the 'Beggars' are among these. It is true that their dramatic progress converges to a moral, rather than anagogical point: in the one a woman is cautioned about her maternal duties, in the other hospitality and kindly judgement are taught. But in both there is an obligato of pastoral imagery that keeps us reminded of the larger charity, and also there is some direct recommendation of the following of Christ. In the grit of the satiric context this slight reference to such a pattern is indeed effective.

Extremists have a way of bringing ridicule and censure on the very things they admire – and admire to excess. In no work does Erasmus show himself more devoted to the blessed mean position than in his *Ciceronianus*, his satire against extreme Ciceronianism. Many years had gone by since in the *Praise of Folly* he had campaigned against the obscurantism of scholastic philosophers and the unlettered folk of that day. Yet the scholastic preoccupation with the minutiae of speculation had in it something in common with this new obscurantism, which too concerned itself with the letter rather than the spirit. The colloquies had denounced the formalism of much that passed for religion at the time, and the *Ciceronianus* too denounces, with obvious ridicule, a kind of formalism, not unrelated to religion, though immediately concerned with letters. Looked at from another angle, however, the intransigent scholastics and the ultra-modern, ultra-classical Ciceronians are at opposite ends of the philosophical caucus, and the opposition is another instance of the old quarrel between the ancients and the moderns.

In the two decades that separate the *Praise* from the *Ciceronianus* (1528), Erasmus had probably changed somewhat too. He had withstood the attacks on the *Praise* and on the colloquies and the editorial works, defended them to some extent, and suffered under the accusations of heresy the monks had levelled against him. The monologues and the colloquies had had their effect too; there was less abuse in places where it had been rife; but other abuses had come to be. Erasmus might have the character of a trimmer but Luther had not, and his ideas were now dividing Christendom. Erasmus had finally written against him, challenging his denial of the freedom of the will, a point not merely academic but heavily charged. Once Erasmus' *De libero arbitrio* (1524) had been published, it is quite likely the clerical disapprobation of him abated somewhat and the tension eased. The tone of the *Ciceronianus* is less sharp than that in many of the other colloquies.

Although Erasmus' quarrel with the Ciceronians is not directed solely against their pseudo-scholarship or literary pretentiousness, it is on these grounds that he first attacks them. Their exaggerated devotion to the letter is death to the true spirit of Ciceronian imitation, and these men, he declares, are not even good Ciceronians. Indeed, the advancement of all literature is enervated by their adulation, for if Cicero had reached a perfection beyond which one cannot go, there is nothing left but imita-

tion, and creative writing is doomed. This is sad; but sadder is
the Ciceronian's injury to good Christian thinking. The extremists
made a god of Cicero so that 'through him and with him and in
him' they had their being. To add irony to the situation, these
extremists were, for the most part, Italian churchmen. Erasmus'
ideal had never been to set classical culture in the place of
Christian, but rather to re-establish a united Christendom,
wherein the best of Greek and Roman thought might be incorporated into a strong and sensitive Christianity, baptized into it.
Who, he might have asked himself, ought to have been seeing
to it that the new learning be assimilated and put to the service
of Christ and the Church? Surely the scholars already dedicated
to the Church. But no, the very churchmen who should have been
concerned to re-establish the primacy of Christian life were all
too ready to subordinate its culture to the reviving embers of a
pagan age, and to assert its doctrine in faint and ambiguous
terms. It was out of such recognition of a cult both unscholarly
and unchristian that the *Ciceronianus* was born.

If Erasmus' satires were to be ranked according to their
excellence, and not according to chronology, *Ciceronianus* might
find place next to the *Praise*. It is a conversation among three
people, one of whom is unreasonably devoted to the imitation of
Cicero, and the other two supposedly (and initially) of the same
mind, but gradually revealing themselves as sound-thinking men
intent on pointing out to their friend the foolishness of his ways.

The dialogue is the form used again. Lucianic in some measure,
for the absurdly pretentious language of Nosoponus is similar to
that of Lexiphanes, its mood is more flexible than Lucian's usually
is, and is rather Socratic in its movement towards a true position.
Discursive rather than episodic, it has the Erasmian kind of plot
and progress: one character does convince another. And since
the victim is allowed to speak for himself and voice his absurd
ideas, the irony is immediate, not remote. The scene opens with
the two right-thinking fellows spying their friend Nosoponus
(Morbid Toiler) dragging his sad and silly self towards them.
Their comments before he appears prepare for his reception, and
he enters with the ground already cut from beneath his feet.

Immediately he begins to speak of his constant study of his model and god, Cicero:

> Now I shall reveal the mysteries. ... For seven whole years I have touched nothing except Ciceronian books, refraining from others as religiously as the Carthusians refrain from flesh ... lest somewhere some foreign phrase should creep in and, as it were, dull the splendour of Ciceronian speech. Also I have enclosed in their cases and removed from sight all other books lest I should sin inadvertently; and hereafter there is no place in my library for any other except Cicero.[35]

Bulephorus marvels: 'I do not wonder!'

The irony is double here, as it was in the *Praise*: it is satiric and dramatic, the conscious irony of the fanatic himself, unaware of his absurdity, and the *double entendre* of the friends' comments. And it is like *Julius exclusus* too, inasmuch as the right-thinking, corrective character obviates the listener's need to make judgement. The folly is immensely exaggerated and the ridicule sharp, but there is no parody, and so easily there might have been. Nosoponus talks about Ciceronianism and of how he cannot express himself in any other style, but the style of his own speaking does not evidence this devotion, for it is not noticeably Ciceronian. Donne's tufftaffatie beau, Shakespeare's Osric, many of the Jonsonian characters are immensely effective because they not only talk of their excessive admirations but are excessively imitative of their idols in the talking; Moria too: the substance of her oration lambastes affectation, while the style and structure of it mimic the pretensions of oratory. But Nosoponus' contributions to the three-cornered conversation are not Ciceronian burblings. Nor is there in the *Ciceronianus* the liveliness of character and situation that was in the *Praise*, though there is a measure of interest in the conversion of the Ciceronian.

---

35 *Dialogus ciceronianus, or A Dialogue on the Best Style of Speaking* ed (with introduction) Paul Monroe; trans Izora Scott (New York 1908) 23. Subsequent references will be to this edition and bracketed into the text.

Towards the middle of the dialogue the speeches of the mentors become longer and more serious. Bulephorus sometimes declaims now for pages at a time with only a perfunctory comment from the others. As the fanatic shows a disposition to learn, they present him with an exposition of his folly and a direct statement of what true rhetoric is. Bulephorus, the mouthpiece of Erasmus' own ideas, remonstrates with those who think every sentence should open with some recognizable Ciceronian opening:

> If anyone should ask Cicero why he began with these words, he would, I think, make the same reply that in the Blessed Isles Homer made to Lucian's query as to why he began the *Iliad* with the word μῆνιν (for this question had troubled Grammarians for many ages). 'Because,' said Homer, 'that word at the moment happened to occur to me.' [49]

He goes on then to show that, without utter foolishness, the sixteenth-century writer can hardly imitate Cicero's words literally, since the places and circumstances vary, and 'he does not even speak well whose language is inappropriate,' and 'we speak fittingly only when our speech is consistent with the persons and conditions of present-day life' (61). Some pertinent rhetorical questions follow:

> Wherever I turn I see things changed, I stand on another stage, I see another theater, yes another world. What shall I do? I, a Christian, must speak to Christians about the Christian religion. In order that I may speak fittingly, shall I imagine that I am living in the age of Cicero and speaking in a crowded senate in the presence of the senators on the Tarpeian Rock? And shall I borrow words, figures, rhythms from the orations which Cicero delivered in the Senate? I must address a promiscuous crowd in which there are young women, wives, and widows; I must speak of fasting, repentance, of the fruits of prayer, the utility of alms, the sanctity of marriage, the contempt of changing things, the study of the Divine Word. How will the eloquence of Cicero

help me here to whom the themes as well as the vocabulary were unknown? Will not an orator be cold who sews, as it were, patches taken from Cicero upon his garments? [62]

A little later he is pointing out that Cicero himself borrowed from the poets. Should the Ciceronian borrow only Cicero, he wonders, or Cicero plus Cicero's borrowings? Nosoponus, the Ciceronian, thinks 'the antiquity of those whose words he quotes has a sort of majesty in Cicero,' and Bulephorus turns his words against him:

> How comes it then that we think the whole oration defiled if from the most ancient prophets, from Moses, the Psalms, the Gospels and apostolic letters we seek the adornments which Cicero sought as a heathen from the heathens? Is it admirable to borrow from Socrates, but blameworthy to borrow from the proverbs of Solomon? ... Do we admire the wisdom of Plato more than the wisdom of Christ? ... Divine wisdom has an eloquence of its own and no wonder if somewhat different from that of Demosthenes or Cicero; for one dress becomes the wife of a king, another the mistress of a braggart soldier. [71]

The assertion that 'divine wisdom has an eloquence of its own' and the illustration of it might have come directly from Augustine; and there are many more instances of such Augustinian thinking.[36] Erasmus' part in the turning of literature to 'language such as men do use' and the sheering away from formalism in rhetoric must surely bear on the new interest in recreating an Augustinian high style wherein speech is the direct projection of thought, and symbolism is organic because 'things are the words of ideas.' The late Professor Ruth Wallerstein,

---

36 Bulephorus insists, for instance, that 'nature ... intended speech to be a mirror of the mind' (12), and rebels against a uniform formalism; he says too (122) that 'each mind has an individuality of its own, reflecting in speech as in a mirror,' and that the writer's chief care should be to 'know the subject which he undertakes to present'; this in itself, he says, will 'furnish him with a wealth of speech and true natural emotions, and with language that will persuade' (122).

however, in her study of this movement and its consequences in the seventeenth century, quite definitely excludes the *Ciceronianus* from this Augustinian impulse, since Erasmus was concerned in that work with classical issues rather than early Christian.[37] It is true that he does not explicitly assert that he is concerned with scriptural figurativeness and its transference to rhetorical or poetical writing, any more than he explicitly recommends the principle of Senecanism, that language is a mode of discovery as much as it is a mode of communication and should show the mind in the process of meditating and discovering.[38] But he does explicitly recommend the kind of writing that Augustine had recommended and that had become part and parcel of Erasmus's own thinking; and this reverence for literary sincerity, whether or not it is consciously Augustinian, is pervasive throughout the work.

Of the possible influence of the *Ciceronianus* on the development of Senecanism, two things may be said: the first is that it has both a negative and a positive value. It must have helped in the clearing away of a too slavish imitation of classical eloquence which was a cult contrary to either Augustinian directness or Senecan impulses; and its positive directives did urge, as the paragraphs above show, that the mind's reflections should show in the writing, which is Senecan in principle. Secondly, Erasmus' place in the new kinds of writing depends rather on his own style of writing than on his prescriptions. There are parts of the *Praise of Folly* that have all the characteristics of Senecanism, not only structurally, but stylistically too.[39]

---

37 *Studies in Seventeenth-Century Poetic* (Madison 1950) 55
38 He implies a great deal, however, when he calls the writings of Grocyn and Linacre 'Attic,' and dismisses them rather shortly, though not without praise for their respect for Ciceronian decorum. He speaks of More's 'Isocratic rhythm and logical subtlety' and calls him a poet in essence. One gathers from the ironic references to himself that he does not at all deprecate the kind of writing which 'hurries along, writing a whole volume at a sitting,' and uses 'theological words and even vulgarisms.'
39 An example might be taken from the last portion of the book: Moria has been talking of the false exegesis of certain passages of scripture,

The reaction against Ciceronianism, while it seems indeed to have begun in the early sixteenth century, did not become a positive directive to style until the end of the century, when the literary movement tied in with the social, intellectual, and economic temper of the new age, an age which had come to have what J.B. Leishman calls a 'disenchanted resolve to be at all costs realistic, to see things and show things as they really were, and to describe them (as Jonson puts it) in "language such as men do use." '[40] The Senecan temper had, by that time, forgotten that it was anything so negative as a reaction, or anything so moderate as a refusal to emulate Ciceronian periods. There was still plenty of imitation in the late years of the century (in spite of Erasmus' efforts), but it was no longer imitation of Cicero. Interest had veered to the writing of Horace, Juvenal, and Persius, and the French and Italian paradoxists.

Nosoponus is almost converted by the end of the dialogue; and as he yields to the persuasion of his two friends, becomes representative of the reader's similar conversion – or perhaps his confirmation in right thinking. The eloquence now is warm and moving, and the last vestige of irony falls away. If Bulephorus is less satisfying than Moria in this climactic part, it is only because he cannot reach the energy of Moria's evolving selves, and because he is never so winsome or buoyant a person as the earlier figure.

This receding from original irony in favour of direct persuasion, rational, moral, or even spiritual, is found in almost all

and uses as illustration a passage from St Luke. But Moria cares less for the point she is making concerning bad exegesis than for proclaiming the right meaning, and with great ease and grace swings the initial argument out so as to include all the positive and pastoral exhortation in a great parenthesis before moving back to the original denunciation (p 11). Or again, in undertaking to advance the claims of self-love and flattery, Moria leads the reader into speculation about the kinship of one trait with another, about faithfulness in man and in domestic animals, spiritual malaise, grief, the care of children, the way of royal princes; and ends up with an image of two mules scratching each other! (62)

40 *The Monarch of Wit* (London 1959) 107

the satires we have surveyed: Moria embraced a folly that was in the end consummate wisdom, wherein all her perplexities found, if not resolution, at least rest. Her praise of the wise folly was the more effective, dramatically effective, for being a surprising revelation of her depth of feeling; the irony in the first chapters had been a means to this finality, not an end in itself. So too with *Julius exclusus*: the last part is entirely given over to St Peter's denunciation of the folly of Julius' ways, and his exhortation to more reasonable and Christ-like behaviour. The *Complaint* began with a fictitious speaker, but the fiction was soon forgotten in the author's own earnest effort to persuade; and the pattern of the colloquies was similar. Obviously for Erasmus the moral lesson (and sometimes the spiritual) is the great thing, the literary devices quite secondary.

Ciceronianus is like the *Praise* in that it does go beyond the merely rational-moral. The discussion of true rhetoric and the adulation of sincerity as the measure of its success lead Bulephorus to more exalted counselling, and when Nosoponus, a bit wilted, asks whether or not he should 'reject Cicero' entirely, his mentor says no:

> No. He should always be in the bosom of the youth who is a candidate for eloquence, but that over-nicety and fastidiousness which causes one to reject a learned and elegant piece of work and to consider it not worth reading simply because it has not been wrought in imitation of Cicero must be absolutely rejected. ... If his eloquence had cost Cicero as much as it costs the Ciceronians he would have left off some of the ornaments from his orations, I venture to say. That is overdone which is bought at so great a sacrifice of time, health, and even at the price of life itself. That is overdone for the sake of which we neglect the branches of knowledge more necessary to know. And lastly, that is overdone which is bought at the expense of piety. [120]

It is not long before Bulephorus is speaking of perfect rhetoric in terms of the perfect life, of the excellent orator as the good and devout man:

But provision must be made, first of all, that youth, in the simple untutored time of life, be not deceived by the illusion of a Ciceronian name and become pagan instead of Ciceronian. For ... that belief in sacred things which is truly worthy of a Christian must first be gained. When this is accomplished, nothing will seem more ornamental than the Christian religion, nothing more persuasive than the name of Jesus Christ, nothing more charming than the words by means of which the great men of the Church show forth her mysteries. Nor will the speech of any one seem charming which is not in accord with his character and not accommodated to the subject in hand. ... He who is so much a Ciceronian that he is not quite a Christian is not even a Ciceronian because he does not speak fittingly, does not know his subject thoroughly, does not feel deeply those things of which he speaks; lastly he does not present his religious beliefs with the same adornment with which Cicero presented the philosophy of his times. The liberal arts, philosophy, and oratory are learned to the end that we may know Christ, that we may celebrate the glory of Christ. [129]

This is the end then: that we may know Christ and celebrate his glory. We are close here to the mood and purpose of the last parts of the *Praise*. Indeed this is perhaps a better piece of theology than Moria gave us, for in her final vision the scholarly life has seemed to be rejected. Bulephorus is on firmer ground and closer to the Augustinian synthesis. This is not to say, of course, that *Ciceronianus* is a better work than the *Praise*. Moria never became a tract: *Ciceronianus* is sometimes just that. Any one of the long speeches of Bulephorus excerpted from the dialogue is a little treatise solidly didactic and sometimes limp under the burden of instruction. If the speaker had been given any individual characteristics or mannerisms, the worth of his words might the more easily have been recognized; if Nosoponus had been a knowable fellow, the reader might have been more interested in his discomfiture, or his redemption. But Erasmus seems to have forgotten in 1528 what he knew so well in 1509: that lessons are

most easily learned through a human fiction and a vicarious
exercitatio.

It may be worthwhile to note, by way of *obiter dicta*, two
points: first, that the kind of folly indicted here is intellectual,
as it so often was in the *Praise* and the colloquies, the choice
between two rights, one of them reaching an extreme and becoming a wrong; it is the motif of excess and moderation; still
more, of signs and things; but most significantly, it is concerned
with the sins of the intellect, not of the will. And secondly,
though, as we noted above, Nosoponus does not talk like a
Ciceronian – even a bad one – Bulephorus, paradoxically, does
use the manner to body forth the matter: with Ciceronian fineness he builds up his case for the Christian Ciceronian. The
speech just quoted evidences his good use of rounded periodic
sentences, of comparison and antithesis, of argument piling up
on argument and rising to a telling climax.

Erasmus' *Ciceronianus* was the first of several essays of its
kind during this century. Indeed the pulse to and away from
Ciceronian discipleship has run through the whole history of
rhetoric from Seneca to T.S. Eliot. But in this sixteenth-century
rebirth of interest in rhetoric, Erasmus may have been one of the
first to draw attention to the limitations of Ciceronian style, even
at its best. Here, of course, we do not see it at its best, but at its
overdone worst, and anything overdone is, as we know, anathema
to Erasmus. This particular extreme is further vitiated by its
usurpation of a wrong place and by its loss of purpose: it tries to
be an end instead of a means; it assumes thingship, forgetting
that words are rooted in signship.

Even at its height, this is what the new Ciceronian prose
tended to do: become more important than the matter it communicated. Erasmus had imbibed too much of the Augustinian
insistence on the kind of expression which issues directly from
thought and will to be content with Ciceronian elegance. Like
St Augustine's, his was a highly persuasive purpose, and the
merely ornamental made no appeal to him. That is why, furthermore, he could not be satisfied with the old paradoxical writing;

it was too far distanced from the essential paradox in life, which had rational and moral significance. Why spend time and effort defending indifferent things – baldness, gnats, fever, gout, when there was excellent absurdity in the sum of all creation, man?

The many things that can be said about Erasmian satire do not lend themselves easily to tidy summary. The following paragraphs make an attempt to group them under four headings.

First, the best of Erasmus' satire can always be enjoyed as a fiction and simply a fiction. Erasmus makes sure of this response to delight before he ensures any other. All the satires we have considered have in them some element of drama or indirection, inasmuch as it is never the author himself who voices the censure; and each of them uses some figurative device to make that first response entertaining and to awaken attention. The devices are both classical and mediaeval, though he uses them in a new and vital way, as he applies them to contemporary issues. The Lucianic *Dialogues of the Dead* and the soberer Socratic dialogues are a classical heritage, the paradoxes and false encomia and declamations are both classical and mediaeval. The classical forms he uses as they are, except that he shifts them to timely themes and invests them with irony and a new purpose; for the mediaeval allegorical figures he does more: he lets them come to life and take on personality, as Moria does.

Whatever forms Erasmus uses he invests with irony, sometimes simple dramatic irony, as when Nosoponus exults in his empty servitude, unaware of its extravagance; sometimes conscious satiric irony, as when Moria, growing wise, uses withering scorn about the vesture of prelate and prince, or when Peter agrees with Julius that indeed he brought honour to his Church. In either case there is inversion of some sort. This irony, like mercy, is twice blessed, blessing both writer and reader. It enables an Englishman to hide his emotion and so is a boon to the English temperament; even the Dutchman was glad enough to disguise what he had to say, letting overtones speak for him, preferring to laugh at himself than let Willibald Pirckheimer, for instance, or even Thomas More, laugh at him. Still, once he has gained a footing and an audience, Erasmus can and does drop the ironic tone, and does what Donne was to say could not be done: let the brittle mood melt into one of persuasion.

For the most part Erasmus uses fiction and all the literary tropes as winsome trifles to betray us into deeds of deeper consequence. Either they prepare the reader for the moral statement to follow (as in the case of the two orations) or they are themselves framework for the message. This is a scriptural technique, this beguiling of the listener's mind as prelude for instruction. With the satirist it has a new twist: the parable had led naturally into moral instruction; but the Erasmian figurative prelude does not, because it is ironic. Rather it involves a reversal, a sudden dislocation of tone. And there is something dramatic about this. It is surprising, for instance, for Folly to become wise and give a sermon, or for a Dialogue of the Dead to include a persuasive talk, or for a treatise on rhetoric to become a eulogy for the good Christian life; and it is both dramatic and paradoxical for irony to become straightforward; the surprise element and the sudden revelation of hidden seriousness is captivating.

This second point shows us Erasmus as a moralist primarily (and this aspect of his work has, I think, been recently overstressed), but he is a moralist with a questioning and sometimes a troubled eye. That is why he finds irony so expedient. There are so many grains of good sense in what is obviously stupid, and so much of uncommon nonsense in what is theoretically good; and wisdom in the practical order is so much more complex than abstract reasoning shows it to be; and man's nature, made for honest things, seems so readily to seek dishonest, even with the best of guidance, that one hesitates to expound or correct, hesitates to 'sing the good tidings' through very confusion or dismay, and resorts to the ironic mood, detached, observant, content to point out and juxtapose, to sit in the wings and pare one's fingernails.

On the moral level Erasmus' interest is in both consciously willed evil and wrongheadedness, deliberate or indeliberate. But the satirist rarely pursues the sinner who sins with 'full knowledge, consent, and advertence' – the ingredients theologians demand for serious sin; he does not pillage murderers, adulterers, and thieves; nor even the proud or passionate man. His chief targets are the hypocrite and the fool. Incidentally, that is perhaps why Julius lent himself so poorly to the satiric dialogue. The satirist's purpose, both didactic and literary, is to needle the awareness, not to persuade the will. He exposes the hypocrite, he teaches the gull, he forces the reader to think. It is not surprising, therefore, that, although Erasmus was later to underline the responsibility of man's own will in determining what he does, as satirist he is more interested in his wrong thinking. Indeed, it is much more complex than that, for although to read what Erasmus has to say to educators and parents one would think he believed quite simply that idea governed action always, and that all manners and morals were the result of patterns of knowing or thinking, the full context of his works shows him well aware that most men can persuade themselves that they think thus and so, or can lull themselves into not thinking at all.

In any case, the emphasis here is on wrong thinking and self-delusion, on the things and signs of St Augustine's deliberations, and the use or enjoyment of those things and signs; and sometimes on extremes, good things gone crazy through excess. The latter preoccupation is natural to Erasmus, the lover of moderation; the former is natural to anyone wide awake in the early sixteenth century, when theology had become limp and philosophy sterile, when canonists were plentiful and intelligent pastors rare, and when ceremony still flourished though the ardor of faith and good works had dropped to a low level. The author of the *Imitation* had voiced the healthy reaction of his time in saying that it was better to know compunction than to know how to define it. He was only half right, for the two knowings, experiential and academic, are not exclusive of each other; but the need to re-signify the signs and re-validate the forms was something that could surely be felt – and with some disturbance of mind. The practical abuses that Erasmus inveighs against are in the monastic order, the educational and literary orders, and the political, with war, of course, or any discord for that matter, as the special object of his invective in the last category.

For all his apparent awareness of conflict and stress within himself, Erasmus' message in these satires is never entirely negative. Towards the end of most of them there is the exposition of the good life, and some exhortation to it. Moria turns to wisdom; Julius, confirmed in unreason, lapses into silence as Peter becomes eloquent; Nosoponus is somewhat chastened and subdued as Bulephorus warms to his subject. And so with most of the colloquies. Time and time again in these we note that the only dramatic action is the achievement of a change of mind and heart, through conviction and persuasion.

The third point is, like the second, concerned with the good life. It is the inclusion within the moral sense of Erasmian satire of the first and final cause of morality – the end for which man was made. This too is a scriptural or homiletic technique, the moving on to the anagogical sense. Not in all the satires, but in many of them we have noted this interest in, and exhortation to, the highest wisdom, involving the life of charity and faith as well as that of reason. This plea for the life of grace is rarely *within* the ironic inversion, but follows it, with the satiric part an effective preparation for it. And once at least, in the *Praise*, the directive is to something more than the usual way of faith: it approaches the unitive way, suggesting a direct or intuitive experience of God. Such a warmth of devotion coming from the ironic and brittle earlier parts is unexpected and rather moving. It is this embracing of the life of reason by the life of grace, of reasoned prudence by the wisdom of charity, that makes Erasmian satire something apart from the classical models he cites and certainly uses in some measure.

❧ …sed rerum potior ❧

FOR THE FINE CARELESS RAPTURES of imaginative writing Erasmus had only qualified admiration; rapturous or not, his writing had to be disciplined and directed to the perception of moral values, the values he believed constituted man's worth. Consciously held convictions do not always entirely explain the written work of any author, but they do illuminate the broad outlines and undercurrents thereof. This chapter proposes to re-assess these beliefs, and specifically, to follow two avenues of enquiry: first to consider what Erasmus affirms to be the end of man, the 'felicity' he hopes will crown the educative process; and secondly, to probe the Erasmian theory of how man attains this *summum bonum*, and how the attainment is promoted by the written word.

That Erasmus regards man as designed for goodness and learning is evident in all he writes. His ideal goodness comprises both moral good and spiritual, and his learning is both intrinsically good and geared to a practical end: the communication of right thinking and well-doing. He is convinced that man is brought to his fullness of being through instruction and persuasion, and that the word, the didactic, persuasive, always eloquent word, is of paramount significance; and that when persuasive instruction is combined with pleasure, it is the more effective. Considered along with some of the influences that moulded the Erasmian ideal of literary excellence, that last item should account for some part of his satiric invention: irony and fiction and the amusing characterization and word-play; a good deal, but not all, for the human mind, even the simplest human mind, cannot be tabulated and explained away; and Erasmus' was an exceedingly complex mind, allured to, and formed by, so multiple a culture that its richness is often rich confusion. Furthermore, his theories about man and his education will not account for the final effect of his writing. To appreciate this, we must consider his ideal of the perfect Christian. He *is* a Christian – that is the first point – and bound to fit himself for an eternity with God; Erasmus' emphasis, it is true, falls rather on man's own efforts, on his good behaviour towards society, and on his constant use of reason, than on the effect of divine grace; and consequently rather on the cardinal moral virtues than on the theological. But this is a question of emphasis only, as has been evident, and will be made still more so. That Erasmus does allow for the activity of grace along with man's responsibility for his free choice is made explicit in the work in which he deals most directly with this question. In the *De libero arbitrio*, his reply to Luther, made at the behest of the pope, he says that, in order to break with sin, one must seek the remedy of penance and solicit in every way the mercy of God, for 'without it the human will remains ineffectual in spite of our efforts' (LB IX 1217D-E).

It might be argued that this is but a grudging concession to the Augustinian position in a work largely devoted to a contrary one; yet in the same work (LB IX 1224A-D) he gives with some evidence of sympathy the Augustinian position that greatly emphasized man's dependence on grace. Again, the *Hyperaspistes* says explicitly: 'Ego, cum Augustino, gratiam jungo cum libero arbitrio' (LB X 1358B).

But this is the consciously and conscientiously theorizing Erasmus: and even in the *De libero*, once the acknowledgement of grace is made, the argument devolves, as indeed it had been designed to do, into a resounding defence of man's responsibility for his own actions, with the author basing his argument sometimes on authority, more often on reason, with a large indifference to the niceties of philosophical thought which Luther himself had not chosen to ignore. The authority Erasmus cites is that of the Fathers, and sometimes of the classical moralists; and the reasoning appeals mostly to man's experience of his own ability to choose – easy to follow and couched in layman's words. The important point here, in any case, is that, not in his explicit theory only, but in all his work, Erasmus puts the emphasis on man's effort as the *sine qua non* of goodness and salvation: his *vir bonus dicendi peritus* would fit Cicero's ideal better, for instance, than would Donne's or Lancelot Andrewes', or even Richard Hooker's. The fact, however, that Erasmus' humanism (and theology) does recognize in some degree the claims of faith, hope, and charity, and the operation of grace enables him to evoke response from the reader on many levels – the response of natural delight in the contemplation of the human situation, and of rational apprehension of the argument, of the ironic devices which clarify it, and of sympathy in the fullness of the devout life, suggested overtly sometimes, oftener by implication.

This inclusiveness is not found wanting in Erasmian satire; and it is this fullness that gives it its place in the literature of true Christian humanism; the emphases detailed above hardly militate against either its Christian or its humanist character. Erasmus is a man who thinks of his words as more useful than symbolic, and of the reader's mind as more responsive to persuasion and instruction than to inspiration; and he is a writer who takes his responsibilities so seriously that he tends to incorporate his moral lessons too overtly into the fiction, to burden the wings of his symbols with precise explanations, to turn his metaphors into similes and his similes into plain comparisons, and to stoop to moralize his song with a vengeance.

Erasmus is convinced that man only reaches the fullness of his stature through education; and it is not difficult to cull from the educational works some idea of his attitudes and theories on how man comes to knowledge and goodness, both actively and passively, for Erasmus' concern is with both teacher and pupil. Already the context of certain satires has led to the mention of the three focal points in his pedagogy. One might readily call them 'nature,' 'reason,' and 'practice'; but one might by such easy translating imperil their varying significances.

The *De pueris instituendis* presents the most explicit statement. In it Erasmus says that man's felicity or fulfilment rests chiefly on three things: *natura, ratio,* and *exercitatio,*[1] and he goes on to expand the terms. He gives the name *natura,* he says, to the deeply ingrafted affinity man has for 'honest things.' *Ratio* he defines as instruction, consisting of counsels and precepts; and *exercitatio* is practice, the repeated using of that manner of thinking that nature implants and education carries forward. Nature, he goes on, has need of education; *exercitatio* follows the instruction that makes nature a reasoning thing, for unless it is guided by reason, it is prey to many perils and errors – and here perhaps he is thinking of it in its broader sense, experience rather than practice or drill.

The *natura,* we note, does not actually include reason, at least not the *ratio* of Erasmus' trilogy.[2] It is a potential, rather, ready to be taught, and so to become reasonable or reasoning. The point is not without importance. This is no Shaftesbury claiming innate ideas for man; nor yet is it Locke finding the mind a *tabula rasa.* Without teaching, man would not be a man, a reasoning creature; but there is a propensity for 'honest things,' by which Erasmus seems to mean both goodness and truth – moral goodness, factual truth. He defines *natura* in his tract on marriage also, saying there that it is a 'certain aptitude for learning what is taught' (LB V 710D).

Erasmus is sometimes thought to be a Pelagian; perhaps it would be truer to say he is sometimes inconsistent. The humanist Erasmus would surely like to think this wonder of creation, man, drawn only to good, but Erasmus the one-time monk and sometime teacher knows man for a fallen and perverse creature, and

---

1 'Tota vero ratio felicitatis humanae tribus potissimum rebus constat, natura, ratione et exercitatione. Naturam appello docilitatem ac propensionem penitus insitam ad res honestas. Rationem voco doctrinam, quae monitis constat et praeceptis. Exercitationem dico usum ejus habitus quem natura insevit, ratio provexit. Natura rationem desiderat; exercitatio, nisi ratione gubernetur, multis periculis atque erroribus est obnoxia (LB I 496F–497A).
2 The first *ratio* is, of course, of a different colour altogether. It is rather like the *ratione* of the title, *De ratione studii,* meaning progress or course.

knows men who are not at all drawn to good, but rather to bad.
Within the gamut of the educational works, where he is following Quintilian and keeping to the natural and rational levels for
the most part, he makes no attempt to explain the mystery of
iniquity and unreason in a Christian way, but merely states the
bewildering facts: the child in these early years, he says, is easily
drawn towards vice, and by some misfortune or other in the
human design (*infelicitate rerum humanarum*), seems to yield
more readily to villainy than to goodness.[3] He does admit, in the
De pueris, that this tendency, so puzzling to ancient philosophy,
'has its key in the Christian doctrine of original sin,' but adds
immediately that we must not minimize the part doubtless played
by faulty training, 'particularly in the first and most impression-
able stage' (LB I 502C). Even granting, as he occasionally does,
that nature does not always tend to good, Erasmus is convinced
that it is easily salvaged, pliable to the very good *ratio* an able
preceptor will present.[4]

It is in speaking of the interrelation of the *natura* and the
ratio that Erasmus' use of the word *ratio* seems to take on shades
of meaning. According to the texts just quoted, *ratio* is the 'doctrine established in counsels and maxims,' and so seems to be
outside the mind; but in another place, it is that which 'judges
what is to be sought and what avoided,'[5] and thus seems to be a
sort of moral guide or conscience, something akin perhaps to
Donne's 'reason, your viceroy in me,' and certainly *inside* the
mind. Erasmus, who cared so little for schoolmen and their neat
precisions, must have meant his *ratio* sometimes to include all the
natura holds in potency, brought to birth by agencies external to
itself, and sometimes the educative process itself, or the matter
taught therein.

3 See also *De pueris ... instituendis* LB I 489C and 495D.
4 He makes this point also in 'The Godly Feast,' when Eusebius gives
   four points to his 'remedy against the unbridled fury of wicked kings.'
   The first is prevention of his rule, the second the limitation of it – but
   the 'best safeguard of all is to shape his character by sacred teachings
   while he's still a boy ...' (The last resource is prayer.)
5 'Ratio praeceptis iudicat quid expetendum quid fugiendum' (*Christiani
   matrimonii institutio* LB V 710D)

More important than the definition of the term is the relation it bears to the pre-eminence of preaching and teaching. Urging the study of eloquence, Erasmus says it is one thing to be naturally gifted,[6] but that 'education prevails over all else'; and again, in the same work, he repeats this idea with greater emphasis: 'It matters greatly how we are endowed by nature, but much more important are the processes and examples by which we are formed and taught from our youth.' In *The Education of a Christian Prince* he makes almost the same claim, in this case assuming that education is moral formation:

> There is no beast so wild, so terrible, that the skill and endurance of his trainer will not tame him. Why then should the tutor judge any man to be so coarse and so forsaken that he will not be corrected by painstaking instruction?[7]

The responsibility of the tutor (and the writer of colloquies and praises is surely a sort of tutor) is consequently great, for the pliable *natura* is wax waiting for a seal, uncut stone waiting for a sculptor, and can be fixed for evil things by an unscrupulous teacher, just as it may be moulded to good by the wise teacher, 'for nature can become better or worse by our own fault or guilt' (LB V 710D-E), he says in the tract on marriage; and still more pithily in the *De pueris*: 'Nature is an efficacious thing, but education, a thing still more efficacious, stands superior to it' (LB I 492A). His own mission to enlighten and teach Erasmus never doubted.

Exercitatio, in its academic sense, is the exercise or drill that follows the outlining of a principle or paradigm in a classroom; in a larger meaning, and linked to the moral life, it is the practical exercise of judgement or choice; and sometimes Erasmus seems to mean by it simply experience. Not to be slighted, it

---

6 'Est aliquid bene nasci: verum educatio superat omnia' (LB V 710C). Earlier in the same work the idea is given just as clearly: 'Magni refert quomodo quis nascatur, sed multo maxime, quibus rationibus et exemplis a teneris formemur et instituamur' (LB V 615C).

7 *Institutio principis christiani* (1516) ed and trans L.K. Born (New York 1936 and 1964) 145; LB IV 564B

nevertheless comes last in point of time. It is a costly teacher, Erasmus insists many times, leading one into pitfalls and dangers 'unless it is guided by instruction' (LB I 487A). Nevertheless, it is this *usus* or *exercitatio* that, in the end, does transform what has been taught into habit, as he explains in the *Christiani matrimonii institutio* (LB V 710B). But vicarious experience may be provided in some measure surely by the wise teacher, who is thus responsible for both *usus* and *ratio*. Such good classroom procedure is outlined in *De pueris instituendis*:

> As for fables and narratives, he learns them more willingly and remembers them better if the subjects of them are cleverly made to appear before his eyes, and the matter of the story shown him in pictures. [LB I 510D]

Elsewhere he urges that the lesson be presented to the ears (by explanation) and to the eyes (by pictures) so that, through such convincing teaching, the good seeds may reach to the very heart (LB V 719B). And surely a good teacher would find in the colloquies 'tongues that speak to the ears and pictures that speak to the eyes,' with eloquence to persuade as well. Delight is a factor in the process of learning, and by it the scholar is best persuaded to the *honestae res*.[8] For it is not enough, Erasmus says, that the teacher be learned and good: he must be suitable in disposition too. Many, he explains, lack gentleness, and some have little forbearance (LB V 715C). He urges the use of games, debates, pictures, and even an easy meting out of praise when encouragement is needed.[9] A long passage in the *De ratione studiorum* urges the tutor to bring in 'tales of the poets appropriate to the

---

8 Erasmus may have culled these convictions from both Christian and classical sources: from Quintilian, for instance, on whose *Institutio oratoria* he leans heavily in the educational works; however, for Quintilian (and sometimes for Erasmus too) the pleasure comes through exciting desire for fame rather than as an intrinsic part of the learning or teaching; see, for instance, I 2:24 and II 4:10–14. Augustine too insists on pleasure as a quality of the most effective and persuasive teaching (*De doctrina christiana* 193–4).

9 'Non enim satis est praeceptorem esse doctum ac probum virum: comitas quaedam et commoditas adsit oportet qua et ferat aetatis, quam tractat,

illustration of human character – for instance, the story of Pylades and Orestes to recommend friendship, and that of Tantalus to arouse detestation of avarice ...' (LB I 527B-C).[10]

And so Erasmus tries to make each of his own instructive works a thing of some delight, putting his vices and virtues and absurdities into fictional form, men-about-town, down-and-outers, good monks and bad, tough old soldiers and ladylike girls – but all of them articulate in some way, often a very amusing way, with banter and posturing and clownish ignorance, and always with energy and vitality. Into their conversation he pours too the cream of his literary valour, his irony, his schemes and tropes, and his vivid imagery, so that the wisdom he wants to teach is made as visible as the pictures he recommends.

The wisdoms and the follies that Erasmus presents have many shapes; and these lead us to reflect on the shape of his interpretation of the *honestae res* or *philosophia* he posits as the end of man's development. The two terms seems to be virtually interchangeable, though perhaps in isolation each favours one aspect of a twofold goal. *Philosophia* must surely include – or at least could not exclude – *eruditio*, or even *eloquentia*; *honestae res* looks rather to moral goodness, sometimes called *virtus* and sometimes *pietas*. The term and concept *sapientia* (used often in the *Praise* and other satires, but less often in the educational works) should comprise the virtues of both mind and will. With Erasmus, however, it seems sometimes to mean simply goodness and sometimes the combination of goodness with knowledge. In the Epistle to the 1518 edition of the *Enchiridion*, for instance, the wise king, teaching his son true wisdom, 'took much more pain in exhorting him thereunto than in teaching him, as who would say that to love wisdom were in a manner to have attained it,' and since the rest of the passage discusses wisdom in terms more

inscitiam, et semet ad illius naturam accommodet ...' (*De pronunciatione* LB I 918D). The *comitas* idea he probably takes from Quintilian (II 5–6).
10 When Erasmus speaks in this vein to or of the instructor, he surely thinks of him as not only instructor (*grammaticus* or *pedagogus*) but as *formator*, one who moulds a boy, now to intellectual acumen, now to moral integrity.

of Christian moral goodness than of intellectual virtue, one gathers that wisdom here simply means the devout and moral life. Later in the same work, however, he assumes the usual connotation of the word but suggests that, in a Christian context, the terms 'malice' and 'foolishness' are interchangeable, and likewise 'virtue' and 'wisdom' (LB V 26D). In the *Antibarbari* (LB X 1733E), he is quite clear about the double nature of wisdom, saying that it is necessary that virtue be joined to liberal erudition if it is to be called 'wisdom'; and the same is implied in a letter to John More (Allen IX 134), where he says wisdom and eloquence must work conjointly.

Although the word *sapientia* may and often does include both moral and mental virtue, Erasmus does not identify the one with the other; and this is remarkable in view of his regard for Quintilian, who does tend to identify them. In his *Antibarbari* he lets Batt epitomize what the *Medicus* (arguing for unlettered piety) has said:

> I see now what you're getting at. Learning that leads to evil is not good. It follows surely that if it makes men bad it is bad. Learning is one thing, virtue another: he who is good is not necessarily learned, he who is learned not necessarily good. [LB X 1723E][11]

Batt, speaking for the youthful Erasmus, will not concede, of course, that profane learning, or any other kind, is injurious to virtue, but his long rebuttal does not gainsay the truth of the *aliud-aliud* of the doctor's thinking. In fact, Batt goes on to support his case with examples of four kinds of men, two good and two bad. One of the two sinners is learned, one unlearned. Batt's question is ' – and which one would you prefer to be?' and not, as it might have been, 'Is this not a contradiction in terms?' Still,

---

11 Further corroboration of this idea can be found in a letter to Maximilian of Burgundy (Allen VII 141): 'Habes ... domi unde duo quaedam praecipua bona consequi possis; pietatem erga Deum, quae sola beatum reddit hominem, ac liberalem eruditionem.' See also a letter referring to the comedies of Terence (Allen IX 401): 'Disciplinae liberales, quae licet per se virtutes non sint, tamen ad virtutem praeparant.'

the whole paragraph comes as a climax to a long passage maintaining at length that, although *pietas* may and does exist and have validity apart from any intellectual acumen, it is in some way incomplete without it, for 'without it, virtue seems to be in some way incomplete.'

All learning, in any case, can be brought back to Christ, and especially literature, which he says, 'shapes and invigorates the youthful character and prepares [it] marvellously well for understanding Holy Scripture, to pounce upon which with unscrubbed hands and feet is something akin to sacrilege' (*Enchiridion* 51; LB V 26E). One is reminded here of another humanist, John Donne, who was to say that even arithmetic, a 'barren thing,' could show forth the glory of God to one of fine perceptivity.[12] But Erasmus' *omnis eruditio* perhaps hardly includes that fine sight that recognizes divine provenance in the immutable laws of mathematics; nor would he be apt to think the polishing and refining of human talent a good in itself – still less the life of speculation. He never urges the pedagogue to probe the abstract sciences; he scorns the philosophers whose work is not geared to the moral life. He was right perhaps in seeing the scholasticism of his day as attenuated wisdom, but the whole carefully accumulated system of thought preceding this extreme of pure speculation he damns as well; and this seems less than good. He laments the theologians' enshrining of Aristotle, though he cites him occasionally; Plato he admires, but not for his speculative thought; rather for his moral teaching – and of course for giving to man the *sanctus Socrates*, who had joined reason to morality and thought to life, who had preferred the study of morality to the study of nature and ultimate reality because *quae supra nos nihil ad nos*.[13] For Erasmus the great science is moral theology through scriptural exegesis, but a close second is rhetoric, a social science, a medium for communicating thought and persuading man to good and moral living, benevolence, and justice to his fellow man

12 *Sermons* IV 2, p 87
13 Erasmus quotes this adage of Socrates in his letter to John Carondelet (1522) and speaks there of his own efforts to do for theology what Socrates had done for philosophy (Allen V 176, 177).

and so to God. And this may explain why in some of the colloquies, the logic is not precise. In the instances noted above (chapter three, pp 125–7), the essential social truth *was* perfectly
sound; but the method of arriving at it was not; the abstract
reasoning mattered so much less to Erasmus than the truth of
its conclusion. In the *Praise* too we delighted in Moria's percipience and the varied aspects of truth she presented. But it was
moral reflection for the most part – the choice of profession, the
social value of scholarship, the pitfalls of pride and of asceticism,
the degrees of prudence, the sham of insincerity. All this is good:
clear vision does underly the moral life, but with Erasmus percipience seldom probes into the precisions of being or knowing,
and only occasionally becomes that *notitia clara cum laude* that
was the high noon of awareness as Augustine saw it.

So too with Erasmus' attitude to beauty. The glory of the
ancient world, its literature and culture, he loved instinctively,
but one wonders whether, outside this world of artefact, he
recognized much beauty. He rarely comments on the beauty of
nature, though, like More and others of his time, he uses the
garden as a *locus amoenus* in some of his colloquies, as if to imply
that a fair environment stimulates thought; and the world of
flowers and trees and birds and animals he draws on again and
again, but only to provide emblems and analogies for his purpose.
Sometimes too he does forgo his moralist manner to admit pleasure in the fine thing itself.[14] But this is rare. More often he shows

14 In the *Oratio de virtute amplectenda*, for instance, he says: 'Etenim quid
quaeso te omnino aliud vox illa hominis dulcis ac tinnula, citraque
omnem asperitatem eminus etiam aures feriens, nisi Phoebea quaedam
cithara, aureis fidibus divinum quiddam insonans? Quis est autem
ingenio usque adeo stupido, fero saxeoque, quem Battica suaviloquentia,
et vel Nestorea illa mellitior, non excitet, non emolliat, non edomet?
(LB V 70E–F). If one may be permitted a footnote to a footnote, it is interesting, and not irrelevant, to draw attention to Erasmus' witty coining of
the adjective 'Battica'; Battic eloquence is, of course, even more admirable than Attic eloquence, when one's reader will be James Batt, Erasmus'
good friend – and a marginal note gives even a dull reader a little hint.
One wonders if Batt would have remembered, as surely Erasmus did,
that Cicero himself had made a similar play on the word in his *Epistula
ad Atticum* (Book I, Ep 13, Section 5). Cicero says there that his speech,

that even his appreciation of the ancient culture is bent to moral purpose: one reads in order to learn the ancient skills of rhetoric and the ancient laws of human behaviour.[15] And not only his appreciation of literature, but also his creation of it, is conditioned, as we have said many times, by this penchant for teaching. For all his directives concerning the recognition of symbols in Scripture and nature, he himself must explain his own or let them turn into metaphors or simple comparisons. His reluctance to confuse the student of Scripture by offering him an obscure reading of the texts is, of course, explanatory in some measure of all this – and is noted in the first chapter of this study; but his attitude to poetry is not irrelevant, and is expressed in a letter to Ammonius in 1513:

> but personally I have always liked verse that was not far removed from prose (albeit prose of the first order) ... I gain peculiarly intense pleasure from an oratorical poem, in the verses of which

now that it has been praised by Atticus, seems far more 'Attic' even to himself. See too Book xv, Ep 1a, Sec 2). There is a small passage in the *De copia* that also bespeaks Erasmus' admiration for beauty in itself, and Huizinga can speak of Erasmus' admiration of classical rhetoric as something pleasurable in itself (*Erasmus of Rotterdam* 105).

What Bainton says of Erasmus' attitude to music might apply to a more general attitude. He notes that Erasmus would have had the liturgy sometimes in the vernacular, and when the Sorbonne argued for the emotive power of the Latin, had insisted that the vernacular would have had equal emotive power; and Bainton comments: 'Had the Sorbonne retorted that the French would not match the notes, Erasmus would surely have called for changing the notes to fit the words. He would subordinate the musical to the didactic. Music has the power to create moods ... but it lacks conceptual precision' (*Erasmus of Christendom* 235).

15 In a recent essay, Maragret Mann Phillips says of Erasmus' attitude to the classics: 'Whole-hearted as his admiration was, it was never subservient, and he saw the classics strictly in relation to the needs of the modern world. Earnest in his struggle to abolish corrupt texts and misreadings, he was yet not a solemn scholar; there was an element of the journalist in his make-up which banished pomposity and made him take the reader aside in a very human way. ... It was crystal-clear to him that the qualities discoverable in the writers of Greece and Rome were precisely those needed to reorientate the thinking of his own time' ('Erasmus and the Classics,' in *Erasmus* T.A. Dorey (ed) [London 1970] 1).

the oratorical style can be detected, or from a poetical orator in whose prose we can see and appreciate poetry. And whereas some other men prefer more exotic elements, my own very special approval goes to your practice of depending for your effects on the bare narrative and your concern for displaying the subject rather than your own cleverness.[16]

Ammonius' poem (a panegyric in praise of Henry VIII) Erasmus praises because it presents a clear narrative of events; he does, however, criticize one of its lines as being too pedestrian, and praises others for their visual imagery.

Emphasis on the moral life characterizes to some extent Erasmus' spirituality too, his very *pietas erga Deum* which he says is the one thing necessary. Throughout the colloquies, the *Enchiridion*, the *Education of a Christian Prince*, the first and satiric parts of the *Praise*, the *Ciceronianus* to some extent, and especially the educational works, religion seems to be the good, moral, reasonable life (as it is, of course, though it is more); and Christ is the great model of that life, the great exemplar (as he is, of course, though he is more). Indeed Erasmus is more interested, one thinks, in the imitation of Christ than in the thought of union with him or love for him.

Yet all of this is, of course, only half true. One cannot make of Erasmus a tidily predictable piece of humanist machinery when he is in reality a complex person caught between two worlds, trying to be loyal to each, and manifesting the conflict and torment all too often, drifting into an unreal over-confidence in man's capacity for, and tendency towards, good, as he adopts perhaps Quintilian's convictions about the admirable tendencies of human nature; yet suspicious, with St Augustine and Colet, of all things natural; deciding with Quintilian and Cicero that definition is the beginning of wisdom, but hesitant too remembering that St Augustine had thought otherwise;[17] and ever and always,

16 Allen I 545. Translation by D.F.S. Thomson (*Erasmus and Cambridge* H.C. Porter, ed [University of Toronto Press 1957] 172)
17 Augustine has said: 'So, when things are known, the cognition of the words is also accomplished, but by means of hearing words they are not

consciously or subconsciously, conditioned by the early influence
of the Brethren of the Common Life, who had given him his first
schooling and who had thought it better to know how to feel the
things of God than how to define them;[18] having felt the influence
too of Colet, who found natural man 'nothing if not weak, foolish,
evil, vain, lost, and nought, his power weakness, his wisdom
folly, his will malicious ...'[19] Erasmus is a complex piece of Renaissance humanism.

Some unacknowledged remnant of the Brethren's influence

learned'; and again, 'Therefore, that the sign is learned after the thing
is cognized is rather more the case than that the thing itself is learned
after the sign is given.' Yet Erasmus is Augustinian enough when he
begins his *De ratione studii* with the recognition of the firstness of words
in the order of learning, for Augustine goes on to say 'Man is only
prompted by words in order that he may learn, and it is apparent that it
is only a very small measure of what a speaker thinks that is expressed
in his words' (*De magistro*, in *Basic Writings of St Augustine* Whitney
J. Oates (ed) ([New York 1949] I 359).

18 Ideas of holy simplicity must certainly have come to Erasmus through
the late mediaeval movement called the *Devotio moderna* and especially
from his schooling at Deventer where the movement flourished. Professor Walter Kaiser reflects that the two writers, Thomas a Kempis, who
wrote the *Imitatio Christi*, and Nicholas of Cusa, author of the treatise
De docta ignorantia, had both been students at Deventer, which Erasmus
was to attend a generation later, and from which he must have imbibed
that *philosophia Christi* which was so much a part of him. Professor
Kaiser notes that, although the *Imitatio* was the more popular book,
Cusanus' *De docta ignorantia* was more important – and certainly more
important to the creator of Moria, who is anything but the 'humble
analphabetic fool' of the middle ages' predilection. 'In the two paradoxical keystones of Cusanus' philosophy, *docta ignorantia* and *coinci-
dentia oppositorum* [says Professor Kaiser] both the philosophical and
stylistic characteristics of Erasmus' *Stultitia* find their first extensive
exposition'; and again, 'Out of the paradoxical concepts of Kempis and
Cusanus, the Renaissance developed the oxymoronic concept of the wise
fool, who embodies these paradoxes and capitalizes upon the equivocation in the word *wit*' (*Praisers of Folly*) 10 and 12). Yet there are passages too – the non-satirical, non paradoxical parts of the *Praise*, of *Dulce
bellum*, the *Enchiridion* – where the sober lauding of unlearned simplicity seems redolent rather of the *Imitation* than of the *De docta
ignorantia*.

19 *Enarratio in primam epistolam Sancti Pauli ad Corinthios* trans. J.H.
Lupton, 247; quoted by Eugene F. Rice, Jr, in 'John Colet and the Annihilation of the Natural' *Harvard Theological Review* XLV (1952) 141

is seen, distorted perhaps, in the celebration now and then in Erasmus' writings of unlearned virtue. Moria's final vision is splendid, but she seems to be beguiled in this part into an astonishing repudiation of knowledge – astonishing because here she is not ironic, though there is a kind of paradoxical irony in the state she describes. Other evidences too of this repudiation of learning could be cited: the *Dulce bellum inexpertis* provides a good example in the passage where Dame Nature has all the wisdom needed, and man's primitive excellence is lauded and the coming of learning shrugged off as being little more than an 'ideal instrument ... for confuting the heretics, armed as they were with the writing of the philosophers, poets, and orators.' At that time, she goes on, and put to such a purpose, learning did have some value, but as time went on it was approved for its intrinsic worth, and then,

> on the pretext of combating heresy, a conceited taste for controversy crept in, which was the cause of no little evil to the Church. Finally things came to the point where the whole of Aristotle was accepted as an integral part of theology ... [*Adages* 331][20]

There is also the famous passage in *Paraclesis*, where it is said that one needs only a pious and open heart imbued with a pure

---

20 A comparable passage occurs in the preface to Hilary: 'Once faith was more in life than in the profession of articles. Soon necessity urged that articles be prescribed, but they were few and of Apostolic sobriety. Next the wickedness of heretics compelled a more exact examination of the divine volumes. ... At length faith was contained in writings rather than in hearts, and soon there were as many faiths as there were men. Articles increased, but sincerity decreased: contention grew violent, while charity grew cold' (Allen v 180–1; translated by John B. Payne in his *Erasmus: His Theology of the Sacraments* [John Knox Press 1970] 15). In an earlier part of this same writing Erasmus comments that nowhere is St Paul's pithy sentence 'scientia inflat, charitas aedificat' better exemplified than in such idle and contentious probing into what does not concern mortal man (Allen v 177). From these two passages it seems clear that it is not knowledge in itself that Erasmus disparages, but a certain kind of learning that keeps man from his proper pursuits and leads him into disunity.

and simple faith to 'read and understand the Scriptures' (LB V 140C). Yet these instances – and there are others – are the exceptions, and rarely is any knowledge, except the speculative branches taught by the schoolmen, disparaged. Usually it is Erasmus' way to speak of learning as the concomitant to virtue, a prime element in man's felicity on earth and ultimate blessedness.

Related in some measure to this pietistic and moralistic emphasis is Erasmus' marked distaste for ceremony and his sometime de-emphasis of the sacraments. Of his indifference to ceremony we have already spoken, seeing it in relation to the lack of congruence between sign and thing signified. It is hard to say whether Erasmus would have given more approbation to ritual if the age had been one of greater faith and virtue and the congruency of the sign untrammelled.

As for the sacraments, as Churchman and apologist for Christian beliefs, Erasmus is not unorthodox, and indeed writes well of the sacraments in many of his works:[21] they are the channels of God's grace, seven in number;[22] they are revered because they have been instituted by Christ;[23] they symbolize, and in

---

21 For instance: *Enchiridion* (LB V 1A–64A), *Paraclesis* (LB V 137D–144D), *Novum Testamentum* (LB VI), *Ratio verae theologiae* (LB V 75A–137C), *Hyperaspistes* (LB X 1249A–1536F), *Christiani matrimonii institutio* (LB V 615A–724B), *Symbolum* (LB V 1133A–1197D), *Ecclesiastes, sive de ratione concionandi* (LB V 769–1098)

22 LB V 1175E–F (*Symbolum*), and LB IX 227C and 338D (controversies with Lee and Stunica respectively). In the last mentioned Erasmus speaks of sacramental grace as coming through the sacramental signs, but usually he thinks of it as a grace that accompanies the sacrament because Christ promised it so (*velut ex pacto*), not because the sacrament is of necessity and intrinsically the begetter of the grace. See Professor Payne's detailed and careful documentation of this in the work above mentioned (pp 96–106, and footnotes thereto; the pertinent texts are: *Hyperaspistes* LB X 1447E and *Christiani hominis institutum* [a poem], LB V 1358D–E, and *Symbolum* LB V 1175E–F).

23 *Praecatio Erasmi Roterodami ad Virginis filium Iesum* LB V 1211E; *Symbolum* LB V 1141A; *Christiani matrimonii institutio* LB V 620A; *Novum Testamentum* LB VI 798D, and *Inquisitio de Fide* LB V 1152B–C; or, in C.R. Thompson's translation (*Erasmus' Inquisitio de Fide* [New Haven 1950] 68–71)

fact are, the fusion of flesh and spirit, of visible and invisible, of the outward and the inward.[24]

But even in the theological and exegetical writings – and still more in the popular works of devotion and fiction – the emphasis is on the individual, personal efforts of man to shape himself to the Christian standard. And the sacraments have their efficacy, not *ex opere operato*, but through the recipient's willed co-operation with the grace therein proffered to him.[25]

In his recent study of Erasmus and the sacraments, Professor John Payne points out that Erasmus' most detailed analysis of what a sacrament is (in the *Christiani matrimonii institutio* LB V 620B) includes the statement that one notes three things in any sacrament: the *imago*, the *arra*, and the *exemplum*. *Imago* denotes the congruence of the sacrament's sign with what it signifies; *arra* is 'the gift of spiritual grace which *velut ex pacto* is in-

---

24 See, for instance, 'The Godly Feast' (*Colloquies* 68–9 especially) where, as Payne points out, both ceremony and sacrament (Erasmus makes little distinction between the two) are disparaged unless they are accompanied by inner conversion and devotion. The point is made again in Erasmus' defense of the colloquies (LB IX 935D–936A). Still, neither of these passages actually refers to the sacrament itself as being a fusion of spiritual and material. There is a clearer statement in a response to a pseudonymous work: 'In order that I might call men forth from visible ceremonies to spiritual progress, I show that in all things there is, as it were, a certain flesh and spirit, that is, something visible and invisible: but the invisible ... is far more excellent than what is seen, just as in man the soul is more powerful than the body; and this catholic opinion I show through all the species of things, the word of God ... and the sacraments of the new law, such as baptism, Eucharist, and unction' (LB X 1562A–B; Payne's translation: 102–3). Professor Payne comments that, although the spiritual meaning is for Erasmus the preferred – and this is especially evident in the *Praise* and the *Enchiridion* – the corporeal aspect is never rejected.

25 See, for instance, *Apologia adversus monachos hispanos* LB IX 1070A, and *Enchiridion* LB V 30B (in the Himelick translation, 110ff). In the same vein are passages in the *Praise* (pp 80, 87–90), the colloquies, especially 'The Godly Feast' (*Colloquies* 68–70) and 'The Fish Diet' (pp 347ff) and in a letter to Jodocus Jonas on Vitrier and Colet (Allen III 526; a translation of this letter is included in *Christian Humanism and the Reformation: Desiderius Erasmus, Selected Writings* [New York, Harper Torchbook 1965], edited and translated by John C. Olin; the passage is on page 185).

fused through the administration of the sacrament'; the *exemplum* refers to 'what in that similitude is commended to us to be imitated.' And Professor Payne comments on where Erasmus puts the emphasis: 'Erasmus places the greatest weight on this third aspect of the sacrament, although he does not leave out of view the gift of grace which comes through – or better, which accompanies – the administration of the sacrament' (p 99).

But it is emphasis, not orthodoxy, we are concerned with; and Erasmus' bent is away from grace and the sacraments – and certainly from ceremony – and towards the good life, moral and devotional. He never tires of recommending proper teaching and education; he speaks eloquently of prayer and knowledge as a happy combination. The formula is good; but many of his contemporaries would have included the sacraments oftener in their exhortations to the good life.

And yet to picture Erasmus as a man forbidding in his rational and pietistic morality would be to caricature him. He would have men render more than mere justice to their fellow-men; he longs for a Christendom united in charity; he urges his reader, as we have seen, to share with his neighbour his all, to act towards him with the greatest benevolence, to tolerate even his violations of law rather than make war on him. His charity is usually more man-ward than God-ward, but not always. And it is because he does sometimes – notably in the *Praise*, but also in several colloquies and in *Ciceronianus* – lift his whole subject beyond the plane of ethics and reason, and does realize sometimes that satire is operative only on the plane of reason, while man is capable of being moved more effectively by other and more positively hortative modes, that he stands out against the limitations of his immediate successors.

Granting then that a man can convert his fellow man to goodness by teaching (even the acid teaching of satire) and persuasion, and given Erasmus' respect for effective words, it is not difficult to see why he gives so much importance and the right of temporal (and pedagogical) priority to the *cognitio verborum*. The thing is known through definition and explanation; its desirability is communicated through eloquence. Therefore, discourse is the means by which the child learns, and is also what he learns. For, humanly speaking, the word is the means by which the restless, distraught world, the unhappy, ignorant, greedy world, can be made regenerate. That is what the word is for Erasmus: not just the glory of man's human perfection, but the custodian of it.

And that is not all. The word has for Erasmus a distinct relation to the will of God; and although his emphases are on the human efficacy of the word, he does recognize the divine parallel too. In the *De ratione concionandi* he refers first to the mind as 'quandam divinae mentis imaginem'; and then, since the mind is the source from which the word springs, he goes on to say that 'just as the unique Word of God is the image of the Father, so too speech is a certain image of the human mind' (LB V 772F).

The emphasis here is significant. There is, of course, more than a hint of the divine parallel – it is quite explicit; but when Erasmus comes to amplifying it, it is noteworthy that he does not really bring man and his word into the divine analogy as completely as he might have. Only one part of the relationship is articulated: that as God is to his Word, so is man to *his* word. The correlative parallel is perhaps suggested, but not made explicit: that as man is to God, so is man's word to God's Word. The human word's ultimate emanation from, and direction towards, the Almighty is something to which Erasmus might perhaps give academic or notional assent, but not a real one. Often he comments on speech as that which raises man above the beast world,[26] seldom on its being the mark of his rising into another world, or on its being proxy to God's Word, channelling the divine message that may engrace the world. The great emphasis is on reason and practical, devout morality, and so the word of the teacher is pre-eminently important and seems sometimes to be the end of education as well as its means.

---

26 In the *De pronunciatione*, for instance, he says: 'Galenus me docuit hominem a caeteris animantibus ... discerni non ratione sed oratione' (LB I 913D). For a text in which he speaks of the *sermo* making man in some way the image of God, see LB V 772E–F.

In his commitment to practical ethics, Erasmus then is wary of symbols, though he recognizes that God himself teaches by these natural analogues. But the burden of convincing the reader is always on him. Even in the *Praise*, where he does trust himself in more adventurous waters than in any other satires, he nearly spoils the three or four potent symbols around which he hovers by over-explaining them. One cannot explain a symbol; if one could there would be no point in using it. Its effect lies in its power to expand the meaning of the plainer statement through association and suggestion, and sometimes by its own history. For the most part, Erasmus finds his symbols either in Scripture or in classical literature. Of the four outstanding metaphors in the *Praise*, the shadows in the cave, the cock, the Silenus box, the play of life, three were not original with Erasmus, and even the fourth, the theatre image, is Platonic and Lucianic in some degree. The fact that they had been used in earlier literature does not at all mar the effect of the symbol. Rather it enhances it, for the writer can draw on associations already formed in the reader's mind, so that he is taught through what he already knows. But the effect *is* marred, or at least diluted, by Erasmus' determination to teach too thoroughly. The reader is seldom left to pick his own precarious way through symbols he only half understands; the excitement of seeing into the heart of mystery is lost: there is no mystery. Everything is well explained. A fair example of this occurs in the *Dulce bellum* where Erasmus speaks of man's body and its fair exterior. All that nature has given man, he says, she has given him as pledge that he was made for love and amity: he has not the crocodile's scales, the porcupine's quills, the boar's fangs, and so on (*Adages* 310–11). And Erasmus wants man to recognize this as a symbol of man's destiny in peace; but he himself prefers not to use the symbol, but only to ensure that man is taught to see it.

St Augustine is pertinent here. Erasmus was strongly influenced by him, and the influence made for simplicity – as did that of St Jerome. Especially was this so in whatever writing aimed at convincing the reader, or moving him. One small point in this connection might be advanced; one cannot say for certain that it has bearing on the way Erasmus uses the symbol, but possibly it has.

In the early chapters of the *De doctrina*, Augustine reflects on the value of symbol or metaphor in devotional or exegetical writing. The saints, he says, have provided excellent examples for man to revere and emulate. Why is it, then, he ponders, that

> when anyone asserts these facts, he affords less charm to his listener than when he explains with the same interpretation that text from the Canticle of Canticles where the Church is alluded to as a beautiful woman who is being praised: Thy teeth are as flocks. ... Does one learn anything more than when he hears that same thought phrased in the simplest words, without the aid of this simile? But somehow or other I find more delight in considering the saints when I regard them as the teeth of the Church.
> [II 6, 65]

Augustine goes on to admit that he cannot explain why the figures give more pleasure, but declares that everyone knows that this is so; and everyone knows too that one learns the more readily through the use of figures. Yet, when Augustine comes in a later part of this work (IV 2, 169) to detail what the eloquent preacher should do to move his hearers, there is nothing about the use of symbol or metaphor, only that the Christian orator must 'please in order to hold attention.'

Erasmus thinks so too, and in the *De conscribendis epistolis* shakes a disparaging finger at theologians who hold the poets suspect, unaware that 'by the splendour of their words they [can] entice the mind of the reader' – to virtue, if the poet so pleases (LB I 408E).

Mindful always of his position as instructor, Erasmus does precisely what Augustine requires. He explains the interpretation of the symbols he finds in the two books of God's revelation, nature and the scriptures. But when he comes to writing his own exhortations, even when they are in the form of fiction, he is reluctant to talk of teeth and flocks when he means the saints of the Church. Teeth are teeth, saints are saints; and to let one stand for the other might betray some 'frothy showiness of style,' such as Augustine had condemned. For the 'flowers of eloquence,' he says in the adage 'Herculei Labores,' a man engaged in a work of instruction should have no time, an opinion for whose defence he calls up Cicero, Seneca, Prudentius, and St Jerome. 'For myself,' he says, in the same work, 'though I don't despise eloquence in other people, I have never much sought it in my own case, preferring, I don't know why, a sensible style to a highly coloured one, as long as it was not vulgar, and really expressed my thought' (p 203; cf. pp 190–209).

Erasmus' belief in reason's capacity to regenerate the moral life of man is surely something to be kept in mind while explaining his satirical work. Knowledge, or reason, may not be quite the same as virtue, but almost. And so man must be made to see the right. Satire at least helps him to see: ridicule shows the wrong as repugnant, and irony, by indirection, makes the right appear desirable. The witty colloquy, for instance, not only exaggerates and reduces to absurdity some wrong-doing; it also provides the pleasure which should, according to Erasmus, accompany good teaching. It does more: it provides a bit of vicarious experience, the needed *exercitatio* which will make right reason active and habitual. In the best of the satires, especially in the *Praise*, of course, but in some of the colloquies too, and in the *Ciceronianus*, in some measure, the teacher moves from the blackboard to the pulpit, reaching out to exhort and quicken his hearer. And that is perhaps why we find Erasmus abandoning his ironic, satiric attitude, and depending more and more on the well-tried, lofty methods of exhortation, and on all the devices that rhetoric and poetry can lend him to move his listener.

For all his satiric disparagement of man's follies and foibles, Erasmus has all the humanist's admiration for man's nature and achievements. His interest is partly historical, for his study of classical writing and of the culture of Greece and Rome has shown him how great is man's potential, and how far he may develop himself by his own effort and even without the aid of revelation; and he is exasperated at the discrepancy between what man is and what he could be. So the dramatic and exaggerated presentation of Tom and Dick and Harry in the very act of misbehaving or being gulled is satisfying; and the fiction combines three elements of good teaching too: it presents the reasonable norm (*in absentia*, but striking in its palpable absence), it delights, because the reader delights in the imitation of action and enjoys the predicaments of fellows stupider than himself, and it provides vicariously some experience: the reader may live in and through the fictional fellow who makes his hapless choices, and so learn by cheap experience.

Because the satiric works are dramatic in form, Erasmus forfeits his right to intrude to suggest analogues or better thinking. But this limitation he overcomes in several ways – some of them more felicitous than others: his Moria grows away from folly and towards wisdom, and is then able herself to point to the right; the non-satiric characters take over the dialogue of the *Ciceronianus*, and Peter out-talks Julius. But sometimes, in achieving this positive purpose, he loses much of the artistry: certainly *Ciceronianus* and *Julius exclusus* are too didactic in the end.

Erasmus' use of irony links easily with his high esteem for reason, and his belief that even the erring man may grasp an effectively presented truth. Irony appeals to the reason, saying what is not true and provoking a fairer judgement. The reasonable in Erasmus was delighted by the irony found in the classical models and, with some tempering, he adopted it. But not for nothing had he given his best efforts to translating and editing the Fathers of the Church. He knew well that irony was not enough, as reason had not been enough when God was making and endowing man.

Although Erasmus rarely provides, as the Fathers had provided, as Dante and the great Christian poets had provided, a text capable of multiple interpretation, in his work as a whole, even in his satiric work, he proffers something for each mode of human sensitivity. He satisfies the imaginative life in the fiction, the moral and rational life in the lessons given, and in the problems and questions and hints concerning the niceties of decision and choice; his spiritual and devotional life is nourished too, for the little plays and bits of make-believe are invariably set in a Christian world where even the fools know that eternal life surrounds their life in time, and where follies and vices are balanced against eventual beatitude. The *quid ad aeternitatem* is seldom spoken, but it is never far from the surface.

In his later life Erasmus came to rely more on exhortation than on satire, and some foreshadowing of that later attitude can be seen in many of the satires. He thinks of man as being brought to right thinking by good teaching, and so justifies the satiric methods he uses, but he uses them rather as prelude to, or concomitant to, the more persuasive ones. Some of the colloquies are totally satiric, but taken as a whole, the hortative element balances the satiric: the *Praise* suggests the right-thinking norm all through and proclaims it loudly from time to time; *Ciceronianus* and *Julius exclusus* both use the ironic method only as prelude to a more earnest and gentle exhortation. And this is Erasmus' usual way of tempering the irony – a kind of tandem arrangement. Only in the *Praise* does he filter into the wry parts of the work (through imagery and allusion) the sweetness and light of the final glory, and even here, the intermingling of moods is slight.

Strangely enough, it is Erasmus' earliest satire that evokes the richest and most complex response. And this, of course, militates against a theory of a developing ironic technique. Rightly so, for a writer does not labour to perfect an instrument – even a good instrument – that he is coming to find less well fitted to its proper end than others that he knows. Erasmus' greatest work was to be in the field of education and exegesis, and it is a paradox that he should be so widely known as the author of the *Praise of Folly*. He had dashed it off in spare moments, whereas he had laboured long to edit the Fathers and translate the scriptures; he had lamented the *Praise*'s popularity, while he thought with satisfaction of his more serious work. Circumstances had made the *Praise* and some of the colloquies a contributing force in an upheaval Erasmus did not quite foresee, and gave them a prominence out of their due proportion.

In spite of this high acclaim given to the satires, and the spate of imitation that followed, little satire that is truly Erasmian appeared in England outside of the theatre, though its isolated elements did occur: moral earnestness in Anthony Mundaye, Edward Hake, and Thomas Heywood, energetic zeal in Thomas Nashe, ingenuity in Daniel Heinsius and the translators of Synesius and Agrippa and the author of the *Mirrour of Madnesse*, and clever irony in Erasmus' friend Willibald Pirckheimer, and in one Robert Turner. But the elements do not amalgamate in any of them, although each of the last two mentioned did write a false encomium somewhat Erasmian.[27]

27 Pirckheimer's *Prayse of Gout* (*Laus podagrae*), circulating in Latin by 1522, but not in English until 1617, praised gout in the way Erasmus had praised folly, its initial light tone moving into one of greater sobriety. It is ironic and with moral purpose, and is delivered by a person, Dame Podagra, as Erasmus' *Praise* was delivered by Moria, so that the guileless little genitive of this title is, like the 'Moriae' of Erasmus', doubly charged. Podagra has not Moria's fullness of personhood, yet she is human enough to forget her ironic tone as she warms into her subject, and to keep coming back to her original flippancy just when we think she has forgotten it.

Erasmus wrote to Pirckheimer in 1525 after reading the *Gout* (Allen VI 47–8) and includes some facetious paragraphs of similar false praise, comparing the distresses and glories of gout with those of the stone from which he himself suffered, and of course finding the stone much more laudable – and more ennobling to the sufferer!

Turner wrote two false praises: *Encomium debiti* and *De laude ebrietatis*. They are undated but probably written towards the close of the century. Dornavius includes them in his *Amphitheatrum* (II, 175–6). The praise of debt is witty but hardly ironic; but the praise of tippling is both ironic and witty, and the combination of fine raillery and good satire is surely Erasmian. Whether or not it was ever translated into English and so provided enjoyment for English paradox-fanciers is another matter – I know of no translation. Turner was an English priest who wrote his fine Latin in France. The *Ebrietatis* begins as if the author were a loyal disciple of Bacchus, and lauds the delights of unbridled drinking for some paragraphs; then the fulsome praise begins to include words and images that betray the satiric intention: 'nausea,' 'stupidity,' 'insanity.' Like the *Praise of Folly*, this praise finally turns to forthright denunciation and then to exhortation, begging the good Christian reader to heed the voice of reason, to recognize the disparity between Christian ideals of self-denial and pre-Lenten surrender to orgiastic indulgence; and the work ends by cycling back to the initial motif and noting that one who is prey to his appetites is not a free man at all and thus is not beloved of even the pagan gods. For a fuller discussion of some sixteenth-century mock eulogy, see my 'Erasmus and the Tradition of Paradox' *Studies in Philology* LXI: 1 (January 1964) 41–63.

What seems so abundantly strange is that those who thought they appreciated Erasmus fully seem to have misread him. Even Sidney, as we noted, classed him with Cornelius Agrippa as being 'equally merry.' Erasmus really *was* merry, and made his readers so, even as he was tearing the false face from a greedy and unthinking civilization, and giving his readers, for good measure, the delight of some nice speculations about the provinces of wisdom and prudence; and Agrippa was not merry at all, but simply wrote an ingenious, and sometimes witty, repudiation of fantastic erudition.

It is all too easy to account for all this by reference to the times – to the religious factioning that split the Christian world in half and then split the halves, leaving the edges too raw for the urbanities of irony; or to point, as some have done, to a kind of 'dissociation of sensibility' that questioned the old mediaeval way of synthesizing the spiritual and the sensible, and encouraged the partitioning mind.[28] But that is matter for a historian's book, or a theologian's, not for mine.

Erasmus himself was not unaffected by the climate, and had his own difficulties in seeing life steadily and whole. His experience too had been such as to set up in him certain oppositions. He had seen and been lured by the natural grace of an old civilization that had not even known the claims of Christianity; and the richer grace of his own era he saw as marred by quite unchristian greed and contention. He had pillaged the ancient culture for maxims and morals he could transfer to his own, for symbols he could baptize. The strength of his own religion he saw as diluted by its over-dependence on symbols and ceremonies which, worthy as they might be when properly related to what they stood for or honoured, had a way of unseating themselves from their true places and becoming for many people things in themselves, and so neither good nor significant. And so he had grown suspicious

28 See, for instance, Michael F. Moloney *John Donne: His Flight from Mediaevalism* (Urbana 1944) 69–104; L.C. Knights *Explorations* (London 1946) 92–3; Malcolm M. Ross *Poetry and Dogma* (New Brunswick, NJ 1954) passim, especially chapters 1 and 2.

of religious symbols, and hesitant even to urge the grace of the sacraments lest foolish men think their easy reception could supply for indifference in moral matters. Even his own symbols, as we have seen, Erasmus distrusted.

Finally, Erasmus had known (with perhaps an understanding more notional than real) that the whole moral activity of a citizen of Christendom must spring from charity if it is to have significance at all, that charity is the plenitude of Christian perfection, its efficient and final cause, and that love of God should inanimate the love of man. But too often he had seen that men dedicated and vowed to the things of God, surrounded with the helps and reminders of virtuous living, could fall short of even average goodness. He himself had been unable, or unwilling, to sustain the restraints that commitment to a religious order would have imposed on him; and this may have operated towards his rationalizing of all such dedication – even his disparagement of it.[29]

For all that, there is a certain wholeness remaining in Erasmus that makes his humanism very Christian and his work evocative on all levels. Satire is not a form that lends itself to fullness of vision, but Erasmus' best satires move from level to level, their final position latent in the preparatory ones; and in even the less satisfying of them there is still some recognition of, and appeal to, the many-sided, complex heart and mind of man, who is little more than animal, yet is made in the image and likeness of God. Perhaps, of all the notions one can predicate about the thinking of Erasmus, that of his reverence for the word is the most significant. The right word he recognizes as the image of the mind; and the mind and its word make a man a man and not a beast. But more than that, its progeniture is parallel to that of the divine

29 He himself would, of course, cavil at any impugning of his ability to tolerate restraint and would attribute his seeking dispensation from his order to the necessities of what he felt himself called to; see, however, his letter of July 1514, to Servatius Rogers, in which he excuses himself from returning to the order. Especially notable are the second paragraph and the last two. Admissions of weakness are here pretty apparent, even sandwiched as they are between the careful reminders of his good life (Allen I 565–72).

Word, and lends a hallowing to it, bringing it into relationship with the *logos* itself. Rhetoric, then, has no small place in the life of faith and hope and charity. Ultimately for Erasmus the great function of human speech is the re-generating of man through re-creating in him the Christian life. It is not surprising that in his later years he turned his gracious gift of language into moulds more flexible and gentle than that of satire.

❧ Bibliography ❧

The following abbreviations have been used:

CL   *Classical Philology*
EHR *English Historical Review*
ELH *English Literary History*
MLN *Modern Language Notes*
MLR *Modern Language Review*
MP   *Modern Philology*
PMLA *Publications of the Modern Language Association of America*
SP   *Studies in Philology*
UTQ *University of Toronto Quarterly*

PRIMARY SOURCES

Henrie Cornelius Agrippa *Of the Vanitie and Uncertaintie of Artes and Sciences* English by Ja[mes] Sa[nford], Gent. London: Henrie Bynneman 1575 (microfilm)

Thomas Aquinas *The Summa Theologica of St Thomas Aquinas* Part II. Trans Fathers of the English Dominican Province. London: Burns, Oates 1922

St Augustine of Hippo *De doctrina christiana* Vol IV of *The Fathers of the Church* Trans John Gavignan, CSA. New York: Cima 1947

– *Basic Writings of Saint Augustine* Vol I. Whitney J. Oates (ed) New York: Random House 1949

Dante Alighieri 'Letter to Can Grande Della Scala,' in A.H. Gilbert (ed) *Literary Criticism: Plato to Dryden* New York: American Book Company 1940

John Donne *The Complete Poetry and Selected Prose of John Donne* John Hayward (ed) Bloomsbury: Nonesuch Press 1923

– *Biathanatos* Reproduced from the first edition. With a Bibliographical note by J. William Hebel. New York: The Facsimile Text Society. Oxford: B.H. Blackwell 1930

– *The Sermons of John Donne* George Potter and Evelyn M. Simpson (eds) 10 vols. Berkeley: University of California Press 1953–62

Caspar Dornavius *Amphitheatrum sapientiae socraticae jocoseriae* ... Hanover 1619. 2 tomes (microfilm)

John Dryden *Discourse on the Original and Progress of Satire* Students' Cambridge edition of *Poetical Works of John Dryden* Cambridge, Mass.: Riverside Press 1909

Elizabethan Critical Essays G. Gregory Smith (ed) Oxford: Clarendon Press 1904

Desiderius Erasmus *Opera Omnia* J. LeClerc (ed) 10 vols in 11 tomes. Leyden: Batavi 1703–6

– *Opus Epistolarum Des. Erasmi Roterodami* P.S. Allen (ed) 11 vols. Oxford: Clarendon Press 1930–8

– *Ciceronianus, or a Dialogue on the Best Style of Speaking* ed with introduction Paul Monroe; trans Izora Scott. Columbia University Teachers' College Series, no. 21. New York: Columbia University Press 1908

– *The Colloquies of Erasmus* ed and trans Craig R. Thompson. Chicago: University of Chicago Press 1965

– *De duplici copia verborum ac rerum* Partially translated by Donald B. King and A. David Rix as *On Copia of Words and Ideas* Milwaukee: Marquette University Press 1963

– *De libero arbitrio diatribe, sive collatio* (1524) Trans Pierre Mesnard, as *Essai sur la libre arbitre* Algiers: Les Editions Robert et René Choix 1945. Also translated by Ernst F. Winter as part of *Erasmus-Luther: Discourse on Free Will* New York: Ungar 1961

– *Dulce bellum inexpertis* (1517) Trans [with introduction]

J.W. Mackail, as *Erasmus Against War* Merrymount, Mass.: The Merrymount Press 1907
- *Enchiridion militis christiani* (1503–18) Trans as *The Enchiridion of Erasmus* by Raymond Himelick. Bloomington: Indiana University Press 1963
- *Erasmi opuscula: A Supplement to the Opera Omnia* Ed [with notes and introduction] Wallace K. Ferguson. The Hague: Martinus Nijhoff 1933
- *Erasmus and Cambridge (The Cambridge Correspondence)* H.C. Porter (ed); D.F.S. Thomson (trans) Toronto: University of Toronto Press 1957
- *Inquisitio de Fide: A Colloquy* C.R. Thompson (ed) Yale Studies in Religion, xv. New Haven: Yale University Press 1970
- *Institutio principis christiani* (1518) Ed and trans L.K. Born as *The Education of a Christian Prince* New York: Columbia University Press 1936. Republished by W.W. Norton and Company, New York 1968, by arrangement with the Columbia University Press
- *Julius secundus exclusus ...* (1513) Trans by Paul Pascal as *The Julius Exclusus of Erasmus*, with introduction and notes by J. Kelley Sowards. Bloomington: University of Indiana Press 1968
- *Moriae encomium declamatio* (1509) Trans Hoyt Hopewell Hudson as *The Praise of Folly* Princeton: University Press 1941
- *Querela pacis* (1516) Trans T. Paynell, as *The Complaint of Peace*, with introduction by W.J. Hirten. New York: Scholars' Facsimiles and Reprints 1946
George Gascoigne *The Steele Glas* Vol IV of *The Works of the English Poets from Chaucer to Cowper* Alexander Chalmers (ed) London: C. Whittingham 1810
Geoffrey of Vinsauf *Poetria nova* Margaret Nims (ed) University of Toronto Press 1967
John Granger *The Golden Aphrodite* (1517) New York: Scholars' Facsimiles and Reprints 1939

Edward Hake *Newes out of Powles Churchyard* (1579) Compiled by E.H., Gent. Ed Charles Edmonds. London: Henry Sotheran, Baer and Company 1872

Sir John Harington *The Metamorphosis of Ajax* (1596) London: Fanfrolico Press, n d

Gabriel Harvey *Ciceronianus* Ed H.W. Wilson; trans C. Forbes. Lincoln: University of Nebraska Press 1945

Lucian *The Works of Lucian of Samosata* Trans A.M. Harmon. 8 vols. London: William Heinemann 1913

Niccolo Machiavelli *The Prince and The Discourses* Modern Library edition. New York: Random House 1950

The Mirrour of Madnes, Maintayning Madnes to be most Excellent Done out of French into English by Ja[mes] Sa[nford], Gent. London: T. Marshe for T. Orion 1576

Sir Thomas More *The Apologye of Syr Thomas More, Knight* A.I. Taft (ed) for the Early English Text Society. London: Oxford University Press 1930

– *The Dialogue Concerning Tyndale.* Vol II of *The English Works of Sir Thomas More* W.S. Campbell (ed), with introduction by A.W. Reed. London: Eyre and Spottiswoode 1931

– *Utopia* Vol IV of *The Complete Works of Thomas More* Edward Surtz and J.H. Hexter (eds) New Haven and London: Yale University Press 1965

Thomas Nashe *The Works of Thomas Nashe* R.B. McKerrow (ed) 5 vols. London: Sidgwick and Jackson 1910

Patrologiae cursus completus Ser. Lat. J.P. Migne (ed) Vol CXIII Paris: Garnier Freres 1880

Philo-Judaeus *Philo* Trans F.H. Colson and G.E. Whitaker (Loeb edition) Vol I London: Heinemann 1949

Willibald Pirckheimer *The Prayse of the Gout* or *The Gout's Apologie* Written first in the Latin tongue, by Billibaldus Pirckheimerus and now Englished by W. Est. London: G. P[urslow] for J. Budge 1617

Quintilian *Instituto oratoria of Quintilian* with an English translation by H.E. Butler. London: Heinemann 1921–2

William Roy *Rede me and be nott wrothe, for I saye no thinge but trothe.* Written by Wm. Roy and Jerome Barlowe. Printed by

John Schott at Strasburg in 1528. London: Arber English
Reprints, no 28. 1871.
Sir Philip Sidney *An Apology for Poetry* Ed Evelyn S. Shuckburg.
Cambridge, Eng.: Cambridge University Press 1891
John Skelton *John Skelton's Complete Poems* Philip Henderson
(ed) London: J.M. Dent and Sons, Ltd 1959
Robert Turner *Encomium debiti seu paradoxon* in Dornavius,
Amphitheatrum q v
– *De laude ebrietatis* in Dornavius, *Amphitheatrum* q v
Thomas Wyatt, 'Of the Sure and Meane Estate,' in *Poetry of the
English Renaissance* J.W. Hebel and H.H. Hudson (eds)
New York: Appleton-Century-Crofts, Inc. 1957

SECONDARY SOURCES

Robert P. Adams *The Better Part of Valour: More, Erasmus,
Colet, and Vives on Humanism, War and Peace, 1496–1535*
Seattle: University of Washington Press 1962
– 'Designs of More and Erasmus for a New Social Order' *Studies
in Philology* XLIII (1945) 131–45
John William Aldridge *The Hermeneutic of Erasmus* Basel Studies
of Theology, no. 2. Joint publication by EVT-Verlag, Zurich,
and John Knox Press, Richmond, Va. 1966
R. M. Alden *The Rise of Formal Satire in England* Philadelphia:
University of Pennsylvania Press 1899
P.S. Allen *The Age of Erasmus* Oxford: Clarendon Press 1914
– *Erasmus: Lectures and Wayfaring Sketches* Oxford: Clarendon
Press 1934
Francis G. Allinson *Lucian, Satirist and Artist* New York:
Longmans 1926
Roland Bainton *Christian Attitudes Towards War and Peace*
New York: Abingdon Press 1960
– *Erasmus of Christendom* New York: Scribners 1969
Marcel Bataillon *Erasme et l'Espagne* Paris: E. Droz 1937
Earle Birney 'English Irony before Chaucer' *University of Toronto
Quarterly* VI (1937) 538–49

R.P. Blackmur 'Dante's Ten Terms for the Treatment of Treatise' *Kenyon Review* XIV (Spring 1952) 286–300
- *The Expense of Greatness* New York: Arrow Edition 1940
Morton W. Bloomfield 'Symbolism in Mediaeval Literature' *Modern Philology* LVI (1958) 75–6
Louis Bouyer *Erasmus and his Times* Westminster, Md.: Newman Press 1959 (translated from the French *Autour d'Erasme* by Francis X. Murphy)
Walter Burghardt 'On Early Christian Exegesis' *Theological Studies* XI (1950) 104–6
W.E. Campbell *Erasmus, Tyndale, and More* London: Eyre and Spottiswoode 1949
F. Caspari *Humanism and the Social Order in Tudor England* Chicago: University of Chicago Press 1954
H. Caplan 'The Four Senses of Scriptural Interpretation and the Mediaeval Theory of Preaching' *Speculum* IV (1929) 282–90
Rosalie L. Colie *Paradoxia epidemica: The Renaissance Tradition of Paradox* Princeton: Princeton University Press 1965
Morris W. Croll 'The Baroque Style in Prose' *Studies in English Philology: A Miscellany in Honour of Frederick Klaeber* Kemp Malone and Martin B. Ruud (eds) Minneapolis: University of Minnesota Press 1929
Henri De Lubac *Exégèse médiévale: Les quatre sens de l'écriture* Paris: Aubier 1959
T.A. Dorey (ed) *Erasmus* London: Routledge & Kegan Paul 1970
R.B. Drummond *Erasmus: His Life and Character as shown in his Correspondence and Works* 2 vols. London: Smith, Elder & Co. 1873
J. Wight Duff *Roman Satire* Berkeley: University of California Press 1936
Robert Eliot 'The Satirist and Society' *English Literary History* XXI (1954) 237–48
T.S. Eliot *Selected Essays* London: Faber and Faber 1932
George Faludy *Erasmus of Rotterdam* London: Eyre and Spottiswoode 1970
J.A. Froude *Life and Letters of Desiderius Erasmus* New York: Scribners 1894

- 'Times of Erasmus and Luther' *Short Studies on Great Subjects* Vol I London: Longmans 1888
Northrop Frye 'The Nature of Satire' *University of Toronto Quarterly* XIV (1944) 75–89
Helen Gardner *The Business of Criticism* Oxford: Clarendon Press 1959
Martha Heep 'Die Colloquia Familiaria des Erasmus und Lucian' *Hermaea* XVIII (1927) 1–74
J. M. Hofer *Die Stellung des Desiderius Erasmus und des Johann Ludwig Vives sur Pedagogik des Quintilian* Erlangen: Jungen 1910
Christopher Hollis *Erasmus* Milwaukee: Bruce 1933
Philip Hughes *History of the Reformation* 3 vols. London: Hollis and Carter 1930–54
Johan Huizinga *Erasmus of Rotterdam* London: Phaidon Press 1952
Bernard F. Huppe and D.W. Robertson *Fruyt and Chaf: Studies in Chaucer's Allegories* Princeton: Princeton University Press 1963
Albert Hyma *The Christian Renaissance: A History of the 'Devotio Moderna' Movement* New York: The Century Company 1925
- *The Youth of Erasmus, University of Michigan Publications in History and Political Science* XX (1930)
John Jortin *The Life of Erasmus* 2 vols. London: Printed for J. Whiston and B. White 1758–60
Walter Kaiser *Praisers of Folly* Cambridge, Mass.: Harvard University Press 1963
Alvin B. Kernan *The Cankered Muse: Satire of the English Renaissance* Yale Studies in English, no. 142. New Haven: Yale University Press 1959
Joseph Lecler 'Erasmus and Christian Unity' *The Month* IV (1950) 155–68
Charles Lenient *La Satire en France ou la littérature militant au XVIe siècle* 2 vols. Paris: Librairie Hachette et Cie 1966
J.H. Lupton *The Life of John Colet*, DD New Edition. London: George Bell and Sons 1909

William F. Lynch *Christ and Apollo* New York: Sheed and Ward 1960

A.E. Malloch 'The Technique and Function of Renaissance Paradox' *Studies in Philology* LIII (1956) 191–203

J.J. Mangan *The Life, Character, and Influence of Desiderius Erasmus of Rotterdam* 2 vols. New York: Macmillan 1927

Gervaise Marc'hadour (ed and trans) *Thomas More vu par Erasme* Paris: 1962

H.A. Mason *Humanism and Poetry in the Early Tudor Period* London: Routledge & Kegan Paul 1959

James Kelsey McConica *English Humanists and Reformation Politics under Henry* VIII *and Edward* VI Oxford: Clarendon Press 1965

H. Marshall McLuhan 'From Eliot to Seneca.' Review of *The Senecan Amble* by George Williamson *University of Toronto Quarterly* XXII (1953) 199–202

Robert H. Murray *Erasmus and Luther: Their Attitudes to Toleration* New York: Macmillan 1920

Middleton Murry *The Problem of Style* London: Oxford University Press 1922

John C. Olin (ed) *Desiderius Erasmus: Christian Humanism and the Reformation: Selected Writings* Harper Torchbook 1166. New York: Harper and Row, Inc. 1965

John B. Payne *Erasmus: His Theology of the Sacraments* New York: John Knox Press 1970

Arthur S. Pease 'Things without Honour' *Classical Philology* XXI (1926) 27–42

John Peter *Complaint and Satire in Early English Literature* Oxford: Clarendon Press 1956

Margaret Mann Phillips *The Adages of Erasmus: A Study with Translations* Cambridge, Eng.: Cambridge University Press 1964

– *Erasmus and the Northern Renaissance* London: Hodder and Stoughton 1949

– 'Erasmus and Propaganda' *Modern Language Review* XXXVII (1942) 1–17

J.-B. Pineau 'Erasme et la papauté: Etude critique du Julius Exclusus.' Thèse complémentaire. Paris 1924
- Erasme: Sa pensée religieuse Paris: Les Presses Universitaires de France 1923
A. Renaudet Etudes érasmienes (1521–1529) Paris: Librairie E. Droz 1930
Eugene F. Rice 'John Colet and the Annihilation of the Natural' Harvard Theological Review XLV (1952) 141–63
- The Renaissance Idea of Wisdom Harvard Historical Monographs no. 37. Cambridge, Mass.: Harvard University Press 1958
Warner G. Rice 'The Paradossi of Ortensio Lando' University of Michigan Publications in Language and Literature VIII (1932) 59–75
R.K. Root The Poetical Career of Alexander Pope Princeton: Princeton University Press 1946
William Schenck 'The Three Circles' Dublin Review 449 (1950) 66–81
R.J. Schoeck and John Meagher 'On Erasmus' "The Godly Feast"' Erasmus in English I: 3 (1971) 10–12
G.G. Sedgewick Of Irony, Especially in the Drama The Alexander Lectures 1934. Toronto: University of Toronto Press 1935
Frederick Seebohm The Oxford Reformers London: J.M. Dent and Sons 1867
Charles S. Singleton 'Dante's Allegory' Speculum, XXV (1950) 78–86
Beryl Smalley The Study of the Bible in the Middle Ages Oxford: Clarendon Press 1941
- 'Stephen Langton and the Four Senses of Scripture' Speculum VI (1931) 60–75
Preserved Smith Erasmus: A Study of his Life, Ideals and Place in History New York: Harper 1923
- A Key to the Colloquies Vol XIII of Harvard Theological Studies. Cambridge, Mass.: Harvard University Press 1927
J. Kelley Sowards 'Thomas More, Erasmus, and Julius II: A Case of Advocacy' Moreana XXIV (November 1969) 81–9

E.L. Surtz 'Oxford Reformers and Scholasticism' *Studies in Philology* XLVII (1950) 547–56
– *The Praise of Pleasure: Philosophy, Education and Communism in More's Utopia* Cambridge, Mass.: Harvard University Press 1957
– *The Praise of Wisdom: A Commentary on the Religious and Moral Problems and Background of Thomas More's Utopia* Chicago: Loyola University Press 1957
James Sutherland *English Satire* The Clark Lectures 1956. Cambridge, Eng.: University of Cambridge Press 1958
Craig R. Thompson 'Better Teachers than Scotus or Aquinas' *Mediaeval and Renaissance Studies* II (1966) Durham, NC: Duke University Press 1966
– *Translations of Lucian by Erasmus and More* Ithaca, NY: Cornell University Press 1958
– *Erasmus: Inquisitio de Fide* Yale Studies in Religion, XV New Haven: Yale University Press 1950
D.F.S. Thomson 'The Latinity of Erasmus' in *Erasmus*, T.A. Dorey (ed) London: Routledge & Kegan Paul 1970
E.N.S. Thomson *The Seventeenth-Century Essay* Vol III of University of Iowa Humanistic Studies. Ames, Ia.: University of Iowa Press 1923
J.A.K. Thomson 'Erasmus in England' *Vortrage der Bibliothek Warburg* ('England und die Antike') IX (1930–1) 64–93
– *Irony: An Historical Introduction* London: George Allen and Unwin 1926
James D. Tracy 'Erasmus becomes a German' *Renaissance Quarterly* XXI (1968) 280–8
F.M.C. Turner *The Element of Irony in English Literature* London: Cambridge University Press 1926
Rosemond Tuve *Allegorical Imagery* Princeton: Princeton University Press 1966
– *Elizabethan and Metaphysical Imagery* Chicago: University of Chicago Press 1947
Hugh Walker *English Satire and Satirists* London: J.M. Dent and Sons 1925

Ruth Wallerstein *Studies in Seventeenth-Century Poetic*
Madison: University of Wisconsin Press 1950

Helen C. White *The Metaphysical Poets* New York, Macmillan
1936

Maurice Wilkinson 'Erasmus' *Catholic Historical Review* n s 3
(1923–4) 190–204

George Williamson *The Senecan Amble: A Study in Prose from
Bacon to Collier* London: Faber and Faber 1952

F.P. Wilson *Elizabethan and Jacobean* Oxford: Clarendon Press
1945

Humbert Wolfe *Notes on English Verse Satire* London: Hogarth
Press 1929

W.H. Woodward, *Desiderius Erasmus: Concerning the Aim and
Method of Education* London: Cambridge University Press
1904

David Worcester *The Art of Satire* Cambridge, Mass.: Harvard
University Press 1940

Stefan Zweig *Erasmus* Trans Eden and Cedar Paul. London:
Cassel 1934

❧ Index ❧

❧ Erasmus Studies ❧

A Series of Studies Concerned with Erasmus and Related Subjects

This book
was designed by
WILLIAM RUETER
under the direction of
ALLAN FLEMING
and was printed by
University
of Toronto
Press